Spectacles of Strangeness

Spectacles
of Strangeness

Imperialism, Alienation,

and Marlowe

Emily C. Bartels

University of Pennsylvania Press
Philadelphia

Frontispiece: John White, *Pictish Man Holding a Human Head*. Courtesy
of the British Museum.

Copyright © 1993 by the University of Pennsylvania Press
All rights reserved
Printed in the United States of America

Library of Congress Cataloging-in-Publication Data
Bartels, Emily Carroll.
    Spectacles of strangeness: imperialism, alienation, and Marlowe / Emily C. Bartels.
      p. cm.
    Includes bibliographical references and index.
    ISBN 0-8122-3193-7
    1. Marlowe, Christopher, 1564–1593—Criticism and interpretation.   2. Alienation
(Social psychology) in literature.   3. Imperialism in literature.   4. Exoticism in
literature.   5. Spectacular, The.   I. Title.
PR2674.B37   1993
822'.3—dc20   92-45865
                                           CIP

To
ANN BAYNES COIRO,
with admiration and love

Contents

Acknowledgments   ix
A Note on the Texts   xi
Introduction   xiii

Part I. Setting the Stage   1

    Chapter 1. Strange and Estranging Spectacles:
            Strategies of State and Stage   3

Part II. The Alien Abroad   27

    Chapter 2. Reproducing Africa: *Dido, Queen of
            Carthage* and Colonialist Discourse   29

    Chapter 3. East of England: Imperialist Self-
            Construction in *Tamburlaine*, Parts 1 and 2   53

    Chapter 4. Capitalizing on the Jew: The Third Term
            in *The Jew of Malta*   82

Part III. The Alien at Home   109

    Chapter 5. Demonizing Magic: Patterns of Power
            in *Doctor Faustus*   111

Chapter 6.   The Show of Sodomy: Minions and
            Dominions in *Edward II*   143

Conclusion   173
Notes   177
Works Cited   205
Index   215

Acknowledgments

This book could not have happened, and happened so deliciously, without the professional and personal support of many institutions, colleagues, and friends, to which and to whom I am much indebted.

Crucial work on this project has been funded by two Rutgers University Research Council Summer Fellowships (1988, 1989) and encouraged by the FAS Office of the Dean. I have also benefited from the resources of the Folger Shakespeare Library and the kindnesses of its staff. Parts of Chapter 2 have appeared in "Making More of the Moor: Aaron, Othello, and Renaissance Refashionings of Race," *Shakespeare Quarterly* 41 (1990) and "Imperialist Beginnings: Richard Hakluyt and the Construction of Africa," *Criticism* 34 (1992), parts of Chapter 3 in "The Double Vision of the East: Imperialist Self-Construction in Marlowe's *Tamburlaine, Part One*," *Renaissance Drama* 23 (1992), and are reprinted in revised form by permission of *Shakespeare Quarterly*, Wayne State University Press, and Northwestern University Press, respectively. Chapter 4 first took shape as an MLA talk given to the Marlowe Society, which has remained a receptive audience, and as an essay, "Malta, the Jew, and the Fictions of Difference: Colonialist Discourse in Marlowe's *The Jew of Malta*" in *English Literary Renaissance* 20 (1990):1–16. I am especially indebted to the editors—Arthur Kinney, Mary Beth Rose, Barbara Mowat, and Arthur Marotti—for their continued interest in my work. Some of the early groundwork for Chapter 5 appeared in *Renaissance Papers 1989*, and I owe thanks to the Southeastern Renaissance Conference for providing me with a congenial forum in which to test this material.

This project began at Harvard under the enthusiastic guidance of Marjorie Garber, who, in introducing me to Marlowe, opened an exotic door and taught me how to explore the "infinite riches" that lay beyond. Rob Watson has been and remained an extremely generous reader and friend, even though (and surely because) I delight in "this Marlowe person." I am indebted, too, to the members of the Renaissance Colloquium of the Harvard English Department, who provided an appreciative audience for early articulations of my argument, especially to Roland Greene, who stepped in as reader, and Naomi Miller, who shared, and so eased, the struggle of trying to figure out just what our dissertations were actually about. Ann Porter and Deborah Carlin were ready on the sidelines to pull me through the most vulnerable moments of this project, and Mary Crane has been indispensable all along, reading my work with a keen critical eye and engaging me in stimulating chats about everything from authority and subversion to the epigram.

At Rutgers, my work found very helpful readers in Maurice Charney and Ron Levao, sustaining moments of encouragement from Jackie Miller and George Kearns, endless enthusiasm from Bridget Lyons and Barry Qualls, and invaluable support from Miriam Hansen. And I have been overwhelmed by the generosity of Angus Fletcher, David Bevington, and David Riggs, who have gone out of their way to help. Thanks go also to Lynda Boose, Julie Solomon, and Tom Cartelli for their continued interest in my work, and to Walter Cohen and several other incisive, anonymous readers for comments that have helped this book take its final form.

I am grateful, too, to several people who stepped in, especially in the final stages, to make a significant difference: to Beth Durkee, who taught me an invaluable lesson in style, Lauren Berlant, an invaluable lesson in titles, and Paulina Brownie Wilker, an invaluable lesson in life; to Laura Knoppers and Alexandra Barcus, who humored me through many crises, Russ Snapp, who helped me cross all sorts of frontiers, and Gordon Teskey, who cheered me on from the other side; and to Margaret Hunt, who, in her own intriguing way, validated everything.

Finally, I am deeply indebted to Ann Coiro, my remarkable colleague and friend, who, with her compelling warmth, brilliance, and delight, has shared intensely in my fascination with cultural stereotypes, as in so much more. Writing this book in the constant company of her friendship has been an extraordinary experience.

A Note on the Texts

Quotations from Marlowe have been taken from J. B. Steane, ed., *The Complete Plays* (Baltimore: Penguin Books, 1975), except in Chapter 5 where I have used Michael Keefer, ed., *Christopher Marlowe's Doctor Faustus: A 1604-Version Edition* (Peterborough, Canada: Broadview Press, 1991). All references to *Tamburlaine* are to Part 1, unless otherwise noted.

Quotations from Shakespeare are from G. Blakemore Evans, et al., eds., *The Riverside Shakespeare* (Boston: Houghton Mifflin Company, 1974), and quotations from other Renaissance plays are from Russell Fraser and Norman Rabkin, eds., *Drama of the English Renaissance* (New York: Macmillan, 1976), unless otherwise noted.

Spellings of some proper names will vary according to the text being cited.

Introduction

The key question underlying this book is why Christopher Marlowe, the sixteenth century's most important playwright after Shakespeare, chose to bring "the alien" to center stage in each of his plays. What made him turn and return exclusively to such subjects, filling the stage with Oriental barbarians, black magicians, homosexuals, African queens and kings, Machiavellian Christians, Turks, and Jews at a time when he was not only making a name and a living for himself, but also helping transform the theater into one of the most popular and powerful arenas for social and political comment and dissent?

The question, though investigated here in terms of Marlowe, turns us to the larger issue of why the alien was such a vital and appealing subject on the Renaissance stage and within Renaissance society more generally. What made figures like Dionysius and Cambyses the choice exemplars of outrageous tyrants in moral plays such as Richard Edward's *Damon and Pythias* or Thomas Preston's *Cambyses, King of Persia*? Why did dramatists such as Shakespeare, who for the most part rejected the stock types inherited from earlier drama in favor of more complex characters, continue to create stereotypical figures such as Aaron, the diabolical Moor? And why were "other," non-European, worlds like Persia, Egypt, Africa, and the East so often the settings on the stage, at least until Ben Jonson gave the urban home front particular prominence there? Why was the market in stock types and foreign affairs so strong?

The answer, no doubt, depends upon a wide range of factors, extending from theatrical to ideological concerns, from the specific circumstances and predilections peculiar to the era to more universal determinants such as the seemingly timeless fascination with the strange. Yet the prevalence of "others" on the stage at this particular historical moment points to, and points us to, a crucial development in the history of the early modern state—the prominent emergence of imperialist ideologies and propaganda. It was not until the mid-seventeenth century and Cromwell that England began to garner its forces and press concertedly toward empire. Because there was no Elizabethan Empire—because the troops were underfunded, disorganized, and disheveled, because the fleet, even and especially after defeating the Spanish Armada, was severely weakened, because cross-cultural voyages were sporadic and uncertain, and evolved under the aegis of adventurous individuals and self-interested (though state-patented) trading companies rather than in the name of official foreign policy—the importance of imperialism to the era has, until recently, been greatly underestimated. Yet it was precisely because there was no established empire that the promotion of the imperialist cause was so crucial. For how was the state to impose its dominance across the globe until the ideological backing was vitally and visibly in place at home?

The Elizabethan period marks a critical beginning in the drive toward domination, evidenced in and dependent upon the plethora of cross-cultural texts emerging in unprecedented numbers at the time. Discussions of the Renaissance's imperialist discourse have for a long time been preoccupied almost exclusively with the Jacobean era, with the travel narratives on "America" and *The Tempest*. Importantly, however, the Elizabethan age witnessed the widespread production and popularity of texts such as Richard Hakluyt's *Principal Navigations* (1589), William Waterman's translation of Joannes Boemus's *Omnium gentium mores* (*The Fardle of Facions*, 1555), John Pory's translation (1600) of Leo Africanus's *Geographical Historie of Africa*, and indeed, Christopher Marlowe's *Dido, Queen of Carthage, Tamburlaine, Parts 1 and 2*, and *The Jew of Malta*—texts deeply invested in supporting or subverting the idea of English supremacy and with it, England's right to the world's resources.

In laying the critical foundation for or against empire building, these representations not only shaped the society's conception of imperialism. They also impacted significantly on conceptions of England itself and the place of the self and the "other" within it. An important part of the support for English superiority and domination was the insistence on the otherness of the other and on what had been or were becoming stereotypical demonizations of such figures as the Turk, the Moor, or the Oriental barbarian. This kind of discrimination did not stop with foreign subjects or cross-cultural discourse, however, for within domestic discourse, the "aliens" at home—"counterfeit" poor, the insane, religious and political heretics, witches, sodomites, and the like—were also being categorized and persecuted, in practice or in print, as signs of what was not "like" or acceptable to "us." Holinshed's chronicle history of Edward II, for example, displays sodomy, paradoxically, as an unspeakable sin and the sodomite as the progenitor of uncontainable corruption, even as he sits beside and on the throne. It is impossible, and finally unnecessary, to know how directly imperialist impulses affected domestic discourse. What is clear is that these kinds of representations, along with those that directly fostered the imperialist cause, contributed to a widespread ideological exploitation of the other, an exploitation crucial (though not limited) to the move toward empire.

The central thesis of this book is that Marlowe's plays, in bringing alien types to center stage, subversively resist that exploitation and expose the demonization of an other as a strategy for self-authorization and self-empowerment, whether on the foreign or the domestic front. To understand the historical and ideological import of his representations is vital to an understanding of the cultural and individual self-fashioning of the Renaissance. For the plays provide one of the most visible, most popular, and most radical voices of resistance to a dominant discursive trend, which was shaping ideas of self and state. As such, they underscore that trend, its impetus, and its widespread cultural currency, while reminding us that its constructs, however powerful and pervasive, were neither uncontested nor unconflicted.

Others, including Reginald Scot, whose controversial *Discoverie of witchcraft* insists that witches are made and not born, were also protesting against these coercive policies and practices. Yet the ruptures within the dominant discourse—the discrepancies between various articulations of a stereotype, for example, or moments when the "difference" of the other shows through as "same"—themselves undermine its terms. Marlowe exposes these ruptures and, in so doing, not only brings the voice of skepticism into a prominent position on center stage. He also dramatizes the means through which and the ends to which alien types and imperialist ideologies, and the self defined by both, were being fashioned. Thus, although this book focuses on Marlowe's plays, by rehistoricizing them in light of England's nascent imperialism it uncovers a larger cultural phenomenon and brings out its unquestionable importance as well as Marlowe's.

My approach has clearly been shaped by new historicist criticism, but in arguing that Marlowe's plays are finally subversive my book offers an important exception to the new historicist tendency, still being reiterated even as it is beginning to be challenged, to read subversive texts as inevitably playing into the coercive ideologies they seem to resist. I also have attempted to historicize the plays in a way that gives a "thicker description" of a complex cultural phenomenon. One of the most often voiced suspicions about new historicism is that it takes an anecdotal approach to history, strategically culling select bits and pieces from the past and reconstituting that past in ways that answer the critic's own politically charged agendas. Whether or not this charge is true, it usefully compels us—particularly as we attempt to situate texts within history—to scrutinize our choices, to justify what texts we are privileging as essential cultural documents and why. In selecting texts from Marlowe's discursive environment, I have chosen texts such as Hakluyt's *Principal Navigations* and Holinshed's *Chronicles* that, with their wide circulation and appeal, offered the most prominent visions of the alien. Importantly, too, their attempts to impose fixed terms of difference on some "other" and to enforce the supremacy of self, state, or status quo over and against that other are disrupted by the kinds of inconsistencies that are characteristically embedded in similarly coercive texts and that make their agendas and representational strategies clear. The conflicts within these representations reflect conflicts between various representations and within the vision of the alien which together they constitute. I have chosen also to contextualize Marlowe's plays in the extra-theatrical more than the theatrical environment, for it is their relation to the former that most clearly demonstrates the extent of their relevance and resistance to dominant cultural and cross-cultural politics and that, ironically, exposes the intense interconnectedness of theatrical and extra-theatrical discourse.

Finally, a word about the author. Perhaps more than any other Renaissance drama, Marlovian drama, in its remarkable uniformity, its singularity of vision and voice, and its unprecedented radicality, creates a sense of a single author, well in control of his texts. Ironically, even at the end of *Doctor Faustus*—after *The Massacre at Paris* the most unreliable text within the Marlovian canon—we are told that "the author ends the play" ("*terminat Author opus*"), and the statement prompts us to agree. Despite recent skepticism about the validity of assigning a text, and especially a play-text, to a single, identifiable author, I tend to believe that there was indeed an historical figure by the name of Christopher Marlowe, who wrote what we know as "Marlowe's" plays and whose alienated subject position, as a homosexual, a spy, and a playwright at the least, affected them.

Yet because of the uncertainties attached to such an assumption, because what we know of Marlowe comes only from "his" poems and plays and from a very limited collection of documents with their own highly charged agendas, and because the production of play-texts may have been more of a collaborative process than we generally acknowledge, the Marlowe we can speak of with most authority, and the one I speak of here (with the exception of some historical speculation in Chapter 1), is the one constructed by these texts. That Marlowe, too, is embedded in history and shaped by the peculiar pressures of the period—a figure demonized by precisely the kind of discourse he was writing against, deeply invested in writing subversively against it. In authorizing his voice and his authorial presence thus, the plays make the discursive exploitation of the "other" compellingly "real." And while we may question whether Christopher Marlowe wrote the plays, there is finally little room to question whether the emergence of imperialism and the discourse of alienation shaped them. It is that which this book hopes to prove.

Part I

Setting the Stage

1. Strange and Estranging Spectacles: Strategies of State and Stage

"But that was in another country."
(*The Jew of Malta* 4.1.43)

Imperialism, Stereotypes, and the State

To enter upon the Marlovian stage is to enter a landscape filled with strangers and strange lands. One after another of Christopher Marlowe's plays focuses on a character type alienated from or marginalized within English society, and several situate that figure within a foreign setting. Their central characters include a Scythian barbarian, a black magician, a Machiavellian Maltese Jew, a homosexual king, and an African queen; their landscapes range from Carthage, to Malta, Persia, Babylon, Egypt, and beyond. Even the European settings seem markedly unfamiliar: England becomes a locus of uncertain authority, ruled by a homosexual king (Edward II) and his favored "minions" and contested by haughty, overpowering, and questionably noble nobles; Paris, a site of riots, massacres, and murders, also ruled by a homosexual king (Henry III); and Germany, a place where felonious, and potentially damnable, conjurations are admired rather than abhorred, and where devils are likely to appear. The extravagant spectacles (which, on one occasion, allegedly scared spectators from the theater), the "great and thundering speech" (*Tamburlaine* 1.1.3) of Marlovian blank verse, as well perhaps as the vernacular itself, which Steven Mullaney has suggested as a "strange tongue," contributed also to the alterity of these alien worlds and figures.[1]

This preoccupation with the "other," coming as and when it does, is no accident. For Marlowe's representations respond to an increasingly dominant cultural obsession with foreign worlds and peoples, emerging with England's nascent imperialism. As society attempted to come to terms with competing cultures and to establish its place beside and above them, it produced a discourse of difference, a discourse that interrogated and enforced the crucial, self-affirming distinctions between self (Europe, England, "representative man," the status quo) and other (foreign cultures, nonconformists, alternative values). Marlowe participates in this self-scrutiny by producing his own "spectacle[s] of strangeness."[2] What makes his plays so remarkable, so subversive, and indeed, so important is that they combat his society's attempts to prove the alien inexorably alien and expose cultural stereotypes and discriminations as constructs, strategically deployed to authorize the self over and at the expense of some other.

While the Spanish and Portuguese began to develop a substantial trade network in non-European countries during the early sixteenth century without England's competitive intervention, the economic depression of the 1550s helped catalyze Elizabethan interest in the new goods, new markets, new jobs, and eventually new homes that such expansionism promised.[3] Though England had no explicit imperialist agenda, the midsixteenth century witnessed relentless searches for north–east and north–west passages to the East as well as for *Terra Australis*, development of trade with Russia, India, the East and Far East, and exploration and colonization of the recently discovered "New World." Figures such as Sir Francis Drake and Sir Walter Ralegh held prominent positions not only on the seas but also in the court, urging the nation forward, or rather outward, to the resources beyond.

Emerging with this impetus was an intensified desire for knowledge of unknown or partially known domains, a desire answered and evidenced by the energetic contemporary production of cross-cultural descriptions. Joannes Boemus's *Omnium gentium mores*, for example, which describes the "auncient maners, customes, and Lawes, of the peoples enhabiting the two partes of the earth, called Affricke and Asie," had circulated throughout Europe in several languages beginning in 1520 and continuing for almost a century after, and was translated into English in 1555 as *The Fardle of Facions*.[4] John Leo Africanus's "famous worke," *The Geographical Historie of Africa*, which details the "exceeding strange creatures" and "notable things" (customs, races and religions, natural resources and material wealth, geographies and histories) of Egypt and Africa, had been similarly disseminated across Europe and was popularized in England and in English by John Pory's 1600 translation.[5] Travel literature also became eminently popular, particularly under the aegis of Richard Hakluyt, whose "life, from 1552 to 1616, paralleled the rise of a larger England" and whose well-known collection of the "principal navigations" undertaken from the 1540s onward and covering a vast array of places—from Russia, to Africa, America, and the Caribbean—vigorously promoted that rise.[6] In addition to these textual collections, displays of foreign artifacts, and sometimes even people (Indians, Moors, and Turks), became fashionable during the mid-sixteenth to mid-seventeenth centuries, as England began to gather the "infinite riches" of the outside world into its own "little room."[7]

Yet as recent studies of colonialist discourse have suggested, the "knowledge" that Europe produced about other worlds, during the early modern period as through the colonialist and even post-colonialist eras, was far from neutral. Instead it was vitally connected with Europe's self-image and self-authorization especially, though not exclusively, as Europe began to move toward empire. Europe's growing expansionism at once required and threatened the crucial gap between self and other that could "justify" the domination of other worlds. Encounters with other cultures, though recorded at times along with longstanding myths about cannibals, "Anthropophagi, and men whose heads / [Do grow] beneath their shoulders" (*Othello* 1.3.143–44) and with "actual" scenes of marvels, unearthed foreign subjects with fairly normal appetites and anatomies, interested like their European "guests" in self-protection and profit.[8] However the levels of difference and similarity were actually experienced (something which is finally impossible to recuperate), cross-cultural discourse insisted repeatedly on difference.[9]

So too on the home front, within Europe and England, where the division between self and other was also in danger of breaking down. In England's case (which is what I am most concerned with here), the pressure to define and display a superior nation produced within domestic texts, such as the chronicled histories, a similar institution of difference, fostering the illusion of a state fully able to separate the "we" from the "they," to effectively identify, contain, and control transgression.[10]

In his seminal study, *Orientalism*, Edward Said introduced important ways in which European colonialist discourse produces its object as "other," creating through projection and negation an inferior and uncivilized "theirs" ripe for the domination of a superior, civilized and civilizing "ours."[11] For Said the other is not real but imaginary, mapped out more by ideology than by geography, though finally bounded as a real terrain by the imperialism promoted through that ideologic mapping.[12] Though eminently useful, Said's world picture is itself bounded by its own ideology, dividing its territory into West and East, self and other, and leaving out the complicating presence of the "third world" of Africa (as Christopher Miller has pointed out) and of a fourth, the "New World," neither of which can be accommodated within a self/other binarism.[13] Nor, as both Miller and Homi Bhabha have argued, does Said's model allow adequately for the ambivalences present in depictions not only of these other "other" worlds, but also of the Orient itself.[14] For though imperialist discourse masquerades as being monologic, stable, and sure, it is marked by significant contradictions.

This is nowhere clearer than in the case of cultural and cross-cultural stereotypes which were vital to early modern England's production of both self and other and to its early move toward empire. Behind each iteration of these constructs lies a will to knowledge and a will to power, a desire to bound off absolutely and so to exploit, dominate, or suppress an identifiable other. As Bhabha has argued, stereotypes produce a kind of "radical realism" and assert, through an excess of signification, a degree of probability and predictability beyond "what can be empirically proved or logically construed."[15] The stereotype seems to fix the other, to consolidate all we know about that other and all we need to know. Yet while these constructs take and give shape under the pretense of precision, fixity, and singularity, they are as polymorphic as they are perverse and contribute to a discursive field that is abstract, unstable, and conflicted.

Consider, for example, early modern conceptions of the Jew, who was sometimes a devil, sometimes (merely) an anti-Christian infidel, sometimes a cunning villain, sometimes a child-murderer, sometimes a usurer, sometimes some of the above, and sometimes none. Though Shylock and his prototype, Barabas, love their ducats at least as much as they do their daughters, Shakespeare's Jew is a usurer while Marlowe's is not. And while Barabas is all too ready to murder his daughter, along with anyone else who gets in his way, Shylock attempts murder only by law, according to a legitimate (though outrageous) contract. The Turk, too, came in various shapes and sizes, appearing as anything from an empire-mongering barbarian to a diabolical villain. On Marlowe's stage alone, Turks range from Ithamore, the Jew of Malta's base and scurrilous slave who has a "more the merrier" attitude toward murder, especially of Christians; to the imperious Calymath (of the same play), who would rather dominate Malta's Christians than kill them; to Tamburlaine's Bajazeth, who displays the villainous excesses of the one and the imperiousness of the other, and stands ever ready to "glut [his] swords" (3.3.164) and "let thousands die" (3.3.138) in the name of empire. To complicate the matter further, these stereotypes had to compete with more positive though less publicized images—of the Jew, for example, as a victim of the state, scapegoated in times of financial crisis, or of the Turk as a masterful leader, whose forces were significantly better organized and equipped than those of the English.[16]

While the stereotype is produced as if it were *the* definitive type, what is clear in representations of these and other others is that the difference they prescribe is as variable as it is familiar. For Bhabha these discrepancies expose a deep ambivalence embedded in colonialist discourse, predicated anxiously on desire as well as fear, defense as well as mastery. Along similar, though deconstructionist rather than psychoanalytic lines, Miller has argued that Europe's bifurcated vision of Africa expresses Europe's own conflicted attitude toward the other, the self, and the possibility of "maintaining an identity in discourse."[17]

These studies, in exposing the disturbances within colonialist representations, usefully complicate Europe's expression of itself and suppression of the other, pressing us beyond Said and the assumption that colonialist discourse is always hegemonically in charge of itself and taking account of psychological and linguistic uncertainties that insistently disrupt self/other binarisms and the stereotypes constructed around them. Yet while the discrepancies within circumscriptions of the other may in part evolve from these pressures, they also serve strategically to further the colonialist cause, to amplify the critical difference between "them" and "us."

For in the first place, because each iteration of a type stands in conflict with a field of others, it produces a figure who is ultimately unknowable. The "other" is pressed out of the grasp of knowledge precisely at the moment that he or (less often) she is given a fixed place within it. The problem is translated not as a gap in "our" perspective or perception but as an incriminating gap in "their" nature. While Shakespeare's Romans repeatedly typecast Cleopatra as a strumpet, Enobarbus offers a far more alluring vision of the erotic Egyptian queen floating upon the Nile on her barge. Yet though his depiction is rich with detail, Cleopatra gets lost amidst it, as an object beyond the forms of art and nature, creating an unfillable and unnatural "gap in nature" (*Antony and Cleopatra* 2.2.218).[18] Throughout as here, the more the characters talk about her, setting one image against another, the less definable she becomes, dangerously evading the Romans'/ "our" language and knowing, like the crocodile Antony describes that is "shap'd . . . like itself," "is as broad as it hath breadth" and so on (2.7.42–43). Though the play alerts us to the gaps within the discourse, it also contributes to them and puts Cleopatra beyond our grasp, a figure a little less than kin and more than kind, who is neither the strumpet Philo and Demetrius create nor the erotic goddess Enobarbus sees, but rather is as erratic as she is alluring.

Beyond unknowability, all that can be known for sure about the "other" points to where the self/other binarism leads: to the idea of the other as abstractly but unquestionably negative. Though stereotypes enlist a specificity that seems to ring "true," the inconsistencies between and within them leave us with only the broadest and most negative outline. In most cases, the only constant among the other's various guises is that he or she is in some way villainous or threatening at the least, whether because of greed, deception, excessive sexuality, murderous actions, or lack of faith (which means, in early modern discourse, Christian or Protestant faith). And it is that constant that prevails.

Indeed, it seems no coincidence that different alien types, such as the Moor and the Turk, the sodomite and the witch, are confused and conflated within early modern discourse, for their abstract negativity matters more than their specific dimensions. Othello, when calling up the ultimate image to condemn himself before his suicide, identifies himself not as a Moor but as a Turk, a "malignant and a turban'd Turk" who "beat a Venetian and traduc'd the state" (*Othello* 5.2.353–54) and whom Othello allegedly killed. In evoking the image, the Moor partially redeems himself, reminding his audiences that he has been a loyal defender of the Venetian state. At the same time, however, he underscores his otherness by "turning Turk" (something he fears), aligning himself with a figure who has been Venice's quintessential other, as if all others are interchangeable and interchangeably malign.

It is impossible to know finally how consciously stereotypes were set in conflict and articulated through incriminating abstraction. Yet the fact that it was happening in domestic as well as cross-cultural discourse, to figures such as the magician and the sodomite who were more familiar and more available for inspection and circumspection, suggests that the insistent obfuscation of the "other" was not just a product of distance. And while part of the confusion may have arisen from mixed feelings, it nonetheless supported the imperialist cause, exposing the possibility of "maintaining an identity"—an alien identity—"in discourse" through and not despite its indeterminacies. From a practical perspective alone, on the home front the vagueness about what constituted various transgressions not only did not impede prosecution; it also aided it. Because sodomy, for example, was cloaked in layers of abstraction and conflated with all sorts of other "crimes," the charge became a useful way of indicting social and political dissidents whose troubling offenses were less easy to criminalize. So, too, in the case of black magicians, who could be produced from radical intellectuals or religious dissenters on fairly specious grounds.

Critics have been hesitant to ascribe racism and homophobia to early modern culture, in large part because the idea of race and homosexuality seemed poorly formed at best.[19] Yet that poor formation enabled rather than hindered prejudicial ideologies. Racism, homophobia, xenophobia, and the like, though they did not yet have a local habitation or name, had their beginnings here, within cross-cultural and domestic discourses whose uncertainties amplified difference, allowing the self to impose its terms of supremacy on the world, over the alien abroad and the alien at home.

Marlowe, Stereotypes, and the Stage

It is from and against this hegemonic circumscription of unstable but nonetheless inalienable "alien" types that Christopher Marlowe writes. Before Marlowe brought his infamous array of aliens to center stage, the English theater was itself threatening to become a place where stereotypes were prominently fashioned and fixed. Early drama (still being performed in Marlowe's day) had built itself on Biblical typology in which the abstract, figural significance of characters mattered more than their specific material embodiments. Even as its characters were humanized with various degrees of local and comic color, that humanization itself served to fashion a type rather than an individual. In the mystery plays, Noah, for example, was given a vociferously unbelieving wife, who became a prototype of the shrew, and though the rash, outrageous Herods of the cycles invoked Mohammed's name and power, in their anti-Christian lust for murder and revenge, they provided material for the stock type of the Jew.[20] To bring such types into the mystery plays was to make divine "truths" familiar and accessible, but it was also to inscribe difference, to give the "other" a place which seemed as real as it was stable.

So too in the case of the moral plays, which gained prominence in the decades before Marlowe and which capitalized on "others" in order to enforce political "truths." In Thomas Preston's *Cambyses*, for example, the "wicked" king of Persia exemplified the Oriental barbarian; as David Bevington has argued, his contemptible excesses served to caution magistrates against tyranny and to school subjects in absolute obedience to their leaders, who presumably could never be as severe.[21] Yet the message was not only that "our" rulers should not and would not be so tyrannical, but that other/Eastern rulers, categorically, would.

It was not just for the purpose of morality but also for the purpose of profit that the alien found such an accommodating home in the theater. Because of its licensed social and geographic marginality, the theater was one of the few and most accessible arenas where a large portion of the populace could safely "see" the wonders of the world.[22] And because what they were looking for were "wonders," the more other the better. In bringing such figures as Cambyses, Muly Hamet, Tamburlaine, and Cleopatra to center stage, dramatists, including Marlowe, capitalized on public interest.[23] In so doing, they reenacted the imperialist appropriations happening around the world, turning difference into spectacle and spectacle into profit.

Marlowe himself was no stranger to spectacle, especially in *Doctor Faustus*, which performed conjurations that were otherwise outlawed and that were assigned "real" effects and "real" devils.[24] *Tamburlaine*, too, is centered on othering displays, not just of words but of excesses of wealth, bloodshed, torture, and death. Indeed, all of Marlowe's plays in some ways put strangeness audaciously before the spectators' eyes.

Yet while Marlowe himself exploited the cultural fascination produced and promoted along with imperialism, he did so in a way that challenged the idea of otherness and helped turn the theater into a place where hegemonic constructs were more often questioned than confirmed, more often subverted than supported. It seems no coincidence that after Marlowe the stock type begins to lose its prominence on the Renaissance stage, except perhaps in the case of women, which is also excepted in Marlowe (and to which I will return). After Barabas, the outrageous Herods of the mystery plays give way to Shylock who, in his controversial set piece (*The Merchant of Venice* 3.1.53–73) at the least, highlights the sameness of the Jew.[25] And though Shakespeare gives us Aaron, the diabolical Moor in *Titus Andronicus*, he later gives us Othello, a figure caught between a discourse on sexuality and a discourse on race and unable to contain or be contained by either. It is only in Jonson that the stock type prominently reclaims center stage, but then as an agent of satire and parody, whose self-conscious fictionality is clear.

Until recently, critics have read Marlowe's "spectacles of strangeness" symbolically, as part of a "sublime landscape of imaginative aspiration," as a sign of the seemingly infinite possibilities that the protagonists—whether successful or unsuccessful, transgressive or compliant, ironically misguided by the self or inevitably defeated by the world—are compelled, insistently and excessively, to master.[26] Yet the plays speak more immediately to an important cultural phenomenon that touched Marlowe himself. As a spy, possibly an associate of the freethinking School of Night (if it existed), probably a homosexual, and certainly a playwright, Marlowe was alienated within his society and demonized by accusations that are by now a well-known part of the Marlowe myth.[27] His fellow dramatist Robert Greene, for example, attacked him for "daring God out of heaven with that Atheist *Tamburlan*," and when Thomas Kyd, Marlowe's one-time roommate and colleague, was arrested for possessing heretical papers, he ascribed them to Marlowe, who was then summoned before the Privy Council and "commanded to give his daily attendance on their Lordships, until he shall be licensed to the contrary."[28] After his death, which followed ten days later and circumvented further indictment, the defamation seemed only to escalate: Kyd accused him of harboring "monstrous opinions," and the informant Richard Baines, in a "note" that was the most incriminating evidence against him, of blasphemy, sodomy, and so on.[29]

What is also an increasingly well-known part of the Marlowe story is that these allegations, in case after case, were self-serving and coercive, if not coerced. Kyd, for example, promoted his colleague's reputation of atheism to escape being indicted for such "vile opinion[s]" himself and had much to gain, theatrically speaking, in seeing this rival playwright put away. And not only was Baines known as "a troublesome, clamorous, and wilful vexer of divers her Majesty's subjects," in the habit of "bringing malicious suits 'to put the said defendants to great costs, wrong, and travail,'" his note, as David Riggs has argued, may have been coerced by the Privy Council who needed a scapegoat for sedition.[30] For Christian moralists, Marlowe's death provided an excellent example of the wages of sin. In the chapter "Of Epicures and Atheists" in the *Theatre of Gods Judgements* (1597), Thomas Beard argued that Marlowe fell because "hee denied God and his sonne Christ," and displayed him with the hope that "all Atheists in this realme, and in all the world beside, would by the remembrance and consideration of this example, . . . forsake their horrible impietie."[31] And the examples go on.

Jonathan Goldberg has suggested that in rebelling Marlowe came to fill the transgressive space that society had constructed for him.[32] What is most interesting about that space is that it, like that of stereotypes, was significantly open-ended, producing a rebel capable of a seemingly infinite array of subversive activities, social, sexual, political, and religious, and providing a living instance of the uses indeterminacy was being put to in the construction of the "other." The Baines note alone makes Marlowe guilty of being an atheist, a papist, a sodomite, an alchemist, and a tobacco addict. If Riggs is right, the Privy Council's real agenda was to blame someone for publicly (in the Dutch Church libel) threatening a massacre against resident foreigners. While the revolt, according to the libel, was to be carried out in *Tamburlaine* style, Marlowe's complicity with it was otherwise unsubstantiated.[33]

The Baines note, with its plethora of charges, provided the perfect remedy, building Marlowe into a figure of such proportions that his criminality, though in no way related to the alleged crime, could not be questioned. Gabriel Harvey, himself not inconsequentially a rival author, defamed Marlowe as a "hawty man" who feared neither God nor the devil and admired only "his wondrous selfe"; to amplify his otherwise specious attack on Marlowe's "toade Conceit," Harvey blurs impiety, if not atheism, into it, conflating and inflating its impact.[34] For decades, critics attempting to locate the "real" Marlowe, have piled charge on top of charge and have made him increasingly unknowable and increasingly other. They have, for example, aligned him with conspiratorial activities of various sorts, including those of the School of Night and of supporters of the Scottish James VI's claim to the English throne.[35] Though such charges were made to stand alone, together they expand Marlowe's subversiveness into uncertain but limitless proportions, making one thing perfectly clear: that Marlowe was outrageously other.

It is impossible to know, of course, how cognizant Marlowe was of his own demonization. That he may have cultivated his infamy is suggested by the "facts" that he (allegedly) voiced "monstrous opinions," kept himself in "the sinister company of men involved in spying or double dealing," and was entangled in at least four public instances of disorderly conduct—one resulting in a murder, another involving two constables, and the last, ending in his death.[36] His plays flagrantly make public spectacles of publicly unacceptable practices (atheism, conjuration, sodomy), successfully "daring" viewers and critics to recognize the transgressive nature of his subjects.[37] Yet however much he participated in the construction of his otherness, his plays suggest a keen awareness of and resistance to his society's manipulations of difference. Whether or not the plays protest against Marlowe's own personal exploitation within an increasingly discriminatory social nexus, as they turn to other worlds they turn against imperialism and expose rather than fulfill the cultural stereotypes enabling and enabled by imperialist endeavors.

Stephen Greenblatt was the first to rehistoricize Marlowe, to set "the acquisitive energies of English merchants, entrepreneurs, and adventurers" in the foreground of the plays and to link Marlowe's fascination with "the idea of the stranger in a strange land" with European imperialism.[38] For Greenblatt, Marlovian heroes share and reflect those energies as they attempt to map the bounds of their own existences, "to invent themselves" against a void of "neutral and unresponsive" space, and, through "a subversive identification with the alien," "to give life a shape and a certainty that it would otherwise lack."[39] As important and enabling, and as grounded in history, as this story of self-fashioning is, Greenblatt's argument moves away from the context of imperialism, suggesting that what the characters face and what the plays address is a sort of existential crisis, an awareness that identity is itself an invention, that we are all, in fact, homeless and alienated and must construct ourselves in order to exist.

While Marlowe's focus includes this identity crisis, it is directed more specifically toward an alienation being imposed from without rather than being experienced from within—an alienation keyed to the historical moment of England's emergent imperialism and given shape through cross-cultural and domestic stereotypes. What problematizes identity under these circumstances is not just that self-defining boundaries dissolve, but that alienating boundaries persist and are reinforced as relentlessly and authoritatively as self-constituting acts. What finally is most subversive here is not the characters' or the playwright's identification with *the alien*, but the insistence that such an identity does not, of itself, exist.

The Marlovian World Picture

Although Marlovian drama centers on a diverse array of landscapes and of heroes, with widely varying means and ends, it employs common patterns of representation that work to expose and resist the processes of discrimination. In play after play, Marlowe places the spectators in an uncomfortable position, intellectually and emotionally, and, by creating significant discrepancies between culturally inscribed meanings and the meanings applicable on the stage, demands that they suspend not only their disbelief but, more importantly, their expectations and biases. He familiarizes unfamiliar worlds and defamiliarizes familiar ones, situates his aliens within contexts in which their signal traits of difference are not different, and at once provokes and frustrates the spectators' attempts to distinguish the established "ours" from the threatening "theirs." In addition, he evokes emotional responses that are "strange" rather than "automatic" by encouraging audience sympathy, if not admiration, for heroes and spectacles which are socially or politically incorrect.[40]

While these manipulations problematize the process of discrimination, the plays also thematize it. In each case, Marlowe's representations of the alien are about the representation of the alien, and the arbitrary, uncertain, and strategic ways in which difference is constructed, deconstructed, and even reconstructed by the "other" as by those who share his or (in Dido's case) her stage in answer to their own self-empowering agendas. In producing a staged world where the meanings that give meaning to the extra-theatrical environment no longer apply and where discrimination itself is incriminated as a self-authorizing ploy, Marlowe sets culturally inscribed terms of difference in crisis and insists that they be questioned if not rejected, reassessed if not reformed.[41]

The representation of place is particularly important to this process and functions ideologically to unsettle spectator expectations, not only through its foreignness, but also through its familiarity. Our understanding of how precisely settings were set up on the Elizabethan stage is thwarted by the sparsity of performance records and artifacts. Some critics, such as A. M. Nagler, have argued for a "realistically" ornamented setting with painted, illusionistic backdrops; others, such as Alan Dessen, for the openness, flexibility, and neutrality of the staged space; and others, such as Michael Hattaway, for a middle ground of scenic illusion created metonymically by portable and nonportable properties.[42]

Yet regardless of how elaborately or sparsely, metonymically or illusionistically, specifically or neutrally settings were signified by scenery and props, the idea of place was largely symbolic.[43] To create a setting was to establish a nexus of nonspatial conditions and preconditions beyond those that could be actually accommodated on stage—to signal time and temporal shifts, historical contexts, general cultural or situational characteristics (a "tavern world" metonymically represented by a tavern, perhaps also represented metonymically by a table and a mug), ideological divisions between peoples and worlds (Capulets versus Montagues, Rome versus Egypt), metaphysical or psychological situations (the alienation of Edward II in prison or of Lear on the heath), and so on.

For Marlowe, the choice of settings from Africa to the Mediterranean to the East turns our attention to the key sites of England's imperialist exploits and so to the issue of imperialism. On a more symbolic level, however, his representation of those settings breaks down the barriers of difference, showing that the worlds out there are not so different from Europe. Greenblatt has argued that in *Tamburlaine* "all . . . spaces seem curiously alike" and that on the Marlovian stage generally "space is trans-formed into an abstraction" that signals its "essential meaninglessness"; although characters attempt to impose shape and significance on it, this backdrop remains "neutral and unresponsive," exposing the vacancy of self that they struggle to overcome.[44] Marlovian space is, in some ways, shape-less, but the lack of differentiation between its worlds functions on a less abstract level to suggest the meaninglessness not of space but of the bounds imposed upon it. The point is not that space is meaningless, but that the differences assigned to it are empty, overdetermined, or arbitrary, at best.

In the decades before Marlowe, the Elizabethan stage witnessed an outbreak of "tyrant plays" such as *Damon and Pythias* and *Cambyses*, which, though they provide a "mirror for magistrates" and their subjects, emphasize and exploit the foreignness of their settings.[45] Other worlds provided a place where tyranny, in particular, could be dramatized in all its excesses and the message of obedience pressed to an extreme. In *Damon and Pythias*, for example, the prologue announces that the unfolding events—the tyrant Dionysius's "cruel" demand for Damon's death, Py-thias's offer to die in his stead, and Dionysius's final reformation, brought about by this extraordinary act of friendship—happened at the Syracusan court, and that "we mean no court but that" (Prologue 40).[46] We are repeatedly reminded that this saga is a "thing most strange" (Prologue 36) in a most "strange" world. By insisting on its otherness, the play brings its lesson home, suggesting that since the oppression at home is much less, the loyalty should be much more.

What makes Marlowe's plays stand out within this context is that their foreign worlds are not only "Englished"; they make a point of that Englishing. *Dido, Queen of Carthage*, for example, announces the resem-blance between its African landscape and England: Iarbas, in a complaint to Jove, makes "all the woods Eliza to resound" (4.2.10)—a phrase that Edmund Spenser will canonize as part of the English literary tradition—bringing out an embedded parallel between Carthage's queen (whose Phoenician name was "Elissa") and England's. That he is an African king complaining to a pagan god and invoking a name that is otherwise suppressed emphasizes the incongruity, as ours and theirs suggestively collide in a space that excludes neither.

Though exotic beings would be expected to appear more readily in Africa than in Europe or even the East, they do not, and the play makes a point of that fact. When Aeneas first steps foot on the Carthaginian shore, his immediate concern is "whether men or beasts inhabit" here (1.1.177). When Venus greets him shortly after, dressed as a Tyrian huntress in "bow and quiver," ready to "overtake the tusked boar in chase," and looking for her "sisters" "clothed in spotted leopard's skin," she evokes the Amazons who figured as "exotic curios" in descriptions of Africa (1.1.184–208).[47] The potential exoticism of the scene is undermined as quickly as it is suggested, however, by the fact that this is only a "borrow'd shape" (1.1.192) transparent to the staged and unstaged audiences. Aeneas, who soon recognizes her, avows that he "neither saw nor heard of any such" (1.1.187), and for the rest of the play neither do the spectators, who are thus alerted to its lack.

The ordinary texture of this and other of Marlowe's other worlds becomes particularly clear in contrast to that of the exotic landscapes within Spenser's *Faerie Queene*, the first three books of which emerged during Marlowe's lifetime.[48] Although part of that difference is necessarily dictated by the constraints of performance and fostered by the license of allegory, the comparison nonetheless reminds us that the playwright's strange lands exclude the monsters and marvels, the giants and dragons and metamorphosed beings, available for the imaginative refashioning of the self.

Reciprocally, Marlowe's European worlds are notably defamiliarized. *Faustus*'s Germany contains not only devils but also a dragons, included on the 1598 property list of the Admiral's Men and possibly brought onstage (or suspended above it) to show Faustus "whirling round" the universe in a "chariot burning bright, / Drawn by the strength of yoked dragons' necks" (3 Prologue 11, 5–6).[49] The exceedingly rapid tempo of *The Massacre at Paris*, with one act of violence following immediately and surprisingly upon another, though perhaps an aberration of the text, creates a sort of Monty Python world picture. And, as I have suggested above, the presence of a homosexual king on the French throne, as on the English throne of *Edward II*, also distances these kingdoms from Elizabethan (though, of course, not Jacobean) England.

Critics have often distinguished *Edward II* (sometimes along with *The Massacre at Paris*, which is more often ignored) from Marlowe's other plays in part because of its English setting and the historical base, which also lends familiarity; in Edward II's England, characters and issues seem "the most naturally human," or, what has been taken as the equivalent, the most "Shakespearean."[50] The "other" worlds, in contrast, are viewed as decidedly other—as, for example, escapist terrains where spectators need not confront otherwise inescapable fears, issues, or selves, at least not at close range.[51] This division resurrects bounds that the plays themselves resist. Indeed the English king Edward has a prototype in Persia, in the figure of Mycetes, who, like Edward, loves his minions. What characterizes Marlovian landscapes is not a one-dimensional cultivation of strangeness or familiarity but an insistent incorporation of the strange within the familiar—an incorporation that proves geographic bounds arbitrary measures of difference and insists that the spectators suspend categorical assumptions about what is ours and what, theirs.

"Which is the merchant here? And which the Jew?"

This suspension is demanded even more forcefully by the representation of character, for Marlowe evokes cultural stereotypes only to set them in contexts that defy the uniqueness of those types. Significantly, each of the plays initially situates its alien figure in a space of difference.

In *Tamburlaine, Doctor Faustus*, and *The Jew of Malta*, the heroes are introduced in all their otherness in the separate and potentially authoritative space of the prologue. Before we see Tamburlaine, we are warned that the "Scythian" will "threaten the world with high astounding terms, / And scourg[e] kingdoms with his conquering sword" (Prologue 4–6). When he appears, he exoticizes himself, throwing off his shepherd's "weeds" to uncover a "cotte with coperlace" and "breches of crymson velvet" beneath and announcing his intention to "be a terror to the world" (1.2.38,41).[52] The Jew of Malta is introduced by Machevill, who unabashedly offers a catalog of his own subversive policies and blasphemous beliefs, and then surreptitiously begs the spectators not to "entertain" Barabas "the worse / Because he favours me" (Prologue 34–35). Though Machevill proves an unreliable narrator (as I argue below), his prologue nonetheless sets the Jew in a space of otherness, and when Barabas is then discovered in a long nose and possibly a red wig and beard (which, after him, became the stock costume of the stage Jew), fondling his "heaps of gold" (stage direction) and declaiming against Christians, that impression is more than reinforced. And while Gaveston gets no prologue, he, in effect, creates his own as he stands on the outskirts of court, anticipating the homo-erotic pageants he will use to entertain his "dearest friend," the king (*Edward II* 1.1.2).

Yet while the plays consciously emphasize these characters' distinguishing types, they place them in contexts in which they are more like than unlike those who share their stage. The fact that *Edward II* offers two "others" (Gaveston and Edward) is only the beginning. Everyone in Carthage seems to be a stranger in one sense or another—from Aeneas who explicitly defines himself as such, to Dido, an exile from Tyre, to Iarbas, the African king. Tamburlaine, the barbarian, is surrounded by barbarians whose desires to rule the universe seem no more moderate than his; and his episodic and incessant engagement in battles creates a sense that there will always be one more conqueror, like one more country, to conquer. Faustus is alone as he makes his choice to study magic, but he is soon joined and tutored by the infamous black magicians, Valdes and Cornelius, and parodied by the unlearned Robin, who uses one of his "conjuring books" to produce "a roaring piece of work" (2.2.2, 11–12). And while Barabas may be the only prominent Jew in Malta, the island is peopled with Machiavels, Christians as well as Turks among them, whose desires for money and property are no less pronounced and whose strategies for procuring them, no less devious, than his.

On the Marlovian stage, where stereotypical traits of difference are marks of sameness, alien status cannot be categorically assigned. For, to borrow Christopher Miller's words, "a state where everything is other is a state where the word 'other' has lost its oppositional power and no longer means anything."[53] The comic elements mixed into Marlowe's tragedies keep them from generating the same darkness that is found on the Jacobean stage, but the pervasive corruption that defines the societies in the plays of John Webster, Cyril Tourneur, John Ford, and the like and that destabilizes the division between right and wrong has its antecedent in Marlowe.[54] Instead of showing us how the "other" half lives, murders, and deceives, Marlowe and his Jacobean predecessors situate the other as the status quo and, without necessarily valorizing or condemning subversive standards, make them the norm against which other values and behaviors must be measured.

While disallowing automatic discriminations thus, Marlowe's plays also set up oppositions that at once prompt the viewers to discriminate and prohibit them from doing so. Each play centers on a confrontation between the alien and some other(s) who are not alien-identified, setting up what seems a "conflictual, hierarchically structured field" but, significantly, without privileging either term.[55] Marlowe refuses to fault Aeneas, as does Dido, for deserting her in her love, or Dido, as do the Trojans, for detaining Aeneas from his duty; to damn Faustus for transgression, as do the devils, or laud his conjurations, as do the heads of state; to deride Edward as weak or tyrannical, as do the nobles, or exonerate him, as does his son. The point is not merely that the plays are ambivalent toward their alien "heroes" but that they make a point of that ambivalence and expose the indeterminacy, relativity, and subjectivity of judgments which do not.

Tamburlaine provides one of the clearest examples of this strategy, for as it shifts from country to country, conflict to conflict, barbarian to barbarian, it makes it clear that in the world of empire, one ruler's establishment is another ruler's other. Part 1 introduces Persia as "the establishment," with Mycetes on its throne and Tamburlaine, the "incivil" (1.1.40) outsider, threatening its borders. Yet it is the king's brother, Cosroe, who first usurps the throne, and when Tamburlaine then conquers him, it is unclear which side we should support, the "sturdy Scythian thief" (1.1.36) or the original traitor. Before we have time to decide, the focus shifts from Persia to the further reaches and rulers of the East, where it is as hard to choose sides as to map them. Though Tamburlaine defeats the imperializing Turkish emperor, Bajazeth, for example, he himself has his eye not only on Persia, Africa, and endless other worlds, but also on "all the ocean by the British shore" (3.3.259), leaving us unsure whether to cheer or regret the victory.

So, too, in *The Jew of Malta*, whose shifting oppositions similarly problematize our allegiance to any one side. The Christian governor, Ferneze, first joins with the Turks, then turns against them; first disenfranchises the Jew, then joins with him, then deceives and destroys him. The Jew first embraces then betrays the Turks, and first betrays and then embraces the Christians, making it as difficult for us to see the sides as to choose between them. Though the oppositions are more stable in *Edward II*, the idea of right is not. The primacy of a legitimate but homosexual monarch is set in competition with that of an established but seditious baronage, and though, in the end, the power of the monarchy is restored, the issue of which faction was at fault for the intervening chaos is never resolved. Once again, as the scene moves from one side and one set of protests and allegations to the other, we are made aware that "contraries" can both be true, even if both cannot be right.[56]

Marlowe complicates this situation further by encouraging transgressive responses that implicate the audience as disturbingly complicitous, whether intentionally or not, in the "unlawful things" enacted onstage, placing the spectators in a compromised position between cultural standards that condemn and responses that condone. The final Chorus of *Faustus* cautions us not to practice but "only to wonder at unlawful things" (Epilogue 6) and suggests our voyeurism is innocuous if not innocent. Yet its warning encourages and even condones a vicarious participation in those things that is neither entirely innocuous nor entirely innocent.[57] Like the German emperor who asks Faustus to conjure spirits, we, too, beg for a show to "wonder at," the more spectacular (even, or especially, if illegal) the better.

Significantly, Marlowe's heroes dominate the staged stage, directing the action, producing the spectacles, claiming the spectacular speeches, and monopolizing everyone's attention. And while their illicit activities "should" invoke our disapproval, their control over the production makes our enjoyment dependent upon them and their exploits, however subversive, illegal, or ungodly.[58] We need Barabas to poison a convent full of nuns or to trick one friar into "killing" the dead body of another for our amusement, even though it aligns us with the fiendish Ithamore, who also delights in (and worships his master's nose for) excessive villainies. And, though an indignity to the idea of monarchy, we need Tamburlaine to bridle captive kings for his chariot and our astonishment.

When these heroes die, we are encouraged to feel sympathy rather than triumph or relief. In representing Edward II's death, for example, Marlowe turns the king into victim by detailing the torture and torment orchestrated by his captors, culling details from an additional source, Stow's chronicles, in order to do so. We might respond to the deaths of Barabas and Tamburlaine with some relief, because, unlike Faustus and Edward who are progressively disempowered and who finally express regrets, Barabas and Tamburlaine continue almost mechanically to deceive and destroy until the last possible moment. The characters who survive, however, promise to give us more of the same treachery or terrorism, but without the same attracting theatricality. Though Ferneze may steal Barabas's final plot and trap him in the cauldron constructed for the Turks, he can never be as cunning, elusive, or intriguing as the Jew.

While our sympathies are drawn toward figures we should love to hate, they are also turned from those figures' victims, particularly in *The Jew of Malta* and *Faustus* where tragedy is heavily mixed with comedy.

Barabas's most egregious crime is the poisoning of his daughter, Abigail, a crime that plays into the belief that Jews ritualistically murdered children. Yet the fact that she is killed along with a convent full of nuns, and almost (if Ithamore had his way) a monastery full of monks, turns the tragedy into farce, our sympathy into laughter. The thinness of her characterization, like that of the friars, Don Lodowick, and Don Mathias, and the cultivated scurrility of Pilia-Borza, Bellamira, and Ithamore, all murdered by the Jew, create a distance between their interests and ours, their victimization and our sympathy. This same distance also emerges in *Faustus*, for the only victims of Faustus's magic (besides Faustus himself) are the comic figures such as the pope and the horse-courser, who seem to get what they deserve. Marlowe's plays do foster an estrangement, not between their exotic worlds and England, but rather, and more subversively, between the viewers and their world, pressing them to question established categories of meaning, to suspend their biases, and to see the other as part of the self, the merchant as the Jew.

The Subject of Alienation

Marlowe's plays not only frustrate discrimination; they also thematize it. The Marlovian world picture is "spectacular" in a literal sense: its spectacles provide a means not just of displaying strangeness, but of exhibiting the ways in which the "strange" is displayed. Though Marlowe refuses to support prefabricated discriminations, the secondary characters do not, and it is amid their conflicting constructions of self and other that the primary characters must negotiate an identity. Our attention is turned, as Greenblatt has suggested, to their self-fashioning, but it is self-fashioning with a difference. Instead of acting against a "neutral and unresponsive" void, each of Marlowe's heroes is surrounded by characters who are constructing themselves against him or her and whose representations the hero constructs himself or herself against.

The singular prominence that the central characters claim within these texts has prompted critics to give them comparable priority within interpretations, to focus on the outstanding aspects that set them apart from or within the staged environment: their hyperbolic language, ambitions, or histrionics, their obsessive desires to transgress or transcend, their repeated attempts to define themselves or a place for themselves in their own self-aggrandizing, though ultimately self-abnegating, terms, and so on.

While such readings do, to some extent, take into account the dramatic transactions between the primary and secondary characters, the dominance that they give, almost automatically, to the hero tends to reduce the importance of the surrounding society.

Yet it is not only the viewers and critics offstage but also the spectators onstage who are preoccupied with the hero, and it is their preoccupation, in addition to and in competition with his or her self-representation, that not only directs our gaze but emerges as the object of it. What emerges under the gaze is the fact that the sometimes aggrandizing and sometimes demonizing discriminations that these characters impose upon the alien are constructed in answer to their own agendas. When Tamburlaine is not exhibiting his "working words" or "sights of power," other characters are commenting on those exhibitions, valorizing them (and him) if they want to join with him and demonizing them (and him) if they want to defeat him. Barabas, too, is surrounded by discourses which attempt to define him as "the Jew" and so to appropriate his money, his daughter, or his schemes. In *Faustus*, when morality figures are not appearing out of nowhere to label the "good or bad" of Faustus's fortunes, rulers, devils, and scholars are. And even though sodomy was an unspeakable sin, Edward II's barons find a way to speak it, to defame the king and his "minions," and so to justify civil war.

Ironically, what the texts (and the wide discrepancies between interpretations of them) make most clear about the heroes is that their underlying motives are ultimately unknowable, even as they articulate and act upon specific desires (Barabas for money, Faustus for magic, Edward II for "minions," and so on) in ways that suggest a uniformity of mind or purpose. Although their professed preoccupations with a certain object initially define their actions, neither their words nor their deeds remain centered on that goal. Instead they "swell beyond" it, as Michael Goldman has argued—not necessarily or exclusively toward "the possibility of entire bliss" as he posits, but rather toward some more elusive end.[59] Barabas seems intent on gathering infinite riches into his little room; yet as he gains more wealth and power than the governor and directs his revenge against allies and enemies alike, he makes us unsure when (or whether) enough will be enough and what is "enough" for him. Edward declares that he will "either die, or live with Gaveston" (*Edward II* 1.1.138), but his quick embrace of the Younger Spenser, coming even before there could be any funeral baked meats for Gaveston, alters our impression of what Edward is and has been after. Tamburlaine is perhaps the most single-minded of the lot, but his thoughts, too, turn from conquering kingdoms to "entertain[ing] divine Zenocrate" (*Tamburlaine* 2:2.4.17) to acting as the scourge of God or terror of the world.

In making his aliens so elusive, Marlowe runs the risk of reinforcing the unknowability that stereotypes themselves produce beneath the guise of absolute knowability. Yet Marlowe uses that unknown as a way of highlighting the instability of the "knowledge" imposed upon it, exposing the discrepancies between and within the terms the secondary characters use to fix the hero's difference, to produce a self-affirming other. In setting the elusiveness of the aliens in conflict with those terms, Marlowe insists upon uncertainty where competing characters write certainty, gaps where they write knowledge.

It is within this context of conflicting discourses that Marlowe's aliens emerge, and from it that they must (and do) distinguish themselves, that they must, that is, create their own terms of difference and identity. In each case, they exploit the terms imposed upon them and use difference as a means to power. Though they, like Marlowe himself, are made to fill the space of subversion that their societies open for them, they also reconstruct that space and, by playing into and against expectations, turn those constructs against themselves. The crucial question to be asked of Marlowe's aliens is not whether they are "good or bad," but how they and others fashion themselves as such, and to what ends. And it is that question that the following chapters will explore.

Neither my study nor Marlowe's plays attempt to recuperate the "subaltern" voice; instead their focus is on the means of appropriation that silence and occlude that voice, creating in its stead an other who speaks of and for Europe.[60] Though such a project can only tell half the story, that half is vital to our understanding of the cultural and cross-cultural transactions that defined the early modern state.

I have divided the plays into two groups: the "imperialist" plays (*Dido, Tamburlaine, Parts 1 and 2,* and *The Jew of Malta*) that deal with non-European subjects and imperialist domination; and the "domestic" plays (*Faustus* and *Edward II*) that deal with European subjects and internal alienation.[61] While this division risks establishing the kinds of categories that the plays themselves undermine, it also highlights what is crucial to them: that discrimination extends across cultural boundaries. In establishing my own boundaries, I mean only to show that in Marlowe both Europeans and non-Europeans figure as the subjects and objects of alienation. In taking on both, Marlovian drama reinforces what each play affirms individually: that what is out there and what is here are not so different after all, despite the plethora of contemporary representations invested in proving the contrary.

Alienated Subjects

Before examining how Marlovian drama works to undermine cultural biases, however, it is necessary first to acknowledge that in some cases these strategies break down and encourage rather than refute such biases, however consciously or unconsciously. For indeed, while in the abstract and for the most part the plays unfix prescribed bounds of difference, in certain instances they do not. Though the problem may derive in part from hazards inherent in their methodologies, it also suggests that Marlowe, despite the radicality of his position, was nonetheless conditioned by his era and partially subject to the prejudicial tendencies he was otherwise subverting. These inconsistencies do not ultimately disrupt the subversive ideology of his plays, but they do show how powerful and coercive were the forces he was resisting and how necessary and remarkable that resistance was.

Methodologically, in producing strange spectacles to show how spectacles were produced to estrange, the plays run the risk of seeming to present the strange for strangeness's sake, despite their familiarizing strategies, and of distracting attention from their ideological purposes. Ithamore's outrageous representations of the Jew, for example, turn our attention from the fact that he manipulates stereotypes to the comic terms in which he does so, as he turns Barabas into a "strange thing" (*The Jew of Malta* 4.4.82), worships his nose, and the like. Despite itself, the play seems to have been highly influential in ensuring that the stage Jew remain a physically and ideologically marked type. Too, the Dutch Church libel's author evoked *Tamburlaine* (along with *The Massacre at Paris*) in order to incite seditious riot, but that riot was itself aimed against foreigners. Thus, while Marlowe seems to have been a code word for subversion, the subversiveness of his representations of foreigners seems, in this instance, to have been radically misread.

The counterproductive afterlife of the plays does not necessarily reflect ideological inconsistencies within them. Their internal typecasting of secondary figures, however, does. Although the Turkish Calymath is not markedly different from the other leaders contending for Maltese rule,

Ithamore fulfills the stereotype of the Turk as an uncivilized, anti-Christian villain, particularly when he boasts of "setting Christian villages on fire," cutting throats, and crippling Christians (*The Jew of Malta* 2.3.208–17). The caricatured characterizations of Pilia-Borza and Bellamira, similarly, reinforce the basest conceptions of Italians, just as those of *Faustus*'s very worldly pope and his impotent friars and *The Massacre at Paris*'s militantly anti-Protestant Duke of Guise do of Catholics.

More problematic are Marlowe's representations of women, not because they are one-dimensional and wooden (as critics have often concluded) but because they are two-dimensional and contradictory, because they reinscribe a difference that they simultaneously resist. As Simon Shepherd's brief though provocative treatment of Marlovian women suggests, Marlowe shows, rather than merely allows, male control over the staged space and over the definition and agency of the women who share that space. His plays demonstrate how "the ideology of what women should be . . . originates in the man" and how women are fetishized beneath the male gaze.[62] Yet Marlowe also participates in that subjugation and objectification. Although Dido uses and exposes the fetishization of objects as a mode of self-empowerment, her erotic self-presentation makes her an object of desire. In *Faustus* and *Tamburlaine*, too, Marlowe represents Helen and Zenocrate as objects fetishized by male characters and in so doing fetishizes them himself, so effectively, in fact, that "the face that launch'd a thousand ships" (*Faustus* 5.1.92) has become its own suggestive icon, quite detached from Helen, Faustus, or the play.[63]

Even as Marlowe exposes male dominance as male dominance, he presents women who, despite initial acts of resistance, are willingly complicitous in enforcing its terms, and who are unaware of or indifferent to the limitations that we see in their circumscribed situations. Although Zenocrate first resists her captivity at the hands of Tamburlaine, after her "offensive rape" she is ready (with Desdemona-like devotion) to "live and die with [him]," "as his exceeding favours have deserv'd" (*Tamburlaine* 3.2.6, 24, 10). She is not the only one taken in by the conqueror's "working words" and deeds; yet, unlike his male competitors and like other Marlovian women, she follows the leader's lead without a competing agenda, and at the expense of self, home, and heritage. When Tamburlaine threatens to attack Egypt, she begs him to "have some pity" for her father, her country, and her "sake" (4.2.123), but she remains beside him even when he refuses. In Part 2, as she offers herself up to her sons as what they should "resemble" "in death" (2:2.4.75) and presents their father as what they should emulate in their lives, she embraces the position that Marlowe and Tamburlaine script for her—as an image that gives life and meaning solely to the world of men.

The Jew of Malta's Abigail eventually rebels against her father, but she escapes to a nunnery (which figures as unfavorably in Marlowe as it does in Shakespeare), to a new position of subjugation beneath those who, if the friars are right, are as corrupt as her father, though in a different (sexual) way. Despite her claims that she can "see the difference of things" (3.3.68) from that position, she becomes a figure of difference, opting for a circumscribed identity and embracing a religion as other to her as to the audience. After her death, as Barabas continues to murder and deceive, she gets lost in the shuffle as little more than "the rich Jew's daughter" (1.2.378), appropriated for his plots and Marlowe's.

While the limitations Marlowe imposes on his Catholic, underclass, and female characters stand at odds with his otherwise liberating agenda, they do not finally disrupt it. Rather, they set off by contrast those instances in which prejudicial expectations are defied. Importantly too, they caution us to recognize that though Marlowe's politics were to some degree ahead of his time, they were also constrained by it. Though the plays stand in radical opposition to dominating discourses, they are also inevitably subject to those constraints. It is Marlovian drama's liminal position between the inside and the outside that finally makes its subversive vision so disturbing, convincing, and compelling.

Part II

The Alien Abroad

2. Reproducing Africa: *Dido, Queen of Carthage* and Colonialist Discourse

"For we are strangers on this shore,
And scarely know within what clime we are."
(2.1.43)

Out of Africa

From the start of his dramatic career, Marlowe looks to other worlds for his subjects and organizes his plots around cross-cultural encounters. In his first play, *Dido, Queen of Carthage*, probably written during his Cambridge years (1585–86), the schema is simple and the event all too relevant for an emergent imperialist state: a representative "European" hero, Aeneas, lands in Carthage, an ancient city in Africa, on his way to found a New Troy and a new Trojan race (which the Elizabethans claimed as their own).[1] His mission is complicated by the desires and demands of Dido, the erotic African queen, which threaten to distract him from his duty. Yet their mythic romance, often depoliticized and scripted as a story of desire, on Marlowe's stage is not simply a conflict of love versus duty; it is also, more importantly, a conflict of cultures and colonizing powers. And what is at stake is not just Aeneas's mission, but Dido's.

In bringing the two together onto center stage, Marlowe makes clear what colonialist narratives habitually occlude: that cross-cultural encounters are two-sided at the least.[2] Instead of telling Aeneas's story solely from a Trojan/European point of view, he sets it in dialogue with another voice, Dido's, similarly atuned to domination and similarly invested in power. Though *Dido* is organized around a binary opposition between self and other of the sort that imperialist discourse was made on, Marlowe takes these terms out of hierarchy and gives them a competitive equivalence. And while Africa does not and cannot speak through Marlowe's text, the play nonetheless opens a place for that speech, presenting the cross-cultural encounter not as a monologic domination of colonizer over a silent and submissive colonized, but as a dialogic competition between two colonizing authorities, each attempting to interpret the event in his or her own terms and to his or her own ends.[3]

This is clearly not the case in the representations of Africa that were most popular and most widely circulated during the early modern period. For in instance after instance, as the "dark continent" was brought into the light before European eyes, the perspective was always singular and singularly that of Europe. The occlusion of the native voice has been well documented in the case of New World discourse, most recently in the work of Peter Hulme, Tzvetan Todorov, and Stephen Greenblatt.[4] What we find again and again, especially, though not exclusively, in travel narratives, is that the possibility of "any transgression on the part of the colonial power" is systematically suppressed and with it, the claims of the native people to their land, goods, selves, and subjectivities.[5] Native resistance is insistently transcribed as hostile, erratic, and irrational, and European aggression warranted.

It is so, too, in the case of Africa, particularly in Richard Hakluyt's widely circulated *Principal Navigations* (1589) and particularly as suppositions or details that might help justify "unfriendly" native behavior are strategically deleted or delayed.[6] Hakluyt's narrators boast repeatedly of the good profits that the English made from merchandise not worth the price, either because of its small quantity or poor quality, but neither acknowledge such profiteering as exploitation nor explain the natives' resistance as an awareness of or a reaction against unfair trade. To the contrary, any lack of cooperation on their part is translated as somehow deceitful or dishonest. In one instance, Africans who refused to bargain for cloth that was admittedly "ill" and "rotten" are criticized in lieu of the English, who intended to remarket it subsequently at a place "better for sale" (p. 199). Another tribe comes under fire for allowing the English a "reasonable good reckoning" one day but "esteem[ing]" their goods "lightly" on the next and offering only small dishfuls of grain, "whereas before wee had baskets full," with the African "Captaine" taking the blame for being "subtile" (pp. 184–85).

In the case of outright aggression, all provocation on the part of the Europeans, when suggested, is underplayed. One account characterizes a certain group of Africans by the "great daggers, some of them as long as a woodknife, which be on both sides exceeding sharpe, and bended after the maner of Turkie blades" that most of them were wearing (p. 197). Yet the narrator, William Towerson, makes no connection between that characteristic and the fact (which he reports with matter-of-fact nonchalance) that the Portuguese had previously taken a man from them, shot at them, and destroyed all their boats and half their town. Similarly, in a subsequent description of a native attack, it is only after detailing the Africans' aggression and creating an indelible impression of their volatility that Towerson gives all the facts: that the English in the previous year had taken "their golde, and all that they had about them," including four men, one of whom was the "Captaines" son (p. 207).

What distinguishes Europe's vision of Africa from its vision of the New World is that while the latter is inscribed primarily as a "discourse of savagery," as Hulme has suggested, the former, as Miller has argued, is bivalent in extremes, including the civil with the savage in one bifurcated whole.[7] Set beside the irrational "savages," who come equipped with "Turkie blades" and volatile aggression, are Moors, who often have impressive names and titles, live in well-appointed courts, write diplomatic letters to the queen, and enjoy entertainments that sometimes include English dogs and English music.[8] From the darkest depths of the "dark continent," figures such as the mythical emperor Prester John emerge to create exemplary Christian colonies, filling the terrain with "priests," "Archebishoppes," and "temples & churches" which are "muche larger, much richer, and more gorgeous then ours."[9] And it is here that we find Dido, allegedly ruling over one of the most prosperous and renowned seats of civilization in the ancient world.

Yet however much this double vision may have been predicated on Europe's own conflicted attitude toward Africa, it finally works to amplify Africa's otherness, to obscure and erase the validity of its voice. For the discovery of both positive and negative extremes within this other world serves not to neutralize the negative but to destabilize the positive, to suggest that at any moment the civil might devolve into the savage, its darker and truer underside. In the popular *Fardle of Facions* (1555), for example, Boemus (who, admittedly, had never been to Africa) offers his book as a compendium of diverse laws and customs, exposing

> the lewde, as well as the vertuous indifferentlie, that using them as present examples, and paternes of life, [the reader] maiest with all thine endevour folowe the vertuous and godlie, & with asmuche warenes eschewe the vicious & ungodly.[10]

Though the text masquerades to some degree as ethnography, at its center is really a narrative of transformation, a story of how a wild and bestial people, "monstrous" in "phisonomy and shape" and cut off from "the knowledge of the true God and all godlie worship," were miraculously reformed by Christianity. Its primary object is to show "how men have in these daies amended the rude simplicitie of the first worlde." Yet that object is gained at the expense of difference: the Africans, though miraculously convertible, are essentially beings of that "first worlde" and embody all that we should "eschewe"—"rude simplicity," monstrosity, "the vicious and ungodly." It is not they but "our" own civilizing efforts that stand forth for emulation.[11]

In Hakluyt, too, though for a more economically motivated end, is Africa's civility distinguished from and blurred into its savagery and the hint of competing and competitive claims obscured if not erased. As a whole the accounts center primarily on and, despite their different narrators, inscribe a consistent difference between two native groups, the Negroes and the Moors, placing them at opposite ends of a spectrum of civility—the Negroes at the lowest, the Moors at the highest. While Negroes, nameless and primitive, pop out of the darkened landscape in loincloths, fierce weapons, and body paint mostly to sabotage trade transactions with unpredictable and inexplicable acts of hostility and violence, Moors, named, titled, and seated in their "courts," act as hosts for European diplomats, engaging civilly and literately with them in sustained negotiations over safe passage and goods, providing for their immediate needs and entertainments, and the like. Yet at the same time as the accounts enforce these differences, they also inscribe incriminating similarities that align the Moors with the Negroes, rendering their civility suspect and their trappings of civilization meaningless.[12]

The Negroes are themselves allowed a degree of civility when they cooperate with the English (as are the natives of the New World). Their behaviors are categorized and evaluated along another civil/savage divide: those who refuse to trade are "wilde and idle" (p. 187) and those who comply, "more gentle in nature" and "goodlier men" (p. 191).[13] Yet these distinctions are deployed and displayed as much in the breach as in the observance, at moments when the "gentle" natured seem to go almost inevitably beserk. We hear, for example, of a group of Negroes originally defined as "civill" who began negotiations with the English as if in good faith, but then turned against them, "laied handes" on the English "with great violence, and tore all their apparell from their backes" and shot poisonous arrows at others (pp. 270, 272). Though we later learn that an English ship "had taken three of their people" three weeks before and that the Negroes intended to rescue their countrymen by taking and exchanging English hostages, it is only after we see the natives as irrational and volatile (p. 273).

The Negroes provide an ominous reflection of the Moors, whose civility is also shown to break down, usually more subtly but often as unpredictably. Moors also appear suddenly (though infrequently) out of the landscape, fragmented into "cruel hands," to place Europeans "in miserable servitude" (p. 294). And just as resisting Negroes are incriminated as unreasoning, so similarly are uncooperative Moors incriminated as unreasonable. As leaders they are produced as cunning and deceptive, threateningly prone to delaying negotiations and detaining European negotiators to their own advantage, as I have argued elsewhere.[14] Descriptions of their apparently hospitable domains are interrupted at several points by images of Europeans in captivity or constraints—of the Spanish or Portuguese under Mully Abdelmelech's rule, for example, forced to greet an English visitor, their heads "hung downe . . . like dogs," suggesting that they were there "more by the kings commandement then of any good wils of themselves" (p. 287). As the dark side of the Moors is pressed through the cover of civility to match the uncovered aggression of the Negroes, we are encouraged to expect the worst—to expect hospitable Moors to turn "cruel" just as "goodlier" Negroes turn "wilde."

Presented thus along these conflicting axes of difference and similarity, Africa becomes a place where degrees of civilization no longer mean anything, where the people, even at their most civilized best, are unquestionably unlike "us." As such it is easily disenfranchised, its Negroes and Moors alike denied a place and position from which to speak. The nameless Africans are located according to—and even as—the geographic and temporal markers of the Europeans' journeys and are readily kidnapped and, in the one case in which a Negro is named ("George, our Negro"), claimed unabashedly as "ours" (p. 217). And while the Moors appear as the titular heads of kingdoms, they are expected to allow the English safe passage through their territories and must be willing to sacrifice Africa's well-being for England, to defend the English merchants "from any thing that may impeach or hurt them" (p. 429), even if it costs African lives or "lackes" (p. 288). If they do not, they lose their civility. No matter how "civilized," within early modern England's Africanist discourse, the African subject is, in effect, taken out of Africa and defined in terms of a civilization in which he or she has no rights, no stakes, and no say.

Virgil and Dido

Dido, Queen of Carthage turns not only to these imperializing exploits and
the world appropriated for them, but also backward, to the classical past
whose "infinite riches" were also being accommodated within English society. Like "other" cultures, classical civilization became a sign of European supremacy, but through assimilation rather than differentiation. It,
with its letters, laws, and literatures, was "inherited" as part of the spectacular achievement of Europe. When Marlowe draws upon that inheri-
tance, however, upon Books 1, 2, and 4 of Virgil's *Aeneid*, he chooses from
it an account which itself is preoccupied with imperialism and the conflicts
it produces.[15]

From classical times onward, the story of Dido and Aeneas had been
told and retold in various forms, predominantly as a love tragedy. In addition to Virgil's version, the most prominent model for medieval and
Renaissance retellings was in Ovid's *Heroides* (Book 7). Ovid records the
tale only through Dido's epistle to the departed Aeneas, presenting the
queen as a deserted lover and the central issue, that of love.[16] Virgil's account is, in contrast, uniquely politicized, with its emphasis centering on
the imperialist mission surrounding and shaping Dido's interaction with
Aeneas. While the text seems ultimately to support Aeneas's cause, it is not
without uncovering the two-sidedness of imperialist exchange and the
need finally to control "how things seem [and] how they are deemed"
(4:225) within such interactions.[17]

Virgil sets the encounter between Dido and Aeneas within an imperialist frame, introducing it as part of a struggle between Juno, who wants
Carthage to become "the capital of nations" and Venus, who hopes to
establish the Trojans "as rulers over sea and land" (1:28−29, 331). Assuring
Venus that her son will triumph, Jupiter prophecies a Trojan future of
domination: Aeneas will

> wage tremendous war in Italy
> and crush ferocious nations and establish
> a way of life and walls for his own people.
>   (1:367−69)[18]

The resulting Roman race will become "masters of all things" (1:394−95),
with "no limits to their fortunes" and "empire without end" (1:389−90).[19]

As we move from the frame to the central encounter, imperialist relations become even more pressing. Hulme has reclaimed the narrative from sentimentalist readings that schematize the encounter as a conflict between love and duty, and has argued that the relation between Dido and Aeneas is not one, primarily, of love but rather one of host to guest. What is at issue, he contends, is "the great colonial theme of hospitality," central to a tradition of colonialist texts.[20] In offering her body and her kingdom to Aeneas, Dido acts not transgressively as lover but appropriately as host; her actions evoke and comply with a code of hospitality that demands reciprocity—in her case, marriage. Because Aeneas has taken advantage of her hospitality (and her body), in leaving he violates "political ties" that oblige him to stay and to marry.[21]

While this reading helpfully recovers the "political dimension" of the myth, the host/guest relation explains only half—the Trojan half—of the picture. In interpreting Dido's demand for marriage as part of her role as host, Hulme defines her in terms of Aeneas's agenda, reinforcing Trojan dominance. The text, however, also assigns Dido a different agenda, a colonialist agenda, which she scripts in terms of marriage and not of hospitality. To legitimize and secure her bond with Aeneas would be to stabilize her kingdom, endangered on all sides by outsiders. When she explains why her men have inhospitably attacked the arriving Trojan ships, Dido emphasizes the precariousness of her rule and the constant danger ("*tanta pericula*" [1:615]) threatening her frontiers. Although she has resolved to abstain from love, she changes her mind when her sister Anna reminds her of the surrounding aggressors and anticipates that her marriage to Aeneas would bring greatness and glory to the Punic realm:

> If you marry Aeneas, what a city
> and what a kingdom, sister, you will see!
> With Trojan arms beside us, so much greatness
> must lie in wait for Punic glory!
>
> (4:64–67)[22]

With this greatness and glory in mind, Dido embraces Aeneas not merely as a guest ("*hospes*") but as a husband ("*coniuge*"), insisting that the consummation of their bond is, in fact, a marriage ("*coniugium*").

Although Virgil remarks that she "covers up her fault" with the "name"—and implicitly, not the rites—of "marriage" (4:227–28), he does not condemn her (as Richard Stanyhurst does in his translation) for "carnal leacherie."[23] Instead he surrounds that "fault" with conflicting judgments and, by refusing to privilege one over another, presents the legitimacy or illegitimacy of the marriage as a matter of perspective and of naming, not of a singular and absolute truth. The bond is not sanctioned by any official human rites, but the "Elemental Powers" enact the rituals of Roman marriage, with Juno, the goddess of marriage, presiding over and sanctioning the event.[24] She, with her hopes for a great Carthaginian empire, does have a vested interest here, but the voice of Rumour, which counters hers, is no more (and is, in fact, less) reliable. Though Rumour defames Dido and Aeneas as "slaves of squalid craving" (4:257), Virgil discredits her authority by noting her tendency to "hold fast to falsehood and distortion / as often as to messages of truth" (4:248–49).[25] In evaluating the consummation, Virgil himself faults Dido not for her passion but for her inattention to "how things seem [and] how they are deemed" (4:225), refusing to fix the terms of how things, in fact, are.[26] The problem is that she, in taking little heed of established conventions, lays herself open to voices like Rumour's that falsify and distort and make "squalid craving" out of unconventional moves of power.

In the end, Virgil brings Dido's and Aeneas's voices together and emphasizes rather than resolves their differences, showing that what is finally at issue within the exchange is not adherence to or violation of a single code of conduct, but the conflict of two separate and incompatible codes. As Aeneas prepares to depart, he acknowledges only that Dido deserves "kindnesses" (4:450) for her hospitality; but in disavowing all intentions of becoming her husband, he betrays his own awareness of an alternative view.[27] Although Dido ultimately has no choice but to accept his actions, she resists his terms and protests that she is forced to "say 'guest'" in parting, only because "this name is all / I have of one whom once I called my husband" (4:435–36).[28] Instead of faulting Dido or Aeneas—of judging one as faithful and the other as faithless to a single set of terms (whether his or hers), as subsequent reinscriptions of the same episode tend to do—the text remains ambivalent. Though the idea of imperialism does not come under fire as directly as it does in Marlowe, Virgil exposes the complexities of cross-cultural exchange and the difficulties of setting the terms. The central problem is, indeed, "how things are deemed," and if Aeneas comes out on top, it is only because his terms dominate.

"What stranger art thou, that dost eye me thus?"

While Marlowe, in taking on this classical, colonialist myth, reenacts the kind of appropriation that was supporting European supremacy, he does so to quite a different end. For his play takes Virgil's dialogic narrative one step further and not only gives Dido a voice of her own but also offers a pointed critique of imperialism.[29] The European position is not just contested internally by a competitor on the stage; it is also contested externally by the play itself, which raises the issue of who really is the stranger in a strange land. Again we are confronted and left with the irresolvable conflict of two mutually exclusive representations of a mutual experience. But what is clearer here is their coercive edge.

Though Virgil allows Dido to have her say, it is finally to no avail; the idea of imperialism remains relatively secure, particularly under the aegis of Jupiter, whose farsighted vision promises the success of a master race, with no limits to its fortunes or empire. For Marlowe, however, before we ever enter upon the Carthaginian scene, the imperialist agenda is contextualized as part of a domestic squabble, voiced by gods characterized more by self-interest than by foresight.[30] No longer the authoritative spokesman of Virgilian legend, Jupiter sits "toying" with Ganymede, his "female wanton boy" (*Dido* 1.1.50–51), engaging in a homoerotic exchange that, though "chastened" and idealized in some classical and Renaissance texts, is transgressively sexualized here.[31] Though Jupiter assures Venus (and us) that "Aeneas' wandering fate is firm" (1.1.83) and "take[s] order" (1.1.113) immediately to effect it, he first appears preoccupied with a private vengeance and animosity. His "play" with Ganymede, however much predicated upon desire, becomes a way of exhorting his power over Juno and putting her in her place (which, if she protests, will be of bondage, halfway between heaven and earth). Juno's interventions in Aeneas's fate derive not from allegiance to Carthage (her "favorite" land in Virgil) and a grand hope for Carthaginian empire, but from her "hate of Trojan Ganymede" (3.2.42), which she displaces onto Aeneas. Even Venus, who does look out for Troy, acts more as mother, concerned for the safety of her son, than as guardian of the Trojan race.

With imperialism appearing thus self-interested and ungodly in the hands of the gods, Marlowe further undermines the stability of the colonialist position by showing not only that outside England the colonizer is the "stranger" but also that the idea of the stranger is a negotiable and manipulable construct, dependent upon position, perspective, and purpose. From England's perspective Dido, the African queen, should figure as the "stranger" here, but Marlowe aligns the Trojans, the representative Europeans, with that role and questions the assumptions imposed on it.[32] When coming ashore, the Trojan Ilioneus anticipates that as outsiders he and his men will be perceived as savage, lawless, and irreligious. He assures Iarbas, the African king:

> We come not, we, to wrong your Libyan gods,
> Or steal your household Lares from their shrines.
> Our hands are not prepar'd to lawless spoil,
> Nor armed to offend in any kind.
>
> (1.2.10–13)

In projecting Trojan/European preconceptions of the alien onto the Carthaginians, as if the two cultures share the same biases, Ilioneus (unwittingly) suggests what Marlowe will repeatedly confirm: that geographic difference does not translate as ideologic or behavioral otherness. Indeed, after this initial interchange, the Trojans are seamlessly assimilated into Carthaginian society, so much so that Aeneas (who has been separated from them) almost mistakes them for "lords of this town" (2.1.39).

The assumption that "they" are like "us" is itself an imperialist fantasy, manifest, for example, in Hakluyt, as the narrators assign African leaders English titles such as "king" or "captaine," and masking the possibility that there might be alternative terms of "civility."[33] Yet in Marlowe, because the terms are reversed, because "we" are like "them," it works to destabilize the bounds between self and other, to deny the transcription of other as stranger that supports the colonizer's assumed supremacy.

Like and even more than his men, Aeneas is also presented as a stranger, and his characterization is used to suggest even more insistently that strangeness is in the eye of the beholder. When he first arrives on shore, he defines himself and is defined by his Trojan identity. After he catalogs the "many dangers" the Trojans have "overpass'd" (1.1.145), claims Fate as his friend, and anticipates the return of "good days" (1.1.150), his companions express their confidence in this "brave prince of Troy" (1.1.152). He himself announces:

> Of Troy am I; Aeneas is my name,
> Who, driven by war from forth my native world,
> Put sails to sea to seek out Italy;

And my divine descent from sceptred Jove.
With twice twelve Phrygian ships I plough'd the deep,
And made that way my mother Venus led.

(1.1.216−21)

When he redefines himself in terms of Carthage, however, he highlights his alien and alienated status. In "these Libyan deserts," he complains to Venus (who has come before him disguised as an Amazon), he is "hapless," "poor and unknown," "all despis'd," and "exil'd forth Europe and wide Asia both" (1.1.227−29). At court Dido also initially emphasizes his status as an outsider, demanding "what stranger art thou, that dost eye me thus?" (2.1.74), and he answers in kind, internalizing geographic dislocation as self-estrangement and lamenting: "Sometime I was a Trojan, mighty queen, / But Troy is not: what shall I say I am?" (2.1.75−76).

Instead of merely reversing the referents of the self/other dichotomy, Marlowe presents the claim to alien status as a product of a rigid, one-dimensional perspective, imposed with reference to the known (here to the Trojan past) and not to the unfolding unknown. Significantly, it is Aeneas, and not Dido or Marlowe, who denies the meaning of Troy, imposing physical (spatial and temporal) limits on a metaphysical signifier (Troy).[34] For Troy does have its place even here—so much, in fact, that Priam is figured in statue outside the city's walls and seems alive and well enough to Aeneas to "wag his hand" (2.1.29). Though Achates insists that it is "nothing" "but stone" (2.1.14), its lifelikeness deludes Aeneas into thinking that Troy lives on, and in a way he is right: Priam and Troy do live on in Carthage in a figurative sense, as a part of the culture's knowledge, legend, and art.

While Dido is unknown to Aeneas and must be pointed out (to her dismay), Aeneas the "stranger" is no stranger here. Despite her initial insistence that he is, she embraces his legendary identity, asserting that "Aeneas is Aeneas" (2.1.84) and urging him, as he speaks of his own estrangement, to "remember who thou art," to "speak like thyself" (2.1.100) and to speak, at length, of Troy. Urging him to "truly" resolve the discrepancies between the "many tales" (2.1.107−8) of Troy's fall, she makes clear that the Trojan past has been a prominent part of the discourse of her court.

In placing Aeneas's alienation thus in his hands, the play uncovers anxieties that colonialist narratives insistently suppress: that the colonizers were themselves "strangers," "poor and unknown," and "all despis'd" in·

the strange lands they "discovered," scarcely knowing "within what clime" they were. Instead of turning the issue into a matter of psychology or role-reversal, Marlowe gives it a coercive edge, suggesting the colonizer's self-assumed estrangement as a strategic pose, a posture of dependence enabling the European "guests" to exploit their native hosts.

The accounts in Hakluyt's *Principal Navigations* often ascribe a similar sort of naive dependence to the English, especially in the face of the more "civilized" natives, making them the powerless victims of the cunning Moorish emperors (who thus appear more cunning), unable to do anything but sit out a series of ominous delays. In one narrative, for example, Edmund Hogan, recording his encounter with Mully Abdelmelech, emphasizes how long he had to wait. Although he mentions that he was provided with "all things necessarie" in the meantime, he also notes, in a muted complaint, that "souldiers environed the tents, and watched about us day and night as I lay there, although I sought my speedier dispatch" (p. 286). In stressing his impotence and impatience, Hogan produces the Moor as difficult and discourteous, at the least, and the English guest as greatly disadvantaged and dependent, the helpless victim of the exploitative actions of the other.

In *Dido*, Marlowe exposes and incriminates a similar kind of narrative strategy, suggesting Aeneas's self-estranging claims as a way of inscribing himself, blamelessly, as a needy guest and of securing necessary aid, using an overwhelming dependence to mask a motivating independence that has a colony as and at its end. This tactic is anticipated twice in the opening act: once when Ilioneus attempts to gain Iarbas's help by emphasizing the "poor distressed misery" (1.2.6) of his men; and before, when Venus enlists Jupiter to assist Aeneas, insisting that he "rests a prey to every billow's pride" and aggrandizing the severity of his plight by presenting the besieging storm as another fall of Troy, scripting the waves as "envious men of war," the winds as Agamemnon and his "fierce soldiers," the night as Ulysses, Aetna's hill as the Trojan horse, and Aeneas's ships as "poor Troy" (1.1.65–70).

Likewise Aeneas, when first seeking Dido's sympathy and support, uses the story of Troy to amplify the desolation of his state. Speaking without Virgilian precedent, he graphically details the impact of the Greek attack on the most helpless and innocent victims, producing a scene of:

Young infants swimming in their parents' blood,
Headless carcasses pil'd up in heaps,

Virgins half-dead, dragg'd by their golden hair,
And with main force flung on a ring of pikes,
Old men with swords thrust through their aged sides,
Kneeling for mercy to a Greekish lad,
Who with steel pole-axes dash'd out their brains.

                                        (2.1.193–99)

Here and throughout the account, his heavy use of participles adds an immediacy to the violence, giving progressive motion to the completed deeds and pressing the extreme hardships of the Trojan past into the Trojan present.[35]

Ironically, his tale of Troy emphasizes and suggests an awareness of the persuasive power of language and its crucial impact on the outcome of a devastating cross-cultural encounter. It was through "honey words" (2.1.137), he tells us, that Ulysses convinced the Greeks to return to Troy, alleging that "the gods would have them stay" (2.1.141) and prophesying success. And it was with a "ticing tongue" (2.1.145) and "enchanting words" (2.1.161) that Sinon adopted a "pitiful" and "remorseful" pose (2.1.155–56) and persuaded the Trojans to receive both himself and the wooden horse, which "had it never enter'd, Troy had stood" (2.1.172). Though we are never privy to Aeneas's linguistic intentions, his "pitiful" posture, which finds its most forceful expression here, in his recounting of his past, resembles and is incriminated along with that of Sinon, whose strategies are clear. And it clearly serves to his advantage, eliciting Dido's sympathies so much that she professes to "die with melting ruth" (2.1.289) and calls for "some pleasing sport" to ease "these melancholy thoughts" (2.1.302–3).

It is by scripting himself into a position of dependency that Aeneas, paradoxically, can impose his own terms and agendas upon Carthage and erase Dido's. For however much his desires come into play, as he vacillates between staying in Carthage or pressing on to Italy, his dilemma is not whether to give himself to love or to duty, but how best to fulfill his duty. Even though he engages Dido in sexual intercourse of both a physical and a verbal sort, he attempts to further his colonialist mission through it and publicly represents his involvement in political terms as that of guest to host. When Dido first inquires how she might "highly pleasure" (3.2.102) him, he asks only that his ships be refurnished with anchors, riggings, and oars for departure, promising to make her the "author of our lives" if she supplies these "piteous wants" (3.1.111–12). Although he muses, after looking at a gallery of her suitors' portraits, on how "happy shall he be whom Dido loves" (3.1.168), his decision to stay in Carthage rather than leave immediately is coupled to her assurance that he is needed "to war against [her] bordering enemies" (3.1.135). When she becomes more explicit in offering her love, Aeneas, though willing, is also resistant; reaffirming his "hapless" condition, he voices doubts that the queen would "look so low" (3.4.41) on one (himself) whose "thoughts dare not ascend so high / As Dido's heart, which monarchs might not scale" (3.4.33–34). And when he does take her up on her offer of love, her kingdom, and her body, promising "never to leave" and "never to like or love any but her" (3.4.51), he first swears by "all the gods of hospitality," and only secondarily by his "fair brother's [i.e., Cupid's] bow" (3.4.44–45).

The guest/host relation does require reciprocity, but Aeneas frees himself of political obligation by denying Dido's political status and political claims, presenting her as lover, reading and rejecting her demands as personal, if not hysterical. Conveniently, he creates an unbridgeable cultural gap, presenting love as the motivating object of her actions and hospitality as the motivating object of his, and so rendering both personal and political obligation, one which applies only to her and the other only to him, moot. At the first moment of crisis—the first time he decides to leave and to colonize elsewhere—he turns Dido into a dangerously alluring other, fearing that if he says good-by,

> Her silver arms will coll me round about,
> And tears of pearl cry, "Stay, Aeneas, stay!"
> Each word she says will then contain a crown,
> And every speech be ended with a kiss:
> I may not dure this female drudgery.
> To sea, Aeneas! find out Italy!
>
> (4.3.51–56)

He does worry that in not saying farewell he "transgress[es] against all laws of love" (4.3.48); yet he places himself as far outside those laws as he places her deeply within them. Although he admits that he is torn by desire, that he "fain would go, yet beauty calls me back" (4.3.46), he defines that desire in material terms, fragmenting and transforming Dido's body into desirable objects (her arms are silver, her tears, pearl) and betraying a telling preoccupation with wealth and acquisition. And although he allows that her words contain crowns, he presents them as tokens of love and not signs of power. In reducing Dido's gestures to "female drudg-ery" and depoliticizing her desires, he places himself beyond obligation, culpability, and Carthage. He "hear[s]" her calling for him from "a-far," offering to

> link my body to thy lips,
> That, tied together by the striving tongues,
> We may, as one, sail into Italy.
>
> (4.3.27–30)

But we hear only him, giving her body (and voice) through his lips and producing a conflict of "striving tongues" monologically in his own voice and terms.

Although Aeneas does give in to Dido's demands and desires, it is always with an eye to his imperialist purposes. The one time he settles most firmly on a future in Carthage, he speaks, as Dido notes, "like a conqueror" (4.4.93) and envisions a future for himself that includes the Trojan race and, in its articulation, excludes her. He vows to revenge the deaths of his kinsmen and of Priam and his fifty sons, claiming that the Trojan race will "flourish" "in me" (4.4.87), as if he alone will generate that race without Dido's help or body. In his most sexually suggestive speech, he maps out the primary object of his stay, the building of "a statelier Troy" (5.1.2), proclaiming:

> Carthage shall vaunt her petty walls no more;
> For I will grace them with a fairer frame,
> And clad her in a crystal livery,
> Wherein the day may evermore delight.
> From golden India Ganges will I fetch,
> Whose wealthy streams may wait upon her towers,
> And triple-wise entrench her round about;
> The sun from Egypt shall rich odours bring,
> Wherewith his burning beams (like labouring bees
> That load their thighs with Hybla's honey's spoils)
> Shall here unburden their exhaled sweets,
> And plant our pleasant suburbs with their fumes.
>
> (5.1.4–15)

With a Tamburlainian emphasis on "will" ("I will grace," "will I fetch"), he reconstructs the feminine space as an object of and for male domi-

nation. Under his command, the "petty walls" of Carthage will be en-
closed within a "fairer frame," covered by "crystal livery," and surrounded
by "wealthy streams." The "new-erected" city will become a place where
the "sun from Egypt" (like the son from Troy) can relieve "his burning
beams," "load[ed]" like the "thighs" of "labouring bees," and "unbur-
den their exhaled sweets." It will be a site of acquisition, where the "exhaled sweets" from Egypt and India can be gathered up, contained, and
consumed.

This colonialist dream-come-true is disrupted only when Hermes, the
god of commerce, intervenes and reduces the projected domination to
subjugation, insisting that instead of furthering his "own affairs" (5.1.30),
Aeneas can only "beautify the empire of this queen" (5.1.28). Tellingly,
Aeneas's thoughts of staying end here too. Enlisting Iarbas's aid in refur-
nishing his ship, he no longer needs Dido and turns irretrievably away,
without acknowledging any obligation to her, her love, or her kingdom.
Although he protests (in Latin) that "it is not of [his] own will" that he
goes (5.1.140), it is difficult not to agree with Dido's complaint that "Aeneas calls Aeneas hence" (5.1.132). In his final moments onstage, he cuts off
her complaints by protesting: "In vain, my love, thou spend'st thy fainting
breath: / If words might move me, I were overcome" (5.1.153–54). Her
words, however, cannot move him and instead are reduced to "fainting
breath."

In the *Aeneid*, this final dialogue is cut short not by Aeneas but by
Dido, who actually faints. Aeneas goes regretfully, lamenting that he cannot "soften, soothe her sorrow / and turn aside her troubles with sweet
words" and "groaning long and shaken in his mind / because of his great
love" (4.540–55).[36] In Marlowe, however, he turns away without remorse
or regret just as Dido begs him to leap into her arms, and then he exits
with his Trojan identity and colonialist mission in tact—and without further word.

The African Queen

Yet he does not get the last word. For the play neither silences nor reduces
Dido's voice, but sets it beside his as a competing alternative—political
but not (primarily) personal, different but not other.[37] Africa becomes in
Marlowe's hands and under Dido's rule a place that has its own claims to
power and possession, a place equally caught up in the imperialist struggle

and equally determined to profit from it. However much Dido may be touched by desire, here, as in the *Aeneid*, her offer of her hospitality, kingdom, and self and her attempts to instate Aeneas as her husband are political moves, constructed to authorize her power.

Importantly, Dido, whose name means "wanderer," is herself an colonizing outsider in Carthage. According to classical legend, she was daughter to the king of Tyre and escaped to Libya with a group of her people when her husband was murdered by her brother. She then bought land from the Libyans to found a new city, Carthage, which became one of the most prosperous of all Phoenician colonies. Pressured, because of this acquisition, to marry the Libyan king, she chose instead to kill herself.[38] Though in the play she leaps into flames for Aeneas's sake instead, Marlowe writes this history into a subplot and puts the African king on the sidelines pursuing Dido, who rejects him, and hating Aeneas, who wins her. In Iarbas's case, the queen maintains a pose of chastity, asserting that she has given "the greatest favours [she] could give" to the point that she risks being "counted light" (3.1.13–14). When it is clear that she will never give in to him, Iarbas represents her colonialist position as one of violation, complaining to Jove:

> The woman that thou will'd us entertain,
> Where, staying in our borders up and down,
> She crav'd a hide of ground to build a town,
> With whom we did divide both laws and land,
> And all the fruits that plenty else sends forth,
> Scorning our loves and royal marriage-rites,
> Yields up her beauty to a stranger's bed.
>
> (4.2.11–17)

Dido's colonialist history tempts us to schematize the events in Carthage as the competition between two imperialists (Dido and Aeneas) over an oppressed African people (with Iarbas at their head)—a three-sided formulation like that around which *The Jew of Malta* is structured, and to which I will return. Yet Marlowe disenfranchises Iarbas, relegating him, like Anna, to a background of relentlessly unsuccessful lovers, who prove the pursuit of passion a comical endeavor at best. His attempts to charge Dido with dishonor are tainted by his own calculating intent: though he condemns her for violating his people's "royal marriage-rites," he himself would do the same if she were willing, and he objects only because she is not.[39] Though in title he is king of Africa, in effect it is she who sits on the throne and provides the alternative voice of power excluded from colonialist discourse.

In positioning Dido thus in Iarbas's place, Marlowe problematically supports the kind of imperialist terms he otherwise resists, making all too clear that what is being recuperated here is not the "real" voice of Africa. Yet the conflict between Dido and Aeneas stands nonetheless as an important protest against the ways that voice was being silenced and alternative agendas were being displaced and erased. Indeed, however dismissive and problematic Iarbas's role is here, it provides us with a comic but foreboding example of how easily that displacement and erasure can occur, even in "politically correct" texts.

Despite its drawbacks, Dido's position as a colonialist alerts us to the importance and precariousness of her power, underlining the political edge of her efforts that Aeneas would otherwise obscure. Though she speaks in terms of desire and marriage and is not as concerned about defending Carthage's borders as is her Virgilian predecessor, her need for Aeneas is as political as is his for her. To embrace him as husband is a way of signaling and confirming her royal rights, autonomy, and control. Edward II (as I argue below) uses his favoritism of his "minions" to impose his own authority over that of the contesting nobility, and though he has a sexual antecedent in *Tamburlaine*'s Mycetes, he has a political antecedent in Dido. While Edward capitalizes on the sexual transgressiveness of his relations, embracing men whom "all the world" loves to hate, Dido exploits the ennobling potential of her bond, embracing a classical hero and using his good fortune and good name to support and exhibit her own.

From the outset, despite her initial resistance to the "stranger," Dido embraces his noble reputation and situates him in a heightened place beside her, as husband and prince, which matches that renown. When he first arrives, she demands that he exchange his "base robes" for her late husband's garments, all the while proclaiming that "Aeneas is Aeneas, were he clad / In weeds as bad as ever Irus ware" (2.1.84–85).[40] After he changes, although she calls him a "guest," she welcomes him as a "brave prince" and directs him to "sit in this chair"—hers or one next to it—"and banquet with a queen" (2.1.83). And while he emphasizes his misery and meanness, she reiterates that it lies in her hands to make him "blest" (2.1.103), to make his fortune even greater than his birth. In so doing, she underscores not only his worth, but also her ability to enrich it.

Her display of Aeneas seems tellingly allied to her treatment of her previous suitors, whom she contains and exhibits within a portrait gallery. Like Aeneas, the pictured men are nobles whom "all the world well knows" (3.1.165), figures whom the Trojans have seen in Troy and Greece, with whom they have sported, traveled, or disputed, and who, she stresses, are kings. Though she reveals the gallery in efforts to entice Aeneas to stay, she also offers it as proof that she is not in love, that she is self-sufficient and unconquerable, "free from all" and "obtain'd" (3.1.153) by none, despite their concerted attempts to "compass" (3.1.156) her. She boasts of "cast[ing] . . . off" the "wealthy king of Thessaly" because she "had gold enough," a "warlike prince" because "weapons gree not with my tender years," and a Spartan courtier and a musician because their "fantastic humours" and music, respectively, "pleas'd not me" (3.1.158–64). These figures are at once signs and subjects of her dominance, objectified, contained, and displayed within her gallery as a measure of her wealth and power.

It is not until Cupid intervenes and casts a spell upon her that her relation to Aeneas takes a decidedly erotic turn, but even then she appropriates the Trojan, like the other courtiers, as an image of her richness.[41] She anticipates that she will:

> make me bracelets of his golden hair;
> His glistering eyes shall be my looking-glass;
> His lips an altar, where I'll offer up
> As many kisses as the sea hath sands;
> Instead of music I will hear him speak;
> His looks shall be my only library;
> And thou, Aeneas, Dido's treasury,
> In whose fair bosom I will lock more wealth
> Than twenty thousand Indias can afford.
> (3.1.85–93)

Just as Aeneas fragments and depersonifies Dido into "silver arms" and "tears of pearl," so too does she fragment and depersonify him into objects for her entertainment, self-adornment, and self-reflection, making him her altar and her treasury, the sign of the infinite excesses of what she can give and contain.

Though she embraces rather than rejects him as she does her former suitors, Dido keeps Aeneas similarly in her power, using two objects—the ship's riggings and her body—literally and figuratively, to at once entice and force him to stay within her command. Though the two might be differentiated along a love/duty divide, the riggings answering Aeneas's call to duty and Dido's body his needs of love, Marlowe (via Dido) refutes the separation here as throughout, using the obvious political significance of her proffering (and withholding) of the ship's equipment to highlight the less obvious practical significance of her offer of her body. In her hands and words, the erotic becomes a crucial tool for containing and control. When she agrees to refurnish the Trojan ships, what she offers is clearly not made for use—at least not the use for which Aeneas requests it. Instead it serves to impede his going, suggestively through allure. She promises:

> tackling made of rivell'd gold,
> Wound on the barks of odoriferous trees;
> Oars of massy ivory, full of holes,
> Through which the water shall delight to play;
> Thy anchors shall be hew'd from crystal rocks,
> Which, if thou lose, shall shine above the waves;
> The masts, whereon thy swelling sails shall hang,
> Hollow pyramides of silver plate.
>
> (3.1.116–23)

Tellingly, her offer is contingent upon Aeneas's consent to stay, and though she later seems to have provided usable riggings, it is only under the condition that they not be used. When Aeneas breaks the contract and prepares to go, Dido reestablishes her control by reclaiming the gear and replacing it (as it was initally presented) with metaphor, leaving Aeneas only her "favours" (4.4.159) for his masts. In the end, he is able to depart only because Iarbas, in efforts to get Dido for himself, refurnishes the ships.

Yet Dido's manipulation of this critical equipment is not merely literal. On a symbolic level, too, her erotic offer puts Aeneas in a subordinate position and suggestively unmans him. The oars that he can have, though of massy ivory, are oxymoronically "full of holes" and the masts, "whereon [his] swelling sails" are hung, though of silver, are hollow. Her promises recall the seduction scene between Jupiter and Ganymede, in which Jupiter seems similarly to proffer his "little love" autonomy and power while instead enforcing attachment. Though Jupiter promises to put "all the gods" at Ganymede's command, he offers instead entertainment, slumber, and sport—Vulcan dancing "to make thee laughing sport," "my nine daughters [to] sing when thou art sad," the "spotted pride" of "Juno's bird" "to make thee fans wherewith to cool thy face," and the like (1.1.30–42). The young lover is delighted, wanting little more than a jewel for his ear, a brooch for his hat, and a chance to "hug with [Jupiter] an hundred times" (1.1.148), but his gains, like his goals, are mere tokens. Aeneas's goals, however, are not, and the parallel between his situation and Ganymede's, as between Dido's promises and Jupiter's, reminds us who has the hegemonic hold on power, and how.

While Dido's literal and symbolic manipulation of these provisions is critical to her power play, so too is the offer of her body, allowing her the means and grounds to keep him in Carthage. From the outset, she uses the consummation of their bond to contain and control his identity and instantiate her own, turning the classical hero into her husband and king and imposing her terms suggestively over him. Before giving Aeneas her body, she first gives him her former husband's name, title, and love tokens (golden bracelets and a wedding ring), insisting that he be called "Sichaeus, not Aeneas" and "the king of Carthage, not Anchises' son" (3.4.59–60). Despite his protests that "a sword, and not a sceptre, fits Aeneas" (4.4.43), she, in her words, "make[s] experience of [her] love" (4.4.64) by making him "king of Libya by [her] gift" (3.4.64) and putting him on display as hers for all the world to see. Although she invests him publicly with the accoutrements of her rule, her crown and scepter, and promises him command of "as many Moors / As in the sea are little water drops" (4.4.62–63), she gives Anna the reins, directing her to "lead my lover forth," "let him ride, / As Dido's husband, through the Punic streets," and "will" her guard to wait upon him (4.4.65–68). Impressed herself by the show, Dido first pauses to "gaze [her] fill" (4.4.44) and then retires to continue her gaze from a tower suggestively above him.

Importantly, too, through this spectacle Dido exhibits her power not only over Aeneas but also over her subjects. When Anna hesitates to proceed for fear that the citizens will object, Dido embraces their resistance as reason to promote the parade. "Those that dislike what Dido gives in charge," she declares,

Command my guard to slay for their offence.
Shall vulgar peasants storm at what I do?
The ground is mine that gives them sustenance,
The air wherein they breathe, the water, fire,

> All that they have, their lands, their goods,
>   their lives,
> And I, the goddess of all these, command
> Aeneas ride as Carthaginian king.
>
> (4.4.71–78)

To present Aeneas as their "sovereign lord" (4.4.69) is to express, exercise, and exhibit her own totalitarian control over the people, to lay claim to "all that they have," from the air to the land to themselves, to prove herself unquestionably "goddess of all these." It is to use a stranger to obscure the fact that she is herself a stranger here, that the ground is not naturally hers.

In the end, when Aeneas's agenda conflicts with hers and he prepares to go, Dido calls upon the consummation of their bodies as leverage to obligate him to stay. Just as Aeneas reads her in private terms to justify and advance his political moves, so too does she read him, to justify and advance hers. Although she has conflated the "marriage" with politics, in attempting to condemn Aeneas for and prevent him from stepping beyond her control, Dido calls upon his duty to their "spousal rites" (5.1.134) and establishes a code of honor (which Aeneas will violate) through them. She presents herself as one who speaks for "love" (5.1.90) and castigates him as a faithless lover, asking whether "Trojans use to quit their lovers thus" (5.1.106). Though Aeneas insists that he leaves at "the gods' behest" (5.1.127), she protests that "the gods weigh not what lovers do" (5.1.131). She brings politics into the picture only to reverse the terms of her power play—to portray herself as the one victimized by love. "Hast thou forgot how many neighbor kings / Were up in arms," she asks him,

>   for making thee my love?
> How Carthage did rebel, Iarbas storm,
> And all the world calls me a second Helen,
> For being entangled by a stranger's looks?
>
> (5.1.141–45)

The strategic nature of her representations becomes increasingly apparent as her terms become increasingly harsh, defaming Aeneas ever more extremely as a "stranger," declaring that his "mother was no goddess" (5.1.156), that he was "sprung from Scythian Caucasus" (5.1.158) and suckled by Hyrcanian tigers.

It is only after he departs that Dido, speaking to herself, her attendants, and us, makes her political objections and objectives clear. In a final (though fatal) gesture of power, she throws herself into a flaming pyre, as a "relic" of his story, attempting to make him "famous through the world / For perjury and slaughter of a queen" (5.1.292–94). It is for his treason, his offense to her royal power and position, that she dies, hoping that her ashes will rise like a conqueror to avenge her death and prove the supremacy of Carthage "by ploughing up his countries with the sword" (5.1.308). Her suicide stands in notable contrast to the two that follow (by Marlowe's invention), two motivated solely and irrationally by desire. Iarbas leaps into flames after her to escape from grief, and Anna follows after him (whom she loves) to honor him and mingle her blood with his. Though she hopes that gods and men will "rue our ends, senseless of life or breath" (5.1.328), the comic senselessness of these suicides seems to preclude that possibility. The spectacle that Dido creates, however, is loaded with power, so much so that critics have questioned whether and in what terms Aeneas, though the representative European, was indeed false.

The question, however, remains ultimately unanswerable, for the play presents the voices of both Dido and Aeneas as equally legitimate (or equally illegitimate). Dido's claims to "spousal rites" are unsupported by official ceremonies and earthly sanctions, as, of course, by Aeneas. They are, however, backed by Juno (as in the *Aeneid*), who concocts a scheme and a storm to join the couple "in marriage" (3.2.74). No one explicitly disputes Dido's claims to "spousal rites" except Iarbas, who labels the couple "adulterers surfeited with sin" (4.1.120) but who is hardly disinterested. Anna's fear that the citizens will rebel if Aeneas rides through the streets as "sovereign lord" calls the public acceptability but not necessarily the legitimacy of the bond into question.[42] And while Virgil's Aeneas states directly that he never committed himself to a marital agreement, Marlowe's Aeneas does not. Instead, he avoids the issue by defining his situation in terms of a host/guest relation. Still, although Dido pulls forth "letters, lines, and perjur'd papers" (5.1.300) that presumably document her story, we have no objective witness to the "truth"; we must take her word for it, or his.

The conflict between these voices creates a problematic indeterminacy for us, preventing us from knowing whose "rites" are right. That indeterminacy, however, is finally the point and not the problem of Marlowe's play, a point which breaks through and breaks up the monologism of imperialist representations. When Virgil's Ilioneus first meets Dido, he chastises her for allowing her men to attack his ships and admonishes her to "consider that the gods / remember right and wrong" (1:765–66), as if right and wrong are absolute.[43] Yet the queen, justifying her followers' actions in terms of her own "hard circumstances" (the attacks of neighboring tribes), offers another "right," another equally valid agenda, and another appropriate response to the same situation. This initiating exchange brings out what Virgil's narrative and Marlowe's play reveal: that there are at least two sides to every cross-cultural encounter.

Marlowe's Africa is not a dark and disenfranchised site of uncertain civility where the colonizer is always right. It too produces kingdoms and queens whose agendas must be accounted for, whose struggles for land, prosperity, and power have a place in the story. In the plays that follow, Marlowe complicates the intersection of cultures and their colonizing terms by bringing more than two worlds and two perspectives into play. Though in *Dido* he targets the uncertainties between self and other, in subsequent plays he turns to the uncertainties within them, at once exploding the stability of those categories and exposing the strategic ways instability is used to confirm them. When Shakespeare calls similar terms of difference into question, he often does so through dichotomized worlds—of Greeks versus Trojans, Romans versus Goths, Corioles versus Volscians. Yet for Marlowe, who was more immediately engaged with imperialist appropriations, binarisms are finally too limited and limiting. Even *Dido* offers, though it dismisses, a third term (Iarbas). It is in the plays that follow, however, that the multivalence of discriminatory discourses comes most clearly through, and it is to them and to that multivalence that the following chapters will turn.

3. East of England: Imperialist Self-Construction in *Tamburlaine*, *Parts 1 and 2*

> "O gods, is this Tamburlaine the thief?"
> (2.4.40)

The "Mould" and Mettle" of the East

The prologue of *Tamburlaine* leads us "to the stately tent of war,"

> to hear the Scythian Tamburlaine
> Threatening the world with high astounding terms
> And scourging kingdoms with his conquering sword.
> (Prologue 3–6)

It opens, then, upon the extensive landscape of the East, starting with Persia, moving across Asia, and extending finally to Egypt and Africa, and introduces a seemingly endless series of struggles, with leader after leader "threatening the world" with "high astounding terms" and "conquering sword[s]." What unfolds is a drama of empire, played out "out there" in the infinite regions of the East, where choosing sides becomes as difficult as defining them. Tamburlaine emerges from this self-consuming landscape to make a singular and spectacular name for himself that will carry against all odds and against all others. Yet while he attempts to create a monologic voice of power, authorized from above and distinguished from all below, the play integrates his voice dialogically into an imperialist interplay, with a series of competitors measuring their own might by demonizing his. Though he triumphs at the end of Part 1 and establishes an expansive empire before he dies in Part 2, the play undermines his illusion of agency, showing us that in the game of empire, supremacy is not given but made—and made, ironically, out of others' visions and voices.[1]

What is at stake here is not only the great divide between West and East, self and other, but also the possibility of mapping out identity, of sustaining a claim to difference that stands apart from cultural and cross-cultural pressures. And what is at risk is autonomy, agency, and individuation. This is a play (as I argue in Chapter 5) that, with its "high astounding" and highly articulate superhero, turned Marlowe into a name subversive in his day; but it is also a play that rejects such singularity, insisting that what's in a name, and particularly in the name of the other, derives neither from self nor other but from the ever-shifting intersection of the two.

Nowhere was this intersection more pertinent during the sixteenth century than in England's confrontation with the East, particularly the Near East, where the state's efforts to develop ties were more vigorous, unified, and sustained than in the less familiar worlds of Africa and the Americas.[2] While the Muscovy Company (established in 1555) was opening up access to the rich terrain of Persia, the Levant Company (patented in 1581) was developing the Turkish trade initiated in the mid-1570s.[3] Beyond economics, what made the East of particular interest was that it housed England's most powerful and threatening non-European competitor for the world's land and wealth: the Turks. Their empire already established and still growing, the Turks remained a key focus of international concern from the fifteenth to the seventeenth century, particularly after they captured Cyprus in 1571, and with few setbacks, continued to wage a seemingly invulnerable campaign. It is not surprising that the Turks figure significantly in two of Marlowe's three "imperialist" plays (*Tamburlaine* and *The Jew of Malta*) and stand ominously in the margins of *Othello*, Shakespeare's play about cross-cultural integration and disintegration, for Turkish imperialism provided a crucial impetus for England's own.

The output of "Orientalist" texts followed suit. Both Edward Said and Raymond Schwab, whose *La Renaissance orientale* (1950) precedes Said's work, present "Orientalism" as an epistemological event emerging in the eighteenth century—for Said, one loaded with the negative, and for Schwab, with the positive.[4] Yet, as both Said and Schwab acknowledge, the Orient's myths and realities had begun to capture, and be captured by, Europe's imaginative and imperialist interests long before Orientalism became a distinctive category of thought.[5] Christianity had always directed attention eastward as well as upward, with its primary text, the Bible,

offering a sacred compendium of Eastern worlds and peoples, its cultivation of relics valorizing and mystifying Eastern artifacts, and its pilgrim-
ages institutionalizing travel to the Holy Land.[6]

In England, the East was also being brought prominently into view
as an "ethnographic" subject in sourcebooks such as Sebastian Muenster's
Cosmography (1544) and Boemus's *Fardle of Facions*, and as a more exotic
site in narratives such as Jean de Bourgogne's popular *Travels of Sir John
Mandeville* (first translated into English in 1496, but probably more widely
known to the Elizabethans in a later reedition of 1568).[7] On the political/
imperialist front, Richard Eden publicized the Muscovy Company's expe-
ditions in his *Historye of Travayle* (1577) and Hakluyt recorded voyages to
Egypt, Asia, and Persia extending back to 337, while Thomas Newton, in
his *Notable History of the Saracens* (1575), traced "Turkishe Affaires" from
their origins to the present.[8]

At court, Queen Elizabeth was financing revels costumes of Turks and
Moors and entertaining a "Masque of Moors" (1560), which would be
followed in Oriental kind by George Gascoigne's "A devise of a Masque"
for the Viscount Mountacute (1571).[9] And on the stage, Marlowe's *Tamburlaine* (c. 1587–89) was preceded by Preston's *Cambyses, King of Persia*
(1569–70) and *Soliman and Persida* (c. 1589–92; of uncertain authorship),
dramatizing a Turkish Sultan's love for a Christian captive, and it was followed by the anonymous *First Part of the Tragicall Raigne of Selimus* (1594),
which promised but did not deliver (as far as we know) a second part, as
by several other "Eastern" plays.[10] The Admiral's Men even kept "owld
Mahemetes head" among their stage properties, according to the inven-
tory of 1598.[11]

While these and other contemporary representations tended to exoti-
cize their subject to some degree, they nonetheless produced an East at
base more civilized, more organized, and more knowable than Africa and
the Americas. The discourse on the East was, as Peter Hulme has suggested, primarily a discourse of "civilization" that contrasts directly with
the New World "discourse of savagery" as with the double vision of Africa.[12] The figures who emerge most prominently from it are, like the
Moors in Africa (but without the incriminating tie to Negro compeers),
leaders, decked in impressive power and forms of power, imposing and
enforcing, despite their own peculiar hang-ups, a fairly organized and unified rule.

Yet just as Europe's ostensibly bifurcated view of Africa was reduced
to a single sight of savagery, so inversely was Europe's ostensibly single

vision of the East opened to difference. On top of the assumption of civilization, Orientalist discourse is also divided against itself, as the differences between Said and Schwab attest, with the East emerging as at once the place and projection of barbarity and fear and of civility and emulation.[13] Its subjects, instead of being obscured into a composite image of savagery, were inscribed in geographically bounded spaces of extremity, as overwhelmingly wealthy, wondrous, and exotic, or outrageously barbaric, with the excesses of each preventing its collapse into the other.

On one side of the picture were figures such as the Persians, sometimes "wicked" like Cambyses (who rules over Cruelty and Murder), but, perhaps because they were in contention with and less dominating than the Turks, known more for wealth and fineries than for imperious leaders.[14] Barabas sits amid "heaps of gold" (stage direction) apparently made from a "venture" "summ'd and satisfied" by "the third part of the Persian ships" (*The Jew of Malta* 1.1.2–3), and thinks of the East as a wonderland of wealth—people by Arabians, "who so richly pay / The things they traffic for with wedge of gold" (1.1.8–9),

> merchants of the Indian mines,
> That trade in metal of the purest mould;
> The wealthy Moor, that in the eastern rocks
> Without control can pick his riches up
> And in his house heap pearls like pebble stones.
> (1.1.19–23)

Beyond such material fantasies, the Persians in particular were also assigned a brand of Mohammedanism that, with its Christian-like cult of martyrdom, was allowed to "stand more upon reason and nature" than were other more "libertine," martial, or "superstitious" Islamic sects.[15]

On the other side of the picture were figures such as, and discursively dominated by, the Turks, ready to "glut [their] swords," like Bajazeth, with "the feeble Persians' [not to mention, Europeans'] blood" (*Tamburlaine* 3.3.164–65), to "sacrifice / Mountains of breathless men to Mahomet" like Callapine (2:3.5.54–55).

It was perhaps largely because the East, with its longstanding, imperializing civilization, was closer to Europe ideologically and geographically that its people (unlike the Africans or Indians) were given differentiated national identities, more like and relevant to "ours." Yet while these various identities remained for the most part in tact, the different Oriental groups were also accorded both positive and negative attributes that complicated but did not erase the civil/savage divide either between the different nationalities or between them and other "others." What resulted were subjects who were to be emulated *and* feared, not because their apparent civility would at any moment devolve into barbarism, but because that civility was also coupled to barbarism. The example of Cambyses emerges not as an exception but as the rule, proving Persians both wealthy and wicked. Rather than generating or expressing ambivalence, these internal differences only furthered the imperialist cause, exposing the need to contain the East because its leaders were more accomplished *and* more barbaric than we, while establishing a variety of fronts on which to do so.

It seems no coincidence that the Turks, the most prominent and threatening figures on the Eastern horizon, came in the widest array of shapes and sizes—as villainous, Machiavellian, lascivious, barbaric, warmongering, anti-Christian infidels, and as masterful military tacticians, able to successfully discipline and organize their troops (as I've suggested above).[16] In instance after instance, both the negative and the positive are called in to give reason for "us" to suppress or surpass "them."

For example, when George Whetstone, in his *English Mirrour* (1586), one of *Tamburlaine*'s key sources, sets out to demonize Islam, he produces Turks who originated in Scythia (Tamburlaine's homeland) "as savadge men" and who, after "robb[ing] and conquer[ing] certaine provinces" in Asia Minor, "(as barbarous infidell people,) receyved the damnable sect of Mahomet . . . which best greed with their wicked customs" (p. 70).[17] It is difficult to know from Whetstone's text which is the cart and which the horse, which the tenor and which the vehicle of the critique, whether Mohammedanism or the Turks (or both). Yet tellingly, when the topic shifts from religion to politics, from the damnable embrace of Mohammed to the glorified project of Empire, those "wicked customs" disappear and we are shown the "worthiness, and wonderfull prowess" of figures such as the "great Emperour" Bajazet, "the most adventrous, the most renowned and the most feared Prince of this time" (pp. 80, 72). In both cases we are to see in the Turks justification for imperializing—and, ironically, imperializing against them, in particular—either because their leadership is so "wonderfull" or their religion so "damnable."

Conversely, when Queen Elizabeth attempts to regulate commercial and political relations with the Turks, her letters, intended both for the Ottoman leaders and the English public, downplay England's longstanding hostility to Islam, presenting herself as "the most invincible and most mighty defender of the Christian faith against all kind of idolatries of all that live among the Christians and falsly professe the name of Christ," and the Turks as an allied nation equally hostile to idolatry.[18] At issue instead are Turkish politics. Though she commends the Turkish "majesties goodnesse" in one letter and thanks him for granting safe passage to a few Englishmen in another, she also criticizes him for admitting only a few and not many (as he did in the case of other foreigners).[19] She also renders his apparent hospitality suspect by entreating him to free her subjects who have been "deteined as slaves and captives in [his] Gallies," "not by any offence of theirs."[20] In her case, it is not religion but politics which is the problem, and politics not religion which is thus condemned. Yet here too, while one side of the picture valorizes the Turkish—and English— attempts to dominate (here to "defend" the world against idolatry), the other side makes clear why "we" had better surpass "them."

Similarly, in the histories of Tamburlaine, the Scythian is represented in conflicting terms (not always in the same text) as both an extraordinary model and an extraordinary threat. In Petrus Perondinus's *Vita magni Tamerlanis* (1551), the other of Marlowe's key sources, he is a "pitiless, destructive, and irresistible barbarian, dominated by an insatiable thirst for power."[21] In Whetstone, he is one of the two "mightiest princes of the world" (with Bajazet the second), who liberated his homeland "from the servitude of the Sarizens and kinges of Persia" and created such "government and order" among his troops "that his campe seemed a goodly City" (pp. 72, 80).

Whetstone's account is particularly telling, for its attempts to turn Tamburlaine into an exemplary hero are unsettled by glimpses of barbarism, and its uneasy and unsuccessful efforts to suppress the latter instead bring out the tension created by the bipolarity within Orientalist discourse. In the subtitle, the *Mirrour* announces its intention: to provide a glass "wherein all estates may beholde the Conquests of Envy."[22] Accordingly, Tamburlaine figures as a scourge of God, "raysed . . . to chasten the kings & proud people of the earth" (p. 82), yet not without the irrepressible taint of cruelty. He appears in the *Mirrour* for the first time in its account of a "Geneowe merchant," who asked him not to kill all the citizens of a conquered town. Although Whetstone mentions that Tamburlaine ignored this advice "in his fury," he diverts attention from that fury by emphasizing instead the merchant's "good counsell." He does implicate the conqueror in his moral, directing "other Princes that have their passions more temperate" to learn from this example "how to keep under their own suspected subjects without dispeopling of their realms" (p. 16).

Yet when Whetstone recounts the event again, in a section on "The wonderfull conquest of Tamburlaine," he exonerates the hero's rashness by pressing it above and beyond the ordinary realm of humankind, recording and accepting Tamburlaine's self-justificatory answer to the merchant: "Thou supposest that I am a man, but thou art deceived, for I am no other then the ire of God, and the destruction of the world" (p. 82). Whetstone fashions his moral around this claim and vindicates Tamburlaine's subsequent slaughter of men, women, and children through it, concluding that "it seemed by his cruelty, that God raysed him to chasten the kings and proud people of the earth." Yet the "facts"—here, the fact that those "chastened" are not "kings and proud people," but men with "wives & children cloathed all in white, having Olive branches in their handes" and "humbly beseech[ing] grace" (p. 82)—refuse to comply, showing us a leader of questionable dimensions and demeanor where the narrator scripts a hero.

The tension within the account reflects at once the extremes of the Eastern world picture and the attempts to press those extremes out of conflict into an instructive clarity, into a mirror of discrete examples for the West's emulation and contempt. Though Africa could be blurred into a savage darkness, the "civilized" East could not: its message, like England's, had to be clear—and, as ever, clearly to England's advantage. And, on either side of the picture, it was. To people the East with barbarians or with the "mightiest princes of the world" was to promote and justify imperialism, to display a contemptible barbarity and an admirable "might" demanding our containment. To produce extremes in Africa was to reduce a double vision into an incriminating singularity; to produce extremes in the East, however, was to foster a polarity that could only be brought under control and into meaning by the prospects and projects of English domination. And it is that process that Marlowe explores, exposes, and subverts.

"What god, or, fiend, or spirit of the earth?"

When Theridamas, acting for the Persian king, angrily confronts and condemns Tamburlaine, Tamburlaine comments sarcastically, "Noble and mild this Persian seems to be, / If outward habit judge the inward man" (1.2.162–63). Yet in Marlowe's East, as here, the outward habit does not "judge" the inward man. Throughout both parts of the play, characters continually assess Tamburlaine, pondering again and again "of what

mould or mettle he be made / What star or fate soever govern him"
(2.6.17–18), "whether from earth, or hell, or heaven he grow" (2.6.23).
Each time, the answer is different. Marlowe builds Tamburlaine's characterization upon a series of inconsistent and contradictory impressions like
those characterizing Orientalist discourse, but (unlike that discourse) refuses to determine whether his Eastern ruler is a barbarous villain or an
awe-inspiring hero. Instead what is on display is how Tamburlaine and his
competitors deploy these contradictory self-constructions in the service of
empire, creating an extraordinarily threatening or extraordinarily admirable "outward habit" around an unknowable "inward man." While the
characters use these terms to create the illusion of supremacy, Marlowe
disrupts the process, showing at once how little difference there is between
these terms and how much difference there is within them.

In Part 1 (my focus in this and the following section) as throughout,
the representation of Tamburlaine is, as critics have often noted, torn between two extremes.[23] The one, a "sturdy Scythian thief" (1.1.36), "with
his lawless train / Daily commits incivil outrages" (1.1.39–40), kidnaps and
"rapes" a soldan's daughter, and (if that is not enough) kills her suitor,
charges on twenty thousand men as a "pretty jest" (2.5.90), treats a captive
emperor as a footstool and a dog, decimates a town, and impales virgins
on its walls. The other entertains aspiring ideas of nobility and beauty and
expresses himself in extraordinary "working words" (2.3.25), displays and
distributes vast amounts of wealth and worlds, and, at a moment when all
hope for his mercy seems hopeless, saves a soldan's life.

The play provides no stable comparative standard through which we
can judge his relative civility or barbarity and situates him instead within
a dramatic landscape that "swarms" with figures whose nationalities (Persian, Turkish, Egyptian, Natolian, and so on) and whose "incivil outrages"
are at least as incriminating as his.[24] The Persian king's brother, Cosroe,
and the Turkish emperor, Bajazeth, followed in Part 2 by Bajazeth's son
Callapine, to mention only a few, share his project for subduing half the
world, regardless of lives lost or tactics used.[25]

Tamburlaine's own self-representations are no help either. What distinguishes him from his competitors, as David Thurn has argued, is his
ability to create stable and stabilizing "sights of power" which sustain a
convincing illusion of "absolute sovereignty" and "virtually banish indeterminacy" from the stage.[26] Yet although Tamburlaine establishes himself
as the most important "sight of power," he does so in ways that cloak the
"inward man" in contradiction and indeterminacy, at least from our per-

spective. Though he is obviously driven by a desire for empire, each time he articulates the desire behind the desire, he articulates it differently, embracing successively a series of all-consuming ends: living "at liberty" (1.2.26); being the "terror to the world" (1.2.38) as well as scourge of god; "climbing," like Faustus, "after knowledge infinite" (2.7.24); possessing "that perfect bliss and sole felicity, / The sweet fruition of an earthly crown" (2.7.28–29); gaining "fame," "valour," and "victory" while "conceiving" and "subduing" beauty (5.2.118, 120) and "fashion[ing]" himself "with true nobility" (5.2.127). All of these goals and aspects might be integrated into a unified "Renaissance man," but Tamburlaine offers them up discretely and discontinuously, betraying them as "outward habits" detached from an "inward man."

Yet this is not merely a classic case of self-fashioning, prompted by the problem of an elusive and illusory self, but a strategy for imperial success. Tamburlaine exploits the differences between his self-images in his rise to power. When he first casts aside his humble shepherd's "weeds," which he "disdain[s] to wear," and displays the "complete armour" and "curtle-axe" beneath as "adjuncts more beseeming Tamburlaine," he uses the contrast to prove that he and his "silly" [i.e., simple] "country swains" will terrorize the world and "make the mountains quake" (1.2.41–49). He tells his followers (as a means of telling his prisoners and us):

> These lords perhaps do scorn our estimates,
> And think we prattle with distemper'd spirits:
> But, since they measure our deserts so mean,
> That in conceit bear empires on our spears,
> Affecting thoughts coequal with the clouds,
> They shall be kept our forced followers
> Till with their eyes they view us emperors.
>
> (1.2.61–67)

On the one hand he dares us, as he does his other captive audience, to read him as disillusioned and distempered; on the other, he discourages us from doing just that by positioning himself confidently against such readings. His followers, compliantly, "see kings kneeling at his feet" (1.2.55) and are ready (hoping to replace those kings) to follow him "even to death" (1.2.59). We, however, see a figure making a show of himself, representing himself in extremes from distemper to divinity, prompting excessive admiration and excessive fear.

Importantly, too, although he presents his selves as self-initiated and self-sustaining, what determines the shape of his "outward habit" is, to a significant degree, his audience. For Tamburlaine tailors his image to the needs and expectations of his contenders, answering their desires and out-doing their resistance. To those who would be wooed and whom he would woo, he displays divinity, nobility, and wealth; to those who would destroy and whom he would destroy, barbarity and ire. In so doing, he places himself beyond containment and contempt, proving himself supe-rior in his competitors' terms and despite their agendas, making them complicit in his triumph.

The two most sustained and contradictory instances of this strategy occur in his interactions with Zenocrate and with Bajazeth—interactions which, in their difference, together underscore and undermine the ex-tremes of his self-constructions. In the case of Zenocrate, Tamburlaine fashions his displays to answer her "mild aspect" and respect for noble stature, which she measures by deeds as well as titles. When she is first captured by his forces, she pleads for her release by appealing to his ap-parent nobility, calling him "lord—for so [he does] import" (1.2.33). She turns also to the gods who, as "defenders of the innocent" (1.2.68), would not support the oppression of "poor friendless passengers" (1.2.70) such as herself. Though Tamburlaine attempts first to woo her with visions of empire, he takes his cues from her pleas and redirects his attention (and hers) to his lordliness and love, presenting himself as a liberty-loving lord in shepherd's clothing and declaring her "person" "more worth to Tam-burlaine / Than the possession of the Persian crown" (1.2.90–91). No longer "measuring the limits of his empery" (1.2.39), he offers her an impressive catalog of exotic gifts to attest to his love and her beauty—garments of Median silk, an ivory sled drawn by milk-white harts, a hun-dred attendant Tartars and five hundred captives and the like. His compan-ion Techelles voices skepticism about, and draws attention to, this abrupt shift in focus, exclaiming, "What now! in love?" (1.2.106). Tamburlaine's response, "women must be flattered: / But this is she with whom I am in love" (1.2.107–8), encourages our skepticism too, betraying his readiness to manipulate his audience, to flatter women who must be flattered, to speak of nobility and love to women who would not hear of empire.

Though others remain wary, his custom-made persuasions work on Zenocrate. Granted, he gives her no choice but to live with him, either "willingly" or as a slave, but although she initially resists, acquiescing only because she "must be pleas'd perforce" (1.2.259), she soon prefers to "live and die with Tamburlaine" (3.2.24). What fuels that desire is that he remains, to her, a "lordly love" whose "talk" is "much sweeter than the Muses' song" (3.2.49–50) and whose treatment of her "is far from villainy or servitude / And might in noble minds be counted princely" (3.2.38–39). In a telling contrast, her companion Agydas objects to their captivity, sees Tamburlaine's actions as an "offensive rape" (3.2.6) and Tamburlaine as "a man so vile and barbarous" (3.2.26), and, consequently, is met by a different figure, one who, in direct response to these cues, "look[s] wrathfully" upon him and sends him a "naked dagger" to (successfully) command his death (stage direction).

Although Tamburlaine matches Agydas's hostility with violence, he meets Zenocrate's aversion to violence, evidenced throughout Parts 1 and 2, with diversions. When he goes off to fight Bajazeth, he first praises her beauty and then leaves her to "manage words" (3.3.131) with Bajazeth's wife, Zabina, as if the real battle will be as mild. The Turk, in contrast, leaves his wife with anticipations of violence, vowing that their sons "will batter turrets with their manly fists" (3.3.111) when they come of age, as he prepares to do now. After Tamburlaine's triumph, Zenocrate is confronted with the results—the corpses of the encaged Turkish leaders, who have brained themselves against their cage, the sight of her "first-betrothed love" (5.2.327), the King of Arabia, fatally wounded by Tamburlaine in the attack, "Damascus walls dy'd with Egyptian blood," "the streets strow'd with dissever'd joints of men," "heavenly virgins and unspotted maids" "hoisted up" on "horsemen's lances" and so on (5.2.259–67). Made "wretched" (5.2.258) by these calamities, she laments that Tamburlaine was "the cause of this" (5.2.258, 274), and at this moment in which her loyalty to him is most threatened, Tamburlaine draws attention from these bloody spectacles by creating an unexpected but much desired show of mercy. He allows Zenocrate to set her father free, praising her as the one "that hath calm'd the fury of my sword" (5.2.376), and then re-presents his terrorist tactics as an "honour, that consists in shedding blood / When men"—who are thus blamed in his stead—"presume to manage arms with him" (5.2.416–17). Cleaning up the bloody pieces of the past, he promises to entomb Bajazeth, Zabina, and the king of Arabia "with honour, as beseems" (5.2.470) him as well as them, letting what Zenocrate would like to see supplant what she has seen.[27] And his strategies work on her and her father, who embrace him as an honorable man, worthy of taking Zenocrate's hand in marriage.

We ourselves become the manipulated subjects of similar tactics when, in a scene whose internal disruptions have received much critical attention, Tamburlaine offers his famous accolade to beauty ("What is beauty, saith my sufferings, then?" [5.2.97–127]), almost immediately after ordering the deaths of the virgins who have come to plead for Damascus's safety. In effect, he distracts us from the "baneful" sight (5.2.69) (possibly staged in some form) of virgins impaled on the city's walls by reminding us of his ennobling conceits.[28] Yet for us, who unlike Zenocrate have seen this shift and what is on the other side of it several times before, Tamburlaine proves himself neither a monstrous barbarian nor an awe-inspiring hero but a strategist, capable of being both, of appropriating nobility to mask barbarity as circumstance—in this case, the circumstance of an audience predisposed to condemn his violence—dictates. The point is not merely that he, as critics have noticed, uses ceremony to cover violence, but that he does so case-specifically, in the face of those who value ceremony over violence.

Importantly, in the case of Bajazeth, who boasts of brutality and challenges Tamburlaine to match it, the terms change, and Tamburlaine, confronted by a thirst for slaughter, becomes a thirsty slaughterer, able to outdo and subdue his aggressive competitor. Before fighting they engage first in a balanced dialogue of one-upsmanship in which Tamburlaine matches the Turk almost word for word. When Bajazeth attacks "the presumption of this Scythian slave" (3.3.68) who "dar'st . . . bluntly call me Bajazeth" (3.3.71), Tamburlaine protests that the "Turk" "dar'st . . . bluntly call me Tamburlaine" (3.3.72, 74). Because the Turk sets out to "let thousands die" and to use their "slaughter'd carcasses" for "walls and bulwarks to the rest" (3.3.138–39), the Scythian responds graphically in kind (presumably not just in words), boasting:

> Our conquering swords shall marshal us the way
> We use to march upon the slaughter'd foe,
> Trampling their bowels with our horses' hoofs.
>   (3.3.148–50)[29]

We are not allowed to see the battle, but instead see the wives "managing words" during it and Tamburlaine caging and tormenting the Turks after it, the latter an act with striking resonances in an era when a monarch (Mary, Queen of Scots) had been confined and executed. This decentering of the combat, though maybe in part a practical solution to staging a scene of so many men and so much gore, draws our attention to the way the contest is framed—to the imitative acts and dialogues that link Tamburlaine's "outward habit" to Bajazeth's own aggression.

Notably, Bajazeth's words provide the precedent for Tamburlaine's responses long after the scene is over. In Part 2, Tamburlaine spectacularly realizes the Turk's threat that the enemy captains "shall draw the chariot of my emperess" (3.3.80) by bridling the captured "stout contributory kings" (3.3.93) he himself has captured as horses for his chariot. And while the sonless Tamburlaine has no recourse in Part 1 when Bajazeth valorizes his three Herculean sons, between Parts 1 and 2 he has three sons (though one is hardly Herculean), and in Part 2 he teaches them the martial curriculum (how to "gripe a warlike lance" [3.3.106] and "batter turrets with their manly fists"[3.3.111]) that Bajazeth has earlier prescribed. In Part 2 as well Tamburlaine takes his cue from Bajazeth's bloody self-slaughter and vows to "knock out" the jailor Almeda's "brains" (2:3.5.143) for turning traitor and setting Callapine free.

That these displays of barbarity are, in fact, custom-made to suit and surpass Bajazeth is reinforced by the fact that Tamburlaine treats other enemies differently. For example, in winning over Theridamas, who disputes his noble pretensions and contests his power but sees fire in his eyes and does not dream of empire, Tamburlaine becomes the severe master of the fates, bound to conquer the East and, with Jove's help, to pay his followers well.[30] In overthrowing Cosroe, who treats his words as oracles but aspires to comparable power, he first pretends to be a subservient though indomitable follower with no eye to greater gains, insisting that "the world will strive with hosts of men-at-arms / To swarm unto the ensign I support" (2.3.13–14) and that their collective success is guaranteed by "fates and oracles" (2.3.7).

These claims to divine sanction further underline the situational nature of Tamburlaine's identities, for like his awesome civility and awful barbarity, his relation to otherworldly influences, which support those postures, shifts also as occasion warrants. Sometimes he is endorsed by the "stars," sometimes by the fates, sometimes by Jove, sometimes by a Christian God—and sometimes he puts his power above and beyond all these, depending on who is watching and why. Although he makes himself master of the fates to win the Persians' confidence, once he usurps the Persian crown, he encourages their allegiance by putting their endorsement above divine sanction, proclaiming that, thanks to them, the crown is "surer on my head / Than if the gods had held a parliament" (2.7.65–66) and placed it there. As he rallies his forces to "fight courageously" against the Turks,

he turns himself into the "scourge and wrath" of a Christian God, enlisted
to free enslaved Christians and to punish those who regularly "make quick
havoc of the Christian blood" (3.3.58). And, in attempting to justify his
overthrow of Zenocrate's native Egypt and father, he places himself and
his mission above the gods, boasting that "the god of war resigns his room
to me" (5.2.389), that "Jove, viewing me in arms, looks pale and wan, /
Fearing my power should pull him from his throne" (5.2.391–92).

The discrepancies between these evocations, as between his self-representations, and the correlations between his spectators and his selves prove
Tamburlaine neither a god nor fiend nor spirit of the earth, but an imperialist, strategically constructing a self of remarkable ignominy or nobility
from his spectators' expectations, showing us that civility and barbarity
are only skin deep. In Part 2, in the midst of a contention with still another
set of kings, Tamburlaine declares that he is not

> made arch-monarch of the world,
> Crown'd and invested by the hand of Jove,
> For deeds of bounty or nobility.
> (4.1.152–54)

Instead, he asserts, he "exercise[s] a greater name, / The Scourge of God
and terror of the world," and so must "apply [him]self to fit those terms,
/ In war, in blood, in death, in cruelty" (4.1.155–58). His assertion not only
recalls the extreme and opposing roles he has assumed throughout Part 1;
it also articulates the way he has done so, continually but discontinuously
applying himself to fit the terms of those around him. The Jew of Malta
will follow suit, becoming the Jew his viewers expect to see in order to
mask his unpredictable villainies beneath a soothing guise of predictability.
Tamburlaine, however, plays to expectations to surpass them, in either a
positive or a negative way, to inspire admiration or terror, and so to conquer, outdo, and subdue the world.

A "monster turned to a manly shape"

Although Tamburlaine's "working words" do work spectacularly against
all odds and against all others, they are, paradoxically, also dialogically
embedded within an imperialist exchange in ways that are finally self-
consuming rather than self-sustaining. For not only does Tamburlaine ap-

ply himself to fit others' terms, his image is significantly shaped by others' articulations of their terms. And what ultimately determines his imperial "mould or mettle" is the ever-shifting intersection of both.

Tamburlaine's "high astounding terms" have almost always gotten all the good (or bad) press, and with good reason, since they are the most prominent, the most eloquent, and the most successful.[31] Yet they are surrounded by others which are different in degree or effect, but not in kind, and which Tamburlaine himself appropriates, whether consciously or not. When Menaphon celebrates Cosroe's newly won victory over Mycetes and anticipates that the new king will now be able to "ride in triumph through Persepolis" (2.5.49), Tamburlaine twice repeats his phrase, as if to savor the sound as much as the idea, using it to garner support for his own attempt at the throne.[32] (He shows no specific interest in Persepolis before or after, though we are told he has been stealing its merchants' goods for some time). His most famous speech, often quoted as quintessential Tamburlaine, celebrating the potential of "aspiring minds" to "comprehend / The wondrous architecture of the world" and climb "after knowledge infinite," ends, incongruously, by reducing these all-expansive desires to a single goal: "the ripest fruit of all, / That perfect bliss and sole felicity, / The sweet fruition of an earthly crown" (2.7.20–29).

His fetishization of the crown, which thus seems notably out of place here, has been put in place by Theridamas, who earlier revels in anticipation of the "kingly joys" of "wear[ing] a crown enchas'd with pearl and gold, / Whose virtues carry with it life and death" and which proves a god "not so glorious as a king" (2.5.57–62). Even when Tamburlaine marks out his own distinctive rhetorical territory, claiming that "*will* and *shall* best fitteth Tamburlaine," he does so after hearing Theridamas "speak in that mood" (3.3.40–41) and applauding him for it. And it seems no coincidence either that he first declares himself the scourge of god after noting that he has been "term'd the Scourge and Wrath of God" (3.3.44) by others.

Yet it is not just Tamburlaine's discourse that is shaped by others' words but his image as well. For while he builds his own incontestable singularity out of and against their predilections, they prove their own supremacy by imposing their own constructions of difference upon him. Circumscribed thus, he becomes not just an imperializing subject of Orientalist discourse but also its imperialized object, a convenient other whose godlike or fiendlike nature can justify his competitors' triumphs or defeats and testify finally to their, rather than his, power.

In the opening scenes, for example, Mycetes first directs attention to Tamburlaine, not because the "paltry Scythian" is a powerful threat to the Persian regime, but rather, it seems, because he is not. Mycetes is overwhelmed by the internal threats of Cosroe and the "swarms" of "vile outragious men / That live by rapine and by lawless spoil" (2.2.22–23), and by the external threats of the resistant Babylonians and the imperializing Turks. Tamburlaine and his "Tartarian rout" (1.1.71), whose worst offenses at this point consist only of robbing the merchants of Persepolis of their spoils from Western trade and dreaming of empire, provide a more containable foe, who seems suited for the "dainty show" (1.1.80) of power which the king is ready and able to carry out. Even though Mycetes clearly underestimates their strength, to his great disadvantage, he uses (or continues) his misreading to his advantage, excusing his failure by their "incivil outrages" (1.1.40), representing Tamburlaine as a "wicked" Tartarian thief who "inveigle[d]" the Persian forces with "gifts and promises" (2.2.24–26). Ironically, like a self-fulfilling prophecy, what Mycetes privileges as the predominant danger to Persia ultimately becomes just that, for Tamburlaine begins his accumulation of military strength with the troops sent from the Persian court. This is perhaps the only instance in the play when Tamburlaine's rise to power seems so directly and materially predicated upon others' reactions. Yet his friends' and foes' responses to him throughout are dictated as much by how they need to read his shows of power as by his shows of power.

Although Cosroe first discounts the Scythian's potential, his attitude changes at a moment marked not just by Tamburlaine's success over Mycetes' men, but also by his own desire to amass an army of "forty thousand strong" (2.1.61), and through it, to dominate the East as well as Persia. Asking Menaphon to depict the "stature" and "personage" (2.1.6) of this potential ally, his request calls for confirmation of the image that he already has in mind, of Tamburlaine as a "valiant" "man of fame," "that in the forehead of his fortune / Bears figures of renown and miracle" (2.1.2–4). Menaphon compliantly provides those figures, using Tamburlaine's "every part" to construct a wondrously motivated and divinely sanctioned conqueror—assigning his height and straight posture a desire that "lift[s] upwards and [is] divine," his fiery eyes "a heaven of heavenly bodies" that "guide his steps and actions to the throne," his "knot of amber hair" "wanton majesty" (2.1.8–29). Cosroe further shapes the "mould and mettle" of this "wondrous man" (2.1.32) by reading Tamburlaine as one who, despite this divinely authorized anatomy, would be satisfied to be his "regent, and remain as king" (2.1.49). Their cohort Ceneus, too, in his only lines and funtion in the play, designs a Tamburlaine motivated solely by "disdain of wrong and tyranny" (2.1.55) and not imperializing ambition, a Tamburlaine, that is, whose actions and motivations can only undermine Mycetes' authority and validate Cosroe's.

When Tamburlaine then betrays them and proves their impressions false, their responses change significantly. They again appropriate him to reinforce their own potency; yet this time it is not as an incontestable ally, but as an incontestable foe. Instead of ascribing their defeat to their own inability to read his imperialistic features, they project their failings onto him, making him essentially unreadable rather than themselves bad readers. Meander insists that "some powers divine, or else infernal, mix'd / Their angry seeds at his conception" (2.6.9–10). Ortygius, seconding this vision, rallies the faction to "be arm'd against the hate of such a foe, / Whether from earth, or hell, or heaven he grow," whether he is a

> god, or fiend, or spirit of the earth,
> Or monster turned to a manly shape,
> Or of what mould or mettle he be made,
> What star or fate soever govern him.
> (2.6.15–23)

In pressing Tamburlaine beyond knowability, into the unknowable realms of the supernatural or superhuman, Cosroe and his allies not only justify their misreading; they simultaneously mystify their own power, making themselves so great that only a "god, or fiend, or spirit of the earth" or "monster turned to a manly shape" could defeat them. In questioning how "this devilish shepherd" dares "to cast up hills against the face of heaven, / And dare the force of angry Jupiter?" (2.6.1–4), Cosroe aligns himself with "the force of angry Jupiter" and "the face of heaven," able to "send this monstrous slave to hell" (2.6.7). And when he faces defeat nonetheless, he saves that face by turning his opponents into "the strangest men that ever nature made" (2.7.40).

Bajazeth also defines Tamburlaine in similarly shifting and self-serving terms. Like Cosroe, he initially discounts his opponent's imperialist ambitions and offers a truce—from what he says, because he hears "one Tamburlaine" "bears a valiant mind" (3.1.3, 32), but from what we see, because he wants to get on with his "dreadful siege" of Constantinople (3.1.5). When this valiant figure emerges as a menacing but potentially conquerable foe, Bajazeth derogates him as a "base-born" "Scythian slave" (3.3.68,95). Yet when the "slave" triumphs, although Bajazeth continues to derogate him as a thief, he also, at greater length, envisions him as one whose sword is influenced by "such a star . . . / As rules the skies and countermands the gods" (5.2.169–70). Unable to beat Tamburlaine himself and unwilling to try further, the Turk anticipates that only the most extraordinary forces could. He hopes that "millions of men" will "encompass" the conqueror and "gore [his] body with as many wounds," that "Furies from the black Cocytus' lake" will enforce him to "run upon the baneful pikes," that "vollies of shot," "every bullet dipt in poison'd drugs," will "pierce through [his] charmed skin," and that "roaring cannons" will "sever all [his] joints" (5.2.152–60). No longer a valiant competitor or a slave, Tamburlaine becomes unbeatably charmed, providing a challenge even to hell. Similarly overwhelmed by Tamburlaine's invincible campaign, Zabina doubts whether Mahomet or any other god or fiend, or any fortune or hope remains to free them from their "infamous, monstrous slaveries" (5.2.178). With Tamburlaine demonized thus, it becomes no wonder that she and Bajazeth have been defeated and finally give up, taking their own lives.

Likewise, the Soldan of Egypt calls Tamburlaine every name in the book, from the "savage Calydonian boar," a wolf, and "a monster of five hundred thousand heads, / Compact of rapine, piracy, and spoil"; to "the scum of men," "a base usurping vagabond," "a sturdy felon, and a base-bred thief"; to "the hate and scourge of God" (4.3.1–21).[33] His depictions, like those of the Turks and the Persians, ultimately exonerate him, creating a figure whose baseness requires and portends his defeat and whose mythological monstrosities or superhuman sanction provide an excuse for his successes. What his terms (like Bajazeth's and Cosroe's) reveal, with all their inconsistencies, is not a "monster turn'd to a manly shape," but a man, turned and shaped by his foes into a monster. When Tamburlaine triumphs at the end of Part 1, offering to invest Zenocrate as Queen of Persia, he asks her whether she will "consent to satisfy" his designs, and she agrees, explaining "else should I much forget myself" (5.2.438–39). To disagree would, in fact, be to forget herself, to forget that her desires, like those of others, are the stuff that Tamburlaine is made on. For the most part, his and others' terms coincide, building a figure of outstanding civility or terrorizing barbarity twice over. Yet that coincidence—because it is, in fact, no coincidence but the product of a dialogic exchange—undermines the agency of everyone involved. In this game of empire, the assertion of difference denies rather than constitutes identity, proving one man's hero another man's barbarian as need be.

The Empire Strikes Back

The second part of *Tamburlaine* traces a second series of battles between a second series of all too similar foes. It is in this part that Stephen Greenblatt's suggestion of Tamburlaine as a "machine" unable to "slow down or change course" seems particularly apt, both for the figure and for the play itself, for the pattern of events initiated in the first part continues here. The Tamburlaine who reappears is still trying amid competitive and contributory kings to fix the difference between himself and them, to "exercise a greater name, / The Scourge of God and terror of the world," and to "apply [him]self to fit those terms / In war, in blood, in death, [and] in cruelty" (2:4.1.155–58). His enemies continue, as they challenge him, to deride him as a "thief of Scythia" (2:3.1.15) and his actions as "barbarous damned tyranny" (2:4.1.141), and, as they suffer from his triumphs and torments, to demonize him as a "vile monster, born of some infernal hag, / And sent from hell"—or sometimes from heaven—"to tyrannise on earth" (2:5.1.110–11).

Here, too, the events of Part 1 seem to reoccur, though with different key players and somewhat different effects, suggesting that imperialist patterns of competition and conquest, if not history itself, are infinitely and inevitably repeatable. The Christian king Sigismund first allies himself with the Moslem king Orcanes and then betrays that alliance when he thinks victory possible, repeating Tamburlaine's strategic embrace and betrayal of Cosroe. In another instance of déjà vu, the Governor of Babylon, like the Governor of Damascus, resists Tamburlaine's forces, despite citizen protest and in face of certain slaughter, to defend his city's autonomy and honor. After what we've seen of Damascus's fate, the result—the drowning of every Babylonian man, woman, and child and the governor's execution on the city walls—comes as no surprise (except perhaps to the governor, who agreed to pay Tamburlaine to spare his life). Similarly, Tamburlaine's capture and seduction of Zenocrate is reproduced twice: first when the imprisoned Callapine seduces Almeda the jailor to free him by "paint[ing] in words what [he]'ll perform in deeds" (2:1.3.10) and proffering a kingship and a catalog of exotic riches; and second, when Theridamas attempts to seduce the captain's wife, Olympia, insisting that she go with him, if not willingly, then by force.[34]

Yet despite this sense that the power play will never slow down or change course, that similar terms and strategies of power will be continually exercised and exploited by one conqueror (or one victim) or another, and that Tamburlaine will continue being Tamburlaine (or various Tamburlaines) from act to act to act, the second part of the play disrupts the illusion of endless repeatability and meaning that Part 1 has fostered. For in Part 2 Marlowe presses the appropriation of difference to an irreversible point of saturation, homogenizing claims to terrorizing looks and deeds, divine sanction, and infinite forces into the status quo, refusing to let anyone dominate and impose meaning on the space of the stage—Tamburlaine included.

Significantly, in the second play Tamburlaine's campaigns are enmeshed more deeply than before within a nexus of imperialist contentions. Although he continues to preside over the scenes in which he appears and appears in approximately the same high proportion of scenes, he is not as much the center of conversation when he is offstage. His initial appearance, too, is tellingly delayed and downplayed. The play focuses first on the negotiation between Sigismund, who is preoccupied with overcoming the Turks and "scourg[ing] their foul blasphemous paganism" (2:2.1.53), and Orcanes, who seeks an alliance with the Christians in defense against Tamburlaine but whom he mentions only once. This decentering of the hero reproduces what happens to some degree in Part 1 when internal dissension in Persia initially takes precedence over Tamburlaine's advances. Here, however, it is more surprising because Tamburlaine at this stage is not merely an aspiring shepherd but the established king of Persia, supported by a "world of people" (2:1.1.67), kings, and wealth at the least.

Callapine's transaction with Almeda also takes chronological precedence over Tamburlaine's exploits and redoes and outdoes the Scythian's first display of "working words," jeopardizing his singularity before he ever appears. While Tamburlaine calls up "a hundred Tartars," "an ivory sled" drawn by "milk-white harts," and "Median silk / Enchas'd with precious jewels" to woo Zenocrate, Callapine promises Almeda "Grecian virgins," a coach "drawn" by "naked negroes," and "a golden canopy / Enchas'd with precious stones." Although Tamburlaine stops after an additional offer of his "martial prizes," himself, and eventually a queenship, Callapine promises much more: "a hundred kings and more" to welcome Almeda home and "a hundred bassoes, cloth'd in crimson silk" to ride beside him; carpeted streets and "cloth of arras" for his "princely eye to pierce"; "a thousand galleys, mann'd with Christian slaves" and ships "fraughted with gold of rich America"; and, as he says, "more than this, for all I cannot tell."[35] Almeda initially protests that he would not betray Tamburlaine "for all Afric" (2:1.3.12), but what he gets of Turkey, a kingship included, seems to be enough. It is not surprising that the jailor eagerly acquiesces and that the soldan's daughter complies at first because she "must," considering how much he has to gain and how much she has to lose. Yet, his readiness to betray the conqueror makes clear that Tamburlaine no longer corners the market on rich fabrics, costly jewels, and exotic servants; in Part 2 desires for "all Afric" can be adequately met by others too.

Nor does he corner the market on accumulated men and nations.[36] Tamburlaine initiates his military campaigns in Part 2 with a ceremonial gathering of kings and crowns that serves for us as for them as an account-taking of all the Persian forces. Theridamas reports in with ten thousand Greeks, forty thousand "valiant men-at-arms" from Argier and Africa, and "five hundred brigandines" (2:1.5.9–11); Usumcasane with "a hundred thousand expert soldiers" (2:1.6.5) from Azamor to Tunis; Techelles, with "an host of Moors train'd to the war" (2:1.6.14), all handing their men with their crowns to Tamburlaine in a gesture that links their sovereignty (and his) to these enumerated forces. It is this measure that Orcanes details at length when he evaluates their potential and decides to embrace his longstanding Christian enemies for self-defense.[37]

Yet these signs of power ultimately prove as unreliable as they are unremarkable. Not only do all of the competing leaders seem to have "numbers more than infinite of men" (2:2.2.18), but also they display these numbers inconsistently, making both the real and the relative military strength of any faction difficult, if not impossible, to determine (particularly for spectators without calculators and maps). Orcanes insists that his Turkey blades could cut the throats, if need be, of "millions of soldiers" (including some giant Greenlanders, "as big as hugy Polypheme"), for he has behind him:

> revolted Grecians, Albanese,
> Sicilians, Jews, Arabians, Turks, and Moors,

Natolians, Sorians, black Egyptians,
Illyrians, Thracians, and Bithynians,
Enough to swallow forceless Sigismund.
                                    (2:1.1.61–65)

Why he nonetheless finds all these supporters "scarce enough t'encounter Tamburlaine" (2:1.1.66) is not clear either from his catalog or from his subsequent claim that when he fights, "all Asia Minor, Africa and Greece / Follow [his] standard and [his] thundering drums" (2:1.2.81–82).

When Callapine gathers his empire against Tamburlaine, he twice calls on his viceroys to tally their forces. During the first round, Orcanes brings forth "a hundred thousand men in arms" (2:3.1.39), sufficient in number "to drink the river Nile or Euphrates, / And for their power enow to win the world" (2:3.1.43–44). If that is not enough, the kings of Jerasulem, Trebizon, and Soria each contribute "as many" (2:3.1.45) from their domains. But that is not enough, at least for Callapine, who meets the messenger's report that Tamburlaine advances with men "in number more than are the quivering leaves / Of Ida's forest" (2:3.5.5–6) by calling for additional troops. Yet although the kings together add many thousands more, finally amassing "six hundred thousand valiant fighting men" (2:3.5.51) and momentarily satisfying Callapine, the meaning of these numbers falls flat when he, faced by Tamburlaine, flees immediately from the conqueror's looks, "like a summer's vapours vanish'd by the sun" (2:5.3.117), without even attempting to fight.[38]

Instead of measuring power, the seemingly infinite numbers of men and nations that Tamburlaine and his opponents continually display no longer mean anything, because of their commonality, the variability of how they are perceived, and their arbitrary relation to triumphs and defeats. The rhetoric of power emerges as just that, a *rhetoric* of power, full of sound and fury, signifying nothing—or at least nothing singular. Theatrically, the conditions of staging automatically highlight the discrepancy between the representation and what it represents; one man must stand metonymically for a thousand, a million, or more. Talk all they want, the kings onstage can only prove their infinite forces in words, and when words reach a point of saturation, these displays of power are emptied of their power and one man becomes as meaningful, or as meaningless, as a thousand men.

This is also the case for divinity, in which everyone now seems to have a stake. Commenting on the proximity of Tamburlaine's death to his burning of the Koran and on the resultant rupture between what seems to "bring down divine vengeance" and what, from an Elizabethan view, should, Greenblatt argues that the effect is "to challenge the habit of mind that looks to heaven for rewards and punishments."[39] What also challenge that habit are the characters' repeated and repeatedly inconsistent and manipulative turns to that authority. Sigismund, for example, the example of a Christian, reads divine law in terms of his will to power instead of reading his will to power in terms of divine law, suiting the Word to the action and not the action to the Word. When his allies press him to break his oath of peace with the Turks, he objects, insisting that such betrayal would instantiate "treachery and violence / Against the grace of our profession" (2:2.1.31–32) and that "the holy laws of Christendom" (2:2.1.36) are fixed and absolute. Yet he quickly gives in, persuaded that his "dispensive faith" (2:2.1.50) should be contingent upon circumstance, that the Turks' lack of "true" (2:2.1.34) faith nullifies his commitment to stand by what he swears by, and that the opportunity to "scourge their foul blasphemous paganism" (2:2.1.53) overrides everything—and, not inconsequentially, promises victory. Ready to "take the victory our God hath given" (2:2.1.63), he pays no further attention to his potential violation of the "holy laws"—not, that is, until his defeat can be blamed on an angry God, as punishment for his "accurs'd and hateful perjury" (2:2.3.3).

Tellingly, too, Orcanes shares his victory over the Christians with Mohammed *and* with Christ. If his conjunction of these two essentially incompatible authorities does not undermine his claims (since, as noted above, Elizabeth herself emphasized their similarities to promote an Anglo-Ottoman alliance), his questioning of whether "there be a Christ" (2:2.2.39) does. Tamburlaine's followers also gain control over their leader's impending death by involving their gods in a contingency plan. Instead of scripting his fate in terms of providential design, they rewrite providential design in terms of his fate, asserting that if Tamburlaine dies, heaven loses not only its "strangely blest" "instrument" (2:5.3.25, 38) and its glory, but itself becomes displaced by hell.

It is impossible to know from these and similar examples precisely where misprision stops and manipulation begins; yet either way, these evocations of divinity stand out as obviously self-serving. Though critics have railed like Robert Greene against *Tamburlaine*'s atheism, overturned here is not the authority of god (of any particular sort) but such self-authorizing appropriations of that god.[40] And what gets subverted and brought down to earth along with them are Tamburlaine's claims to divine right and purpose, which no longer mean anything in a world where everyone—and consequently no one—has dibs, conveniently if not strategically, on such sanction. In the world of empire, Marlowe insists, even and especially with infinite numbers of crowns, nations, men, and gods easily at hand, it becomes impossible for anyone, including a Tamburlaine, to make a difference, to escape the homogenizing blur of imperialism, or to single out a self (or other) with its terms.

"And shall I die, and this unconquered?"

It is within, if not because of, this homogenizing context, where the excesses of language defy rather than defend singularity, that Tamburlaine is forced to spell out the terms of his sovereignty and close the gap of indeterminacy that his strategic postures have opened. Yet the more he does so, the less his power means. Tamburlaine's character is more unified and predictable in Part 2, his over-saturated language notwithstanding, but it is no more outstanding, and, in fact, is even less. For even these individuated terms are caught in the nexus of cross-cultural negotiation and appropriation, their meaning and difference denied. In Part 2, the imperialist discourse, which so confidently distinguishes self and other in Part 1, proves unable to sustain either.

Though in Part 1 Tamburlaine claims various titles of sovereignty after usurping the Persian throne (which then seems the least of his conquests), in Part 2 he identifies himself more prominently than ever as King of Persia. It is as Persia's king (and not as the emperor of Africa and the East) that he plans to demand tribute from "all Africa" (2:5.1.164) to finance a citadel in Babylon. After drowning all the citizens of Babylon, he can think of nothing more fitting to do than to "depart to Persia / To triumph after all our victories" (2:5.1.210–11).[41] Whetstone's narrative uses this national allegiance to allot Tamburlaine a noble and successfully fulfilled desire to end the tyrannies and strengthen the power of the Persian empire, which had placed his nation in servitude. In Marlowe, however, Tamburlaine's emphasis on his role as King of Persia only blurs him further into an imperialist interplay in which to be a king is no longer to be half, or more glorious than, a god. For clearly, crowns are a dime a dozen here, commonly held and frequently bestowed. In perhaps the most telling return to Part 1, Callapine replays Tamburlaine's crowning of Zenocrate to make a king of his jailor Almeda. Like Tamburlaine, the Turkish leader delays and exploits the promised investiture as an occasion to exhibit his power; yet this gesture of sovereignty is no longer a climactic, show-stopping event. As the King of Jerusalem tells him, "'Tis naught for your majesty to give a kingdom" (2:3.1.78). Even Almeda is not impressed, declaring his unorthodox rise in status "no matter" since "Tamburlaine came up of nothing" (2:3.1.74–75) and simultaneously turning Tamburlaine's self-authorizing precedent into a display of "no matter."

Similarly, as Tamburlaine defines his role as scourge of God more precisely, the validity and singularity of his cause become less clear. Which god he serves remains as questionable here as (if not moreso than) it was in Part 1. He swears "by sacred Mahomet" (2:1.4.109) on the one hand and challenges that authority on the other, seeking "another godhead to adore" (2:5.1.198). As before, for most of the play that other godhead is Jove, who, he claims, invested him. Yet Tamburlaine's final say on the matter is as skeptical as it is ambiguous. He allows "the God that sits in heaven, *if any god*" to be "God alone, and none but he" (2:5.1.199–200; emphasis added). What makes his link to divine authority different in Part 2, however, is that although he does not settle *whom* he is scourging the world for, he defines *what* he is scourging the world of: pride.[42] His self-proclaimed mission is "to scourge the pride of such as Heaven" (whoever sits there) "abhors" (2:4.1.151).

Yet the closer he gets to delineating the difference between himself and others, the clearer the lack of difference becomes. For Tamburlaine is at least as culpable of pride as those who share his stage. Appropriately, he has been given a much deserved space within a recent collection of essays on "Narcissism and the Text"; as Peter Donaldson (who puts him there) notes, he "always wants to be *looked at*" and "tends to think of every victory as a forcing of admiration."[43] The problem, in fact, seems heightened in Part 2. Tamburlaine's most spectacular and memorable gesture of power comes in this play, when he demands that the "pamper'd jades of Asia" (2:4.3.1) draw his chariot, audaciously displaying the "figure of [his] dignity" (2:4.3.25) while ostensibly harnessing theirs, and refusing to let his son (who wants to harness up the extras) share in the spoils.[44] No longer satisfied to "ride in triumph through Persepolis," he anticipates, in much more extravagant terms, that he will "ride through Samarcanda streets,"

> like Saturn's royal son
> Mounted his shining chariot gilt with fire,
> And drawn with princely eagles through the path

> Pav'd with bright crystal and enchas'd with stars
> When all the gods stand gazing at his pomp.
>
> (2:4.3.125–30)

Even the gods are to watch. It is no wonder that Callapine emerges to scourge the pride of "cursed Tamburlaine" (2:5.2.30), though he, with his hopes of being the incontestable monarch of the world, is implicated also.

Further, although previously Tamburlaine defined his devices and desires in shifting and discontinuous terms, some material and some ethereal, in Part 2 a dismembering martial violence is all. While his decimation of Damascus stands out as singularly severe in Part 1, such extremity now becomes his ruling philosophy. In teaching his sons his modus operandi, he asserts:

> he shall wear the crown of Persia
> Whose head hath deepest scars, whose breast most wounds,
> Which, being wroth, sends lightning from his eyes,
> And in the furrows of his frowning brows
> Harbours revenge, war, death, and cruelty.
>
> (2:1.4.74–78)

It is "in a field" "sprinkled with the brains of slaughter'd men," he insists, that his "royal chair of state shall be advanc'd," and anyone hoping "to place himself therein, / Must armed wade up to the chin in blood" (2:1.4.79–84). And he lives up to his terms. Where once "working words" took the place of swords, now swords take the place of words, in ways that far outdo Bajazeth. It is not Tamburlaine but Orcanes and Sigismund who decide (at least at first) to "parley for a peace" (2:1.1.50) in lieu of fighting. By the final act he has "sack'd and burnt" "brave cities," "made waste" of kingdoms, and "drunk a sea of blood" (5.2.26, 13), calling up a rhetoric of dismemberment and destruction all the while. With good reason Olympia, the Captain of Balsera's ill-fated wife, fears the "barbarous Scythians" (2:3.4.19) and Moors "will hew us piecemeal" (2:3.4.21) at the least.

Yet while these are the signs Tamburlaine uses to make a name for himself, they are also the signs of the times. Though his terms and tactics have turned consistently bloody, even they prove nothing worth. Orcanes, too, hopes that his forces will "sprinkle" the Scythian's "poison'd brains" "through the tainted air" (2:3.1.67–68) and that the god of the underworld will "hal[e] him headlong to the lowest hell!" (2:4.3.42). The King of Jerusalem looks to heaven to "pour down blood and fire on [Tamburlaine's] head, / Whose scalding drops will pierce [his] seething brains" (2:4.1.145–46), while Callapine anticipates "invent[ing] some pain / That most may vex his body and his soul" (2:3.5.98–99). And the examples go on.

To some extent, in increasing the violence done (or hoped to be done) to bodies and body parts, Marlowe is guilty of demonizing the East— perhaps not in small part in order to capitalize on the seamier side of life and sustain the interest of spectators who have already witnessed five acts of predominantly G-rated conquest. Indeed, Part 2 contains more suggestions not only of barbarity but also, though less prominently, of lust. Turkish concubines replace Damascus's virgins as the helpless victims of Tamburlaine's campaigns, prostituted rather than impaled as punishment, and, in contrast to Tamburlaine's frigid seduction of Zenocrate, his son Calyphas voices fantasies and fears of "a naked lady in a net of gold" (2:4.1.69) coming to his bed, without the net.[45]

This play, too, unlike *Dido*, peoples the African and Asian continents with exotics. Techelles, for example, boasts of finding and overthrowing "the mighty Christian priest, / Call'd John the Great," (2:1.6.60–61), confronting "Amazonians" "with whom, being women, [he] vouchsaf'd a league" (2:1.6.65–66), and conquering the "negroes" (2:1.6.74) in Cubar. That Theridamas extends this exoticism to Europe and reports finding and burning the Black Forest where devils dance underscores the strategic edge of these claims, as of the play's and its characters' display of violence.[46] For just as these men discover exotics to boast of their prowess, so too do the characters throughout exhibit violence to instantiate their power.

Instead of equating the East with barbarism, the general darkening of this Eastern world picture signals the beginning of the end—the irreversible collapse of individuating terms and tactics. The rhetoric of dismemberment effectively dismembers identity, of self and other, bringing the process initiated in Part 1 to a head and the constructs repeatedly deployed to an end.[47] It is, not coincidentally, within this context that Tamburlaine loses control over his "sights of power" and is no longer able to make sign and referent meet. His attempts to establish his sons, literally a product of himself, as a image of his own singular and spectacular martial prowess fail completely. Amyras and Celebinus do "love the wars" (2: 1.4.47) and follow him in his words and deeds of conquest; but Tamburlaine, proving his own valor by stabbing his arm, must dress them artificially in his blood to make them fit the imperial part he has prescribed.[48]

Even worse, the doomed Calyphas, who prefers card games to battles, has, as Tamburlaine argues, a "form not meet to give that subject essence / Whose matter is the flesh of Tamburlaine" (2:4.1.114–15), a form Tamburlaine himself eradicates. On his deathbed, he hands Amyras the signs of his power—his crown, scourge, and "royal chariot of estate" (2: 5.3.179)—but the "scourge" is no longer an awe-inspiring or terrorizing persona but a mere prop. Amyras takes hold of the "silken reins" (2:5.3.203) reluctantly, dwelling on the "inward powers of [his] heart" (2:5.3.197) rather than on empire. Historically, instead of continuing the project of imperialism, the sons, plagued by their own "envy and discord," caused its division and dissolution.[49] Although the play gives no suggestion of this outcome, in disabling Tamburlaine's terms of power, it presages a similarly bleak future.

Tamburlaine's sudden death places a final and telling limit on his gestures of power, with Marlowe creating a gap between sign and referent that Tamburlaine is unable to bridge and using the self-abnegating difference inevitably embedded within language to undermine the self-affirming differences espoused by imperialist discourse.[50] Although Tamburlaine becomes distempered after explicitly challenging Mahomet's authority and burning the Koran, neither the play nor any of its characters make a definitive link between the two.[51] The First Physician's diagnosis is no more satisfying than a religious or moral explanation; after doing the necessary lab work, he decides that a "substance more divine and pure" than the body's elements "is almost clean extinguished and spent" (2:5.3.88–89)—a substance that he cannot specify beyond the "lively" and life-giving "spirits" of the soul (2:5.3.94).

Despite the burned Koran and the doctor's otherworldly diagnosis, all that Tamburlaine's death can ultimately signal to us as to him is that "sickness prove[s]" this figure who has "been term'd the terror of the world" "now to be a man" (2:5.3.44–45). The point here is not simply and humanistically that "man" is no more than this, but rather that discourse is—that while mystifying and aggrandizing terms can construct a differentiated, sovereign self, they ultimately cannot sustain it. When Tamburlaine attempts to talk himself out of being proven just "a man" by ascribing his fate to some "daring god" (2:5.3.42), Theridamas advises him to "leave these impatient words" (2:5.3.54), betraying the ultimate meaninglessness and undeniable limitation of Tamburlaine's claims to power, sovereignty, and singularity. In the end, he fades into an unfinished map of conquest, feeling "no sovereign ease" (2:5.3.214) and affirming that Death is the only true "monarch of the earth" (2:5.3.217).

   The two-part production of Tamburlaine, then, constructs an Oriental leader who is neither an insatiable barbarian nor an awe-inspiring hero
nor a scourge of god, but a figure whose strategies of self-authorization
prove him to be a "man," strategically shaped of sovereignty or monstrosity by himself, his allies, and his foes. While Renaissance discourse
emptied Africa of voice, disenfranchising its people of their individuality
and autonomy, it filled the East with conflicting voices, with Persians and
Turks, nobility and barbarity, promise and threat. And while in representing Africa, Marlowe opens a space for the silenced voice that imperialist
discourse leaves out, in representing the East he amplifies what that discourse fills in, bringing its conflicting voices together and exposing its
contradictory impulses as two sides of the same strategy, two sides which
in their contiguity unfix the critical differences that they attempt to fix.
   While *Dido* insists that the difference on which imperialism depends
is relative, *Tamburlaine* insists that it is constructed, not just in all or nothing terms, as either self or other, but also, paradoxically, in all and nothing
terms, as self and other. That paradox seriously undermines the dichoto-
mization vital to imperialist self-fashioning, whether acted out on Africa
or the East, proving the difference between self and other as slippery as it
is essential. In *The Jew of Malta*, Marlowe complicates the vision further by
adding a third term to the schematization, reminding us that the world of
empire could not be divided, literally or symbolically, through simple binarisms, and that while England might apply itself to fit those terms, those
terms not only did not hold, they did not apply.

4. Capitalizing on the Jew: The Third Term in *The Jew of Malta*

"Tush, who amongst 'em knows not Barabas?"
(1.1.68)

The Jew in Myth and History

To turn from *Dido* and *Tamburlaine* to *The Jew of Malta* (which may or may not have been the next of Marlowe's plays) seems to be to move away from imperialist themes and events toward a more domestic situation, where the center of focus is the conflict between Christians and Jews, or rather between Barabas, the infamous Jew, and any Christian who happens to get in his way. The prologue fosters this illusion, as Machevill, after launching into a diatribe on his political gains and strategies, stops short, remembering that he has come not

> to read a lecture here in Britain,
> But to present the tragedy of a Jew,
> Who smiles to see how full his bags are cramm'd.
> (Prologue 29–31)

As the prologue gives way to the play, we see Barabas, costumed in a long nose and possibly a red wig and beard, fondling the "infinite riches" crammed within his "little room" (1.1.37), enjoying "the blessings promis'd to the Jews" (1.1.107), and declaiming against the "malice, falsehood, and excessive pride" which he sees as the only "fruits" (1.1.118–19) of Christianity.[1] Accordingly, critics have often centered on the play's Semitism or anti-Semitism, debating whether it is the Jew's race, religion, or villainy that is really under fire.[2]

Yet it seems appropriate that when *The Jew of Malta* was initially performed in London, it was being produced alongside *Mully Mullocco, The Spanish Comedy, The Spanish Tragedy, Orlando Furioso*, and *Sir John Mandeville*, all plays that center on foreign themes, characters, or interests.[3] Marlowe's play, too, looks to the world outside and how it was being shaped by and giving shape to the European inside. Marlowe sets Barabas on an island in the middle of the Mediterranean, a key site of cross-cultural commerce and conflict, demanding that we consider what it means to be "of Malta" while deciding what it means to be "the Jew."

And what it means is domination. Like Tamburlaine, Barabas at once represents himself and is represented by others in terms of difference that promise singularity and power. Yet unlike Tamburlaine, he is not an imperialist but a capitalizing victim of imperialism, caught within a struggle between two contending powers. Although the Jew is not exonerated for his manipulative acts, others' exploitation of him shows that in the game of empire, nothing finally is sacred.

In presenting "the tragedy of a Jew," Marlowe complicates the terms of cross-cultural competition, bringing three rather than two (or in Tamburlaine's case, a series of two) terms into play and recuperating a third, another "other" outside but nonetheless appropriated into the contest of self and other. Whereas *Dido* effectively displaces Iarbas, the disenfranchised African king, from its dichotomized conflict, *The Jew of Malta* entertains triangulation, making clear that imperialist politics are not as straightforward as they seem, that the "other" under fire is not always the other at stake. Here, too, Marlowe couples imperialism more explicitly to profit, bringing the "infinite riches" that stand as adjuncts or agents of conquest in *Tamburlaine* and *Dido* into the foreground as a dominant goal. In Malta the will to profit stands beside, if not above, the will to power— a will that, because it was only questionably virtuous, had to be cloaked beneath statements of other more civilized and civilizing purposes.[4] Although the focus on "a Jew" seems out of place in a drama of empire, what figure could better instantiate the dispossessed in a country that had exiled its Jews and in an era that refused to admit them still? What figure could better point to financial oppression in a country that had turned its Jews into usurers and its usurers into devils while feeding off the profits?

What is so striking in the period's historical discourse, and commonly ignored in studies of early modern representations of the Jew, is that this history of oppression is not erased, at least not totally, as if because the Jews' dispossession was so complete and their presence (*in absentia*) so slight that they did not have to be so exhaustively maligned.[5] When religion was called into play, Jews were of course demonized as the Antichrist or devil, and accused of carrying out ritual murders, especially of Christian children, desecrating the Christian host, blaspheming, and the like. On the economic front, they were criminalized as usurers; on the social front, they were assigned a variety of vices and misdemeanors, such as cheating, or having a peculiar smell (*Foetor Judaicus*).[6]

When they figure as political/historical subjects in the chronicles, however, particularly in Holinshed but also, to some degree, in Stow, they emerge as scapegoats, taxed, fined, or attacked (and their money taken) when the state's treasury was low or political tempers were high.[7] As modern historians have argued, before their banishment from England, the Jews served the Crown primarily "like a sponge, sucking up the floating capital of the country, to be squeezed from time to time into the Treasury," especially under the reigns of Henry III and Richard I.[8] And it is that story the chronicles tell, despite occasional references to ritual murders and occasional excoriations of their "detestable usurie," "crueltie," and "malicious purpose."[9] When Henry III decided "to rid himselfe out of debt," Holinshed tells us, "he caused the Jewes to give unto him a great portion of their goods, so that they were greatlie impoverished" (2:419). When the nobles then revolted against the king, robbing those "whom they knew to be against their purpose," according to Stow, they too targeted the Jews for their purpose.[10] We also hear of a group of Jews who were slain because one of them asked for too much interest.[11]

Though the critique is often muted, these accounts repeatedly make clear that the punishment levied against the Jews rarely fit the crime and that the occasions singled out to justify attacks against them were, in fact, just that—occasions singled out to justify attacks. Holinshed acknowledges that Jews were sometimes punished "by the pursse," and "gréevouslie punished," and at least once excused of alleged murder because they could "buy their peace" (2:387). Most striking is his account of Richard I, who gave official protection to the Jews despite his country's widespread anti-Semitic sentiment, and whose temporary absence from the realm on one occasion allowed that sentiment to surface in "wild" and incriminating ways. With the king away, "the heads of the common people began to wax wild," Holinshed writes,

> and fain would they have had some occasion of raising a new tumult against the Jewes, whome (for their unmercifull usurie practised to the undooing of manie an honest man) they most deadlie hated, wishing most earnestlie their expulsion out of England. Herupon by reason of a riot committed latelie against them, . . . other people in other parts of the realme, taking occasion

hereat, as if they had beene called up by the sound of a bell or trumpet, arose against them . . . and robbed and bet them after a disordered and most riotous maner. (2:210)

Although the usurious Jews are by no means let off the hook, neither are the riotous Christians, their heads "wax[ing] wild," their actions "disordered and most riotous," their occasion taken from some other otherwise irrelevant example of riot, and they themselves spurred on, like Pavlov's dogs, as if "by the sound of a bell or trumpet."

Here and elsewhere, Holinshed is particularly critical of the practice of usury, despite the fact that with the move toward a money economy, usury was becoming more and more a part of the status quo, so much so that it was officially decriminalized (though still condemned) by the end of the sixteenth century.[12] As William Harrison writes in his *Description of England* (1587), though usury was "a trade brought in by the Jews," it was "now perfectly practiced almost by every Christian and so commonly that he is accounted but for a fool that doth lend his money for nothing."[13] Even Philip Stubbes, in his infamous *Anatomie of Abuses* (1583), which is elsewhere harshly anti-Semitic, aims his attack against usurers also against Christians, arguing that "an usurer is worse then a Jewe," since the Jews, unlike the Christians, "will not take any usurie of their brethren."[14]

Like Stubbes, Holinshed, even though he condemns the Jews for usury, also makes clear that they were not the only offenders. He is equally hard on the "Caursini" (or, as he calls them, the "locusts of Rome"), who came to lend the English money, with interest, during the reign of Henry III, when the pope demanded an otherwise unpayable payment of one tenth of England's wealth (2:364–65). The Jews' similarity to "the popes merchants" (2:379) would hardly win them any favor from antipapist Elizabethan readers. Still, it not only disrupts the easy equation of usurer and Jew; it also points to a glaring double standard in the punishment of usury (which Holinshed records with some pause), with Jews being slain and Catholics tried for the same offense. In one instance, the bishop of London tried to excommunicate Catholics on the grounds of usury, but was himself tried by the court of Rome and made to "cover his fathers shame" (2:379). When the king, Henry III, still "in great néed of monie," later imposed a heavy tallage on the Jews, they, "sore impoverished with gréevous and often paiments excused themselves by the popes usurers." Henry, however, disallowed the excuse and, as Holinshed criticizes, "fleeced the Jewes to the quicke," ultimately procuring for himself "the name of an oppressor and covetous scraper" (2:435).

Though in the historical record Judaism as a religious practice does not get much mention, it does not get much direct condemnation either, and never reaches the extremes it held on pageant wagons in the raving caricature of Herod, for example.[15] Both Holinshed and Stow record an almost legendary incident in which Judaism was publicly mocked, but significantly, both back away from judgment. They write of a Jew who fell into a "jakes" on a Saturday and refused to be rescued "in reverence of his sabboth." Hearing this, the presiding Earl of Gloucester refused to pull him out on Sunday, deciding that "the christians should doo as much reverence to their sabboth." Consequently, the Jew was left until Monday, when he was "there found dead," probably to no one's surprise.[16] The target of mockery of the narrative is much less clear than the target of mockery within it, but the similarity between the Jew and the Christian, forced by the Earl of Gloucester, seems more incriminating to the Christians. If the Jew's faith is peculiarly and dangerously inflexible, so also is the Christian's, but with the added edge of hyprocrisy and cruelty.

When Stubbes retells the tale, he clarifies, and highlights by clarifying, the mixed moral message, refocusing hostility more exclusively on Judaism. The Earl of Gloucester drops from view entirely and we hear only that the Jew chose "rather to dye in that filthie stinking place (as by other morning he was dead in deede), then to breake or violate the Lord's Saboath." Stubbes uses the way the Jews "are but too scrupulous, and overshoote the marke" as a contrast to show how "we are therein plaine contemptuous and negligent, shooting shorte of the marke altogether."[17] Though the Christians are under fire here, with the earl's retaliation erased, the Jew stands out as incomprehensibly inflexible in the matter of religion. Stubbes's loaded message underscores what is notably absent in the chronicles in which religious difference has only a minor place. Their decentering of the issue suggests what is evident throughout: that though the Jews were ostracized as Jews, their Judaism was a secondary part of the problem, if that. To the contrary, it was finally their religion that helped foster renewed toleration in the late sixteenth and early seventeenth centuries, as the Reformation's emphasis on the word of God began to bring the Old Testament and Hebraic studies into a more favorable position and to pave the way for England's readmission of the Jews.[18]

The chronicles leave a telling gap in recording England's final solution to the "Jewish problem" and offer no rationale for the state's ultimate, unprecedented act of discrimination against the Jews—their banishment under Edward I. In Holinshed, mention of the decree is followed not by explanation but first by a condemnation of the "wicked," "fradulent and mischeevous dealing" (2:492) of certain mariners who caused the Jews they were deporting to drown, and then by a description of the king's attempts to get money for a trip to the Holy Land. The first positions the Jews as victims, strikingly at a moment when they would best (for the exoneration of the state's policy) appear as victimizers. The second brings economics back into play, reminding us that the Jews had provided a vital source of capital that now would have to be met in other ways.[19] When so many explanations (usury, ritual murder, and so on) had been conjured up to justify less serious actions against the Jews, the lack of an explicit explanation here, or in the decree itself, betrays the Jewish problem as something more complicated or evasive than those explanations could accommodate—something that says incriminatingly more about the self than about the other.[20]

Though England's historical record does not and could not erase the more diabolical socioreligious profile disseminated beside (and in some places within) it, it nonetheless displays the Jews as the offended and as the offenders, used by as well as using the state in "gréevous" and "wicked" ways. Both Stow and Holinshed were deeply invested in supporting the status quo and came down hard on other others such as sodomites, as I will argue in Chapter 6. This "tolerance" for the Jew, instead of constituting a radical, counter-cultural gesture, seems to underscore the extent of the Jews' disenfranchisement from England's political and economic scene— to suggest, that is, that the other who had been successfully contained and expelled and who, from that position, no longer mattered, could be in part redeemed and called in from the space of the other—but only in part.

Malta, Spain, and Turkey

In Marlowe, however, where the Jew emerges in bold-faced diabolic shape, the figure is reclaimed more fully from the space of alienation and set in the middle not only of the Mediterranean but also of an imperialist competition in which discrimination, of the sort that marks Jewish history so prominently, provides the means for political and economic survival. The play is structured around a crucial parallel between the external domination of outside forces over Malta and the internal domination of Christians over Jews, with both Malta and the Jew called into an opposition that does not otherwise involve them. And it is through the parallel that

Marlowe turns colonialism into capitalism, and the Jew into a site of struggle for profit and power.

In *The Jew of Malta*, more than in *Dido* or *Tamburlaine*, setting plays a vital role in directing us toward the play's center of interest. Renaissance plays, even those set in England, often associated their Jews with foreign worlds. In William Haughton's *Englishmen for My Money* (1598), for example, Pisario, the Jew, is quick to point out that though he now resides in England, he comes from Portugal, one of England's chief rivals in the international marketplace. In Robert Wilson's *The Three Ladies of London* (1592), Gerontus, the Jew, resides in Turkey, and in Robert Daborne's *A Christian Turn'd Turk* (1612), the Jews are found in Tunis. While this choice allowed for historical accuracy, reflecting the long absence of Jews in England, it also served to amplify their otherness. It is no coincidence that Italy, a locus allegedly crawling with corruption, became a favored setting for Shakespeare and others who subsequently brought the Jew to center stage. In *The Travels of Three English Brothers* (1607) by John Day, George Wilkins, and William Rowley, the travels of the brothers extend across the East, but Zariph, the Jew, is found (demanding money) in Venice.[21]

Marlowe, however, chooses Malta, a place important throughout Europe and the East as a strategic post for both trading and war. Europe's interest in the island was heightened by the unsuccessful Turkish siege of 1565, which, if it had succeeded, would have given the Turks a threatening control over Mediterranean commerce and defense. In response to this event, England launched an "ideological campaign" against the Turkish "aggressor," taking on Malta's cause with an eye to England's own national security, with the self-interest of this support betraying itself two centuries later when England annexed Malta as a colony.[22]

Subversively, Marlowe rewrites history and lets the Turks triumph in their siege and, in so doing, turns Malta into a place defined and delimited by domination. When Ferneze, the Governor of Malta, first appears, his rule is being overridden by the dictates of the Turkish Calymath, who demands that Malta pay a tribute established by his father. Although Ferneze initially acquiesces, he quickly changes his mind when the Spanish vice-admiral, Del Bosco, reminds him of his Christian mission. "Remember," Del Bosco cautions,

> that, to Europe's shame,
> The Christian Isle of Rhodes, from whence you came,

Was lately lost, and you were stated here
To be at deadly enmity with Turks.

(2.2.30–33)

Del Bosco's directive calls up the historical prototype for Ferneze and his knights, the Knights of St. John. Though originating in the twelfth century as "Hospitallers" to care for weary pilgrims in Jerusalem, the order, populated by nobles from countries all across Europe, took on the mission of defending the Christian world against the Turkish "infidel." Like Ferneze's knights, they too were driven in their campaign from Rhodes and (in 1530) to Malta, their last and most permanent outpost. Because they were Catholic crusaders, England's support for the Knights dwindled significantly after the Reformation. Yet the English langue of the order was not completely dissolved until the mid-sixteenth century, almost certainly because it provided a useful ally against the Turks. Indeed, one of the few references to the Knights in the chronicles comes in the description of a confrontation in 1572 (during Elizabeth's reign) between an alliance of Christian/European forces (Catholics and Protestants, the Knights and the English among them) and the Turks. Under such circumstances, Holinshed urges, Europe's various factions should "emploie their forces against the common enimie, to the benefit of the whole christian world, which (the more is the pitie) they have so long exercised one against another, to each others destruction" (4:264). Even after the Reformation, in the face of Christianity's "common enimie," there is room and reason for Catholics and Protestants to join together and, importantly, for the Knights to exist.

Both history and Del Bosco prompt us to view Malta as a valued Christian stronghold set in contention with the "barbarous misbelieving" Turks (2.2.46), and it is perhaps because these terms seem to fit so well with historical biases that critics have endorsed them. J. B. Steane, for example, applauds Ferneze's overthrow of Calymath and Barabas as the triumph of "Establishment" over "Outsider," suggesting a simple referentiality between Malta and Establishment as between Turks (not to mention Jews) and Outsiders.[23]

Yet the facts of this play, like Marlowe's others, resist such organization, for not only are the Turks neither the quintessential nor the only Outsiders here, but Malta is not an autonomous Establishment. *Tamburlaine* should make us skeptical both of the absolute designation of Establishment versus Outsider and of the demonization of the Turks. If not, *The Jew of Malta* does. The Turkish Calymath, instead of seeming as "barbarous" and "misbelieving" as Del Bosco suggests, acts on a law established by his father. While his basso, Callapine (whose name recalls the aggressive son of Bajazeth in *Tamburlaine*), insists that Ferneze pay up immediately, Calymath extends "a little courtesy" (1.2.23) and grants the governor a month to collect the payment.

More important, however, is the fact that it is not just the Turks but also the Spanish who are imperializing over Malta (and in the "real" early modern world, threatening England). Del Bosco appears in Act 2 as envoy for Spain and announces to Ferneze that the Spanish king "hath title to this isle, / And he means quickly to expel you hence" (2.2.37–38). Editors, uncomfortable with this bold-faced imperialism, have substituted "them" (meaning the Turks) for the quarto's "you." [24] Yet "you" seems no mistake but a telling signal of Spain's intent to use rather than protect Malta. Although Del Bosco claims that, in staying, he intends only to set Malta free, we see another, opposing, story. Notably, Spain is in competition with the Turks and, ironically, over Mediterranean trade and territories, with Malta foremost among them.

Tellingly, Del Bosco arrives with a shipload full of "Grecians, Turks, and Afric Moors" (2.2.9) to be sold as slaves, ominously associating him with the business of taking captives and making profits. What prompts him to object to Ferneze's league with the Turks is that it interferes with his profits, prohibiting Malta from buying his captured Turks. In disrupting the league, he establishes a new alliance and a new contract of trade between Malta and Spain. In addition, he also creates a new opposition, between Malta and Turkey, which works to ensure Spanish—not Maltese—supremacy. Having just done battle with the Turks at Corsica, who attacked as his ship left without "vail[ing]" to them (2.2.11), and recalling how "their hideous force environ'd Rhodes" (2.2.48) and left no survivors "to bring the hapless news to Christendom" (2.2.51), Del Bosco is clearly reluctant to engage them again. In mobilizing Malta against the Ottoman forces, he gains a crucial ally, if not substitute, in what has been and promises to be a grueling contention.

For centuries, the Knights of St. John served Europe in its war against the Turks in a similar capacity, receiving in return special privileges such as exemptions from certain tithes and rights of self-government. Although they were allowed to create an independent state, that state was critically dependent upon outside support not only for its membership but also for its acquisition of a permanent home. Charles V of Spain offered up Malta in 1523, with the stipulation that the Knights would also occupy nearby Gozo and the northern coast of Africa, and "provide the first line of defence in [his] battle with the Turks for control of the central Mediterranean."[25] While the order was officially allowed its neutrality, it remained thus a crucial middleman in Europe's imperialist campaigns. In setting up the Turks as Outsiders and Malta as the Establishment, Del Bosco puts Malta in a similar position, using the opposition to further Spain's own vested interests in the island and the struggle and, to that end, to mask Spain's imperialist position outside the former and inside the latter.

Moreover, Malta's position as Establishment, which Del Bosco asserts, is anything but established. Historically, before the coming of the Knights, the island had been under the rule of Sicily, but it had exchanged hands so frequently (being ruled successively by the Greeks, Carthaginians, Romans, Goths, Arabs, Germans, and Spanish) that it had become a multinational melting pot.[26] Likewise, in Marlowe's Malta are there no true-blooded Maltese. The governor himself comes from Rhodes (at least, most recently) and the citizens are of such diverse or undetermined nationalities that it is impossible to know who, if anyone, has prior claim to the island. When Ferneze calls the Jews together as the representative (i.e., taxable) "inhabitants of Malta" (1.2.21), Barabas protests that they are "strangers" (1.2.61). Both claims ring hollow, however, for everyone—from the Christians and Jews, to the Italians and Turks—seems to be a stranger here. When Barabas subsequently disguises himself as a French musician to undermine a plot against him, although his "French" is absurd (as such phrases as "Must tuna my lute for sound, twang twang first" [4.4.42–43] or "*Pardonnez moi*, be no in tune yet" [4.4.63] attest), his disguise fits right in. For to be "of Malta" really means not to be, originally, of Malta.

Del Bosco's attempts to define Malta as the archenemy of the Turks, Calymath's attempts to claim it as an indebted ally, or worse, a subjugated territory, and even Ferneze's attempts to rule it as his own, then, stand at odds not only with each other but also with the identity that we see. Malta on its own is a place of difference, not in relation to some Other (as Del Bosco would have us believe), but within itself, a place whose plurality defies a singular definition and whose inscription within a self/other, Establishment/Outsider dichotomy can only ring hollow, and ring of exploitation—as indeed it does.

The Jew, the Christians, and the Turks

The characterization of the Jew not only emerges from this context, but is also shaped around a similar play of negotiation and appropriation. For just as Del Bosco rewrites the conflict between Spain and Turkey as a conflict between Malta and Turkey, so too does the Christian governor, Ferneze, rewrite the conflict between Christians and Turks as a conflict between Christians and Jews. And just as Malta figures as the appropriated third term, given oppositional meaning by characters who have as much to gain from that meaning as Malta has to lose, so too does Barabas.

From the moment Marlowe calls up the stereotype of the Jew, he frames it as a subject of domination. When Barabas enters, he seems already to be "trailing clouds of ignominy," not only because of his "Jewish" costume and demeanor, but also because of his resemblance to Machevill, who, in the prologue, has already begged us not to entertain Barabas "the worse / Because he favours me" (Prologue 34–35), and so, encourages us to do just that.[27] Given what we know about the doubling of roles, it seems likely, too, that the same actor played both Machevill and Barabas. Yet these clouds of ignominy are simultaneously dispersed, making way for a Jew who is caught up in a larger political conflict. For instead of giving him an unfavorable fixed definition, the prologue sets up a pattern of discrimination and domination that becomes the focus of the play.

Machevill's prologue is in some ways a "false start," its exclusive rights to the Jew denied.[28] Malta is filled with hard-core policy-making Machiavels, as critics have noted, and Barabas stands out as the least Machiavellian among them, having little or no interest in the citadels, Caesars, and public/political policies that interest Machevill.[29] Although Machevill insists that the Jew's money "was not got without my means" (Prologue 32), Barabas ascribes his gains more convincingly to cross-cultural mercantilism, which has already won him "credit in the custom-house" (1.1.58) and which places him comfortably amid the company of merchants, who are the first characters to appear with him. Machevill also warns us that he "weigh[s] not men, and therefore not men's words" (Prologue 8). Instead of typecasting the Jew, the prologue functions to typecast the Machiavel, as a figure who wants to impose his name everywhere, to take credit even for the deeds of those who "hate [him] most," "speak openly against [his] books," and "cast [him] off" (Prologue 9–12). What is not "false" about this start is that it tags the Jew as a subject of domination, singled out to give another a voice and a place on the stage.

Although Barabas first appears as a greedy Jew, fondling his money bags, his career is initiated by an event that sets him in the middle of the ensuing imperialist competition between Christians and Turks and makes clear that this "tragedy of a Jew" is not just about a Jew. Before he has a chance to gather up his newly arrived fortunes from Egypt and the bordering isles, he is interrupted by the news that "a fleet of warlike galleys" (1.1.149) has come from Turkey and that the Jews must report to the senate house. In *Othello*, the threat of the Turks starts as the impetus for the political action but, thanks to a fortuitous storm, quickly becomes a meaningless event—all too meaningless for Othello, who would otherwise define himself through it. In *The Jew of Malta*, the situation is reversed, and what starts as an annoying interruption in commercial affairs becomes the defining event, not only for the citizens of Malta, but also for the Jew. Barabas foresees that eventuality and attempts to protect his assets from it, assuring his fellow Jews that all is well while hiding his money and admitting to us his fears that the Turks have come for a tribute they know Malta cannot pay and intend "to seize upon the town" (1.1.188).

Yet on this island, it is impossible to escape; for like Del Bosco, Ferneze is a colonialist, concerned with maintaining his authority over Malta and ready to use its Jews, like Del Bosco uses him, to his own profit. The "real" Knights, though subjugated by the European powers, were themselves guilty of the same, in Malta as in other temporary bases. The order was officially committed to preserving native rights, but their domination often devolved into dictatorships.[30] By the mid-eighteenth century, the Maltese in particular were denied "all positions of authority" in their state and were totally subject to "the arbitrary rule of the grand master." And it was not until the end of the century, until they rejected the order in favor of Napoleonic "liberation," that the Knights' domination of Malta ended.[31]

The play, in its inscription of Malta as an island of strangers and its focus on the Jew, is clearly not a reenactment of the historical conflict between the Knights of St. John and the Maltese, but its example alerts us to the fact that Malta's knights are colonizers as well as the colonized. Unwillingly exiled from Rhodes, Ferneze has taken charge of the Maltese government as if it were his own, and before Del Bosco intervenes, he is ready to tax the "inhabitants of Malta" (1.2.21), strategically pinpointed as the Jews, to obviate a confrontation with the Turks. His money, he tells us, has been used up in the wars, and now theirs must be contributed to "a common good" (1.2.102)—a "common good" that clearly does not extend to the Jews, who must give up half of their estates, become Christians, or, refusing either, lose all. The expediency with which Ferneze produces his decrees (immediately after the Turks leave and the Jews gather), and the fact that he has summoned the Jews to court before conferring with Calymath, suggest that the Turkish demand allows rather than provokes what seems a previously calculated policy against the Jews. After all, Barabas's "goods and wares" alone "amount to more than all the wealth in Malta" (1.2.136–38), and the wars, to more than Ferneze, admittedly, can finance.

Ferneze's most pointed and prominent appropriation of the Jews is directed, however, toward the Turkish situation, which he and Malta have been put in the middle of. Just as Del Bosco situates Malta conveniently between the Turks and the Spanish, so too does Ferneze put the Jews between the Turks the Christians, evoking the time-honored religious conflict between Christians and Jews and scripting the Jews as "infidels" as a convenient excuse for exploitation. Historically, such circumscription served the Knights' purposes well, especially during the Crusades (when anti-Semitism was at a high), since one could argue that "it was not right to allow Jewish infidels to enjoy their ill-gotten riches undisturbed at home, while the soldiers of the Cross were facing untold dangers to combat Moslem infidels overseas."[32] Clearly here, as in the play, what gives rise to the Jews' status as the faithless is their wealth. Ferneze declares them "infidels," "accursed in the sight of heaven," and argues that his tolerance of their "hateful lives" has led to the "taxes and afflictions" of Malta (1.2.65–68). Yet, as we have seen, those "taxes and afflictions" have absolutely nothing to do with religion or the Jews and everything to do with politics and the Turks.

That the religious signifier, Jew, carries only secular meaning under Ferneze's regime is all too obvious. His laws define the Jew solely in terms of money: if a Jew refuses to pay the required tax, he "shall straight become a Christian" (1.2.76–77): no longer a source of money, he can no longer be a Jew. While the governor refers to the "profession" (1.2.149) of Christianity as established belief, he defines the Jews' "profession" (1.2.124) only as money-making (implicitly, via usury).[33] The inconsistency may have been especially striking to Elizabethan viewers because the secular meaning of "profession" had only entered the language in 1541.[34] Since everyone on the island—from the Turkish slave, to the courtesan and "her man," to the friars, to the governor's son, to the governor himself—is driven by "desire of gold" (3.5.4), religion becomes the only way to make a difference (and a profit) where there is none. It is only because Ferneze can defame Barabas for his usury and covetousness that he can also, with impugnity, direct him to "live still" in Malta, "where thou gott'st thy wealth / . . . and if thou canst, get more" (1.2.105–6). Although from our perspective, it is difficult to tell "which is the merchant here, and which the Jew" (*The Merchant of Venice*, 4.1.173), by imposing a religious signifier on top of a secular signified, Ferneze attempts to make that difference absolute and clear.

His attempt to defame Barabas as "the Jew" is incriminatingly parodied when Barabas's slave attempts to do the same, under circumstances in which profit, too, rules all. Encouraged by Pilia-Borza and Bellamira to extort money from the Jew, Ithamore capitalizes on the occasion to aggrandize his own self-image (and as well his power and his purse) at his master's expense. When Barabas comes to the brothel, dressed as a French musician, Ithamore immediately asks if he knows "a Jew, one Barabas" (4.4.77). When the "musician" responds that he thinks Ithamore to be the Jew's "man" (4.4.79), Ithamore "scorn[s] the peasant" and constructs "a strange thing of that Jew" (4.4.80–82). He accuses Barabas of "liv[ing] upon pickled grasshoppers and sauced mushrooms," of "never put[ting] on a clean shirt since he was circumcised," and of wearing a hat that "Judas left under the elder when he hanged himself" (4.4.82–90). It is ironic that he treats these alleged characteristics as something to scorn here, in the company of Pilia-Borza, "a shaggy, totter'd, staring slave," whose face (if we can believe Barabas) "has been a grind-stone for men's swords," whose

> hands are hack'd, some fingers cut quite off,
> Who when he speaks, grunts like a hog, and looks
> Like one that is employ'd in catzery
> And cross-biting; such a rogue
> As is the husband to a hundred whores.
>
> (4.3.6–14)

Although Ithamore attempts to pass himself off to Bellamira as Jason and Adonis, we know from him and from Pilia-Borza that he, too, looks and creates villainies "like a man of another world" (4.2.8–9) and, as a Turk, is probably circumcised as well. Like Ferneze's, the Turk's demonization of the Jew emphasizes differences that not only have nothing to do with his Jewishness but also are not different within this context. Both representations, too, are clearly motivated by a will to profit, more incriminating to the subject speaking than to the subject spoken about.

Taken out of Machevill's hands and put into Ferneze's (and Ithamore's), the Jew figures, then, like Malta, as a third term outside another's power play, strategically brought into an antagonistic position within it, as the established self (in Malta's case) or other (in Barabas's) to another established other (in the Turks' case) or self (in the Christians'). What is suggested in the process is not only what is embedded less boldly in the chronicles, that the demonization of the Jew was a part and product of political and financial exploitation. Exposed also, and even more subversively within an imperialist state, is the illusion that the circumscribed subjects of colonization are not necessarily its objects.

In *Othello* one thing that proves the Turks Turks is that they create a deceptive "pageant" to keep the Venetians "in a false gaze" (1.3.18–19), and pretend to head toward Rhodes while really targeting Cyprus. That pretense had become such a familiar Turkish strategy off the stage that "it was holden a mocke and a by-word in many places, that the Turke would goe to besiege Rhodes." [35] Though the Turks in Marlowe's play do go for their true targets, the Spanish and the Christians do not, proving themselves incriminatingly like the Turks and their imperialist constructs part of pageant for keeping all in a false gaze.

"Is not that the Jew?"

To be "the Jew" in Marlowe's play is not only to be the object of colonization, taxed by others' projects of domination; it is also to be the subject of capitalizing exploits—exploits that link profit all the more closely to cross-cultural power and cross-cultural power to profit. It is no coincidence that imperialism and capitalism emerged concurrently in early modern England, when overseas exploits were providing a prolific supply of merchandise, or that the subject of capitalism found a prominent place on the stage, in plays such as *Volpone, Bartholomew Fair, The Comedy of Errors, The Merchant of Venice, Timon of Athens, A New Way to Pay Old Debts*, and of course, *The Jew of Malta*. Although not all the plays centered on capitalist exchange centered on the Jew, the Jew, with his reputation for usury, provided an obvious subject for the exploration of mercantilism at home and abroad, with all its promise and problems.

In a vital study of the relation between the theater and the marketplace, Jean-Christophe Agnew has argued that a crucial problem with merchants and the idea of the merchant was that they necessarily marketed themselves as "artificial persons," strategically misrepresenting what they represented in the name of profit.[36] Their transactions were aligned not only with Machiavellianism, but also with usury, which by the seventeenth century had "become at times a catchword for any inequitable bargain."[37] What allegedly made the usurer, and the merchant, so successful, so indistinguishable, and so dangerous, as Thomas Lodge cautions in his *Alarm Against Usurers* (1584), was that he operated by insinuating himself within every "secret corner" of his victim's heart, and "framing his behaviour to the nature of the youth."[38] And so in the case of Barabas who, whatever else he may be, is above all a capitalist selling himself as "the Jew" to gain advantage over and take advantage of others. What Tamburlaine does for power, Barabas does for profit (which is sometimes in bodies and sometimes in gold), though by playing into rather than beyond expectation. And what *The Jew of Malta* dramatizes is not the criminal history of a diabolical Jew in a less diabolical Christian society, but rather the strategies of negotiation and domination in an international marketplace, where imperialism and capitalism inevitably collide.

Though Tamburlaine moves between two extremes of barbarity and civility, the Jew appears in so many postures that his character seems to consist more of what he is not than of what he is. Barabas is clearly a villain in a way that Tamburlaine, with his high ideals and high astounding terms is not, but critical assessments of him are comparably wide-ranging, discovering at one extreme a sympathetic and praiseworthy hero, "conscious of being hated and want[ing] to be loved," and at the other, the "quintessential alien," or worse, "a mere monster brought in with a large painted nose to please the rabble."[39] Clearer than anything is that he is not "the Jew."

Although he attempts to define himself in terms of Judaic doctrines and heritage, his terms are as unconvincing as they are unsustained.[40] He makes frequent reference to Old Testament wisdom, but in each case perverts or rejects the teachings that he invokes, equating his private fortune to "the blessings promis'd to the Jews" and "old Abram's happiness" (1.1.107–8) and dismissing Job's example as an irrelevant model of patience, since all he had and patiently lost was a mere

> seven thousand sheep,
> Three thousand camels, and two hundred yoke

Of labouring oxen, and five hundred
She-asses,

(1.2.186–89)

small husbandry compared to Barabas's "infinite riches."[41] His language, however loaded with proverbs, is not, as Greenblatt has noted, "the exotic language of the Jews but the product of the whole society, indeed, its most familiar and ordinary face."[42] Barabas does place himself within an international community of famous Jews—Kirriah Jairim in Greece, "Obed in Bairseth, Nones in Portugal," "some in Italy," and "many in France," who "have scambled up / More wealth by far than those that brag of faith" (1.1.124–29)—but what secures his place (and theirs) on the roster is wealth, and not religion. Tellingly, too, he is clearly disinterested in identifying himself with the less wealthy Jews in Malta and, while assuring them that he will look out for "our state" (1.1.175), tells us that he will look only to himself, his daughter, and his wealth—as indeed he does.

In looking out for his daughter, he, in fact, turns her and her Judaism into an exploitable commodity, sending her as a convert into a convent to retrieve his hidden gold and marketing her as a "diamond" (2.3.141)—appropriately, in the middle of a slave market—to lure her suitors into a fatal competition with each other. Abigail herself, in the pattern of her father, appropriates religion, converting "for real" in order to be saved not by Christ, but from the Jew, seeing "no love on earth, / Pity in Jews, nor piety in Turks" (3.3.53–54) and, therefore, by what seems a process of elimination, turning Christian. Although Barabas is outraged, the source of his discontent is not that she "varies from [him] in belief" (3.4.10), but that she, "unknown and unconstrain'd of [him]" (3.4.1), might betray his villainies.

Part of the problem in knowing who Barabas is is that he seems to be "always acting, always disguised," not just to those onstage but also to us.[43] He declares himself "of finer mould than common men" because "a reaching thought will search his deepest wits, / And cast with cunning for the time to come" (1.2.224–27). Yet the play continually provokes and frustrates our attempts to follow that "reaching thought" and foresighted "cunning." We do not know, when Barabas laments over his loss of wealth, that he has a hidden store at home. Like the characters onstage, we can only be surprised when he suddenly dies a "very strange" (5.1.54) death, and even more surprised when he rises again (explaining belatedly that he had drugged himself). And while he uses his partnership with Calymath to overthrow Ferneze, when he then switches allegiances and vows to "set Malta free" (5.2.96), we cannot second guess his "policy" or know "to what event [his] secret purpose drives" (5.2.123–24). (Del Bosco has also vowed to free Malta, rendering such promises suspect.)

Even when Barabas is defining his motives, his terms continue to shift. Although he seems always after material reward, as Tamburlaine is after empire, his actions are prompted by varying and elusive impulses. What begins as a desire for money, his "soul's sole hope" (2.1.29), explodes into desires for revenge, power, "absolute play," and impromptu deception.[44] And even as he follows through on any one of these goals, the original motive seems to get lost along the way. His revenge, for example, is initially directed against the governor and his son, but somehow multiplies as quickly and inexplicably as his wealth, and before three acts have passed, Barabas has engineered the deaths not only of the son but also of two friars, Mathias, Abigail, a convent full of nuns, Ithamore, Pilia-Borza, and Bellamira. While each act has its "reason"—the Christian Mathias wants to marry his daughter; his daughter joins a convent; the friars know his guilt; Ithamore betrays him, and so on—together they have none.

And, in the matter of politics, although Barabas works his way into the governorship, it is never clear why he does so. At the outset of the play, he rejects the promise of power as untenable, insisting that Jews "come not to be kings" (1.1.131) because their only access to crowns is by force, and "nothing violent," he has heard, "can be permanent" (1.1.134–35). Knowing that "Malta hates [him]" (5.2.31), he gives power back to Ferneze almost immediately after attaining it. And at the end of the play, he asks us whether his is not "a kingly kind of trade, to purchase towns, / By treachery, and sell 'em by deceit?" (5.5.50–51). Historically, this "kingly" trade was the only way Jews could profit from real estate: they could act as middlemen to buy and sell land, but could not own it.[45] Yet while Barabas suggests that he is after financial profit, his simultaneous celebration of his treachery makes us wonder whether profit alone has been the goal, particularly since it is unclear what, materially, he could have gained had his final betrayal of the Turks succeeded. When he is finally trapped, he vows to all above that he "would have brought confusion on you all" (5.5.90). That, in effect, is what he has done. With all this shifting, deceiving, and acting, how can we know the player from the play, the protagonist from his pretense?

The point is that we cannot—that Barabas becomes, in effect, an "artificial person" whom we can never second guess. The disjunction within his characterization—and, since his actions dictate the action, within the play—has led some critics to fault the text, to blame Marlowe for an unintentional unevenness, or to locate a gap between Acts 2 and 3 and ascribe the last three acts to another author.[46] Rather than signaling authorial inadequacy, however, the discontinuity functions strategically and complements what Marlowe's representation of Malta's situation has shown: that the identity which others give to the colonized is, indeed, given—and in this case given in part by the Jew.

The Jew, like Malta, emerges here as a representational space without a circumscribable identity. Like Malta, he is endlessly cosmopolitan. Although we do not know where he is from, he has connections across the globe. He has a hat from the Great Cham (the ruler of the Mongols and Tartars, or the Emperor of China); he has learned in Florence "how to kiss [his] hand" and "duck as low as any bare-foot friar" (2.3.23–25); and he has fornicated "in another country" (4.1.43). He emerges as a cross-cultural capitalist, as he collects goods and establishes his credit throughout Persia, Egypt, India, Africa, and other parts of the East. These imperialist exploits place him in the company of Ferneze, Del Bosco, and Calymath and, like their own, do not stop with merchandise. Barabas, too, creates an other to secure his own position, and that other, ironically, is "the Jew."

"Credit in the custom-house"

Throughout the play, instead of *being* the Jew, Barabas strategically *plays* the Jew—or rather, the various Jews—which others fabricate. His tactics mirror those of Tamburlaine, but with a difference. For while Tamburlaine creates an illusion of unknowable and uncontainable difference, Barabas creates an illusion of knowable and containable difference. And while Tamburlaine's strategies work by placing the spectators in a vulnerable position of uncertainty and awe, Barabas's work by placing them in what proves an equally vulnerable position of certainty and confidence.

The Jew that Barabas becomes not only meets his audience's expectations but also reflects their preoccupations. From an offstage perspective, the link between the two reminds us that discrimination is allied to projection: that what we discriminate against in others is what we would deny in ourselves. Onstage, it enables Barabas to evade suspicion and garner trust. By making himself familiar even as he emphasizes his difference, he lulls his victims into a false sense of security that they can know him and the extent of the "many mischiefs" (1.2.291) he can do, and he creates the illusion that he is easily contained and mastered, the colonized rather than the colonizer. To borrow Ithamore terms, "the meaning" that Barabas constitutes for himself "has a meaning" (4.4.106), and it is one that smacks of profit.

This pattern works itself out most clearly in the case of Ithamore who, though he himself fulfills a stereotype, does not know one when he sees one. After buying the slave, Barabas attempts to gain his loyalty and nefarious cooperation both by promising him gold and by selling himself as Ithamore's villainous "fellow" (2.3.219). In a now well-known passage, he claims an outrageous criminal history, boasting,

> I walk abroad a-nights,
> And kill sick people groaning under walls;
> Sometimes I go about and poison wells;
> And now and then, to cherish Christian thieves,
> I am content to lose some of my crowns,
> That I may, walking in my gallery,
> See 'em go pinion'd along by my door,

and so on, concluding with a series of crimes that allegedly gained him "as much coin as will buy the town" (2.3.179–205). Critics have accepted this speech as quintessential Barabas, and with good reason: it moves from goal to goal, at one point privileging revenge, at another money, and it shows a murderous cunning that marks his deeds throughout.[47] In other ways, however, the speech betrays itself as uncharacteristic and inauthentic.[48] When do we ever see Barabas "content" to lose even one coin, after all?

Moreover, although Barabas represents himself as a rash and impulsive villain, who enacts murders almost spontaneously as he "walk[s] abroad" at night, his schemes throughout are consistently more calculated (though we are not always in on the calculations) and more subtle. He boasts of leaving victims "pinion'd" by his door or hanging in public view with "a long great scroll" that tells how he "with interest tormented" them, but, in effecting deaths onstage, does everything to keep himself and his involvement from view. It is Ithamore, not he, who carries the poison to the nuns, significantly a poison that will not appear for forty hours. It is Ithamore, not he, who carries the letter ("a challenge feign'd from Lodowick" [2.3.379]) to Mathias, to initiate their confrontation, and

Lodowick and Mathias who conveniently do themselves in. While Barabas helps his slave strangle Friar Barnardine, he does so with "no print at all" (4.1.154), leaving Friar Jacomo to take the blame. And when Barabas comes to the brothel to poison Ithamore and company, he disguises himself (successfully) as a Frenchman.[49]

After offering his criminal history, Barabas encourages his slave to

> make account of me
> As of thy fellow. We are villains both,
> Both circumcised. We hate Christians both.
>
> (2.3.218–20)

And indeed, the "fellow" he constructs is tailored to produce the kind of exaggerated villainous, anti-Christian murderer suited to Ithamore's tastes and expectations of the Jew. It is, in fact, Ithamore, whom Barabas must school to "be not rash" (2.3.383), whom the caricature matches best.[50] When Barabas produces a feigned letter for Mathias, Ithamore is eager to "have a hand in this" (2.3.373), sure that the letter is poisoned (which it is not). Not satisfied with poisoning a convent full of nuns, when the slave sees "a royal monastery hard by," he implores his "good master, let me poison all the monks" (4.1.14–15) and is dissuaded from doing so only because Barabas assures him that the monks will die with grief anyway, since the nuns are dead.

In addition, although Barabas defines himself as categorically anti-Christian, instructing Ithamore to "smile [in principle] when Christians moan" (2.3.177) and claiming to have victimized generic "Christian thieves," it is Ithamore more than he who has a blanket policy against Christians, who has spent his time "setting Christian villages on fire" (2.3.208), "strew[ing] powder on the marble stones" beneath Jerusalem's pilgrims to "rankle" their knees, and "laugh[ing] a-good to see the cripples / Go limping home to Christendom on stilts" (2.4.214–17). Barabas, in contrast, targets not just any Christian, and not just Christians, but those who have offended him, including Italians as well as Turks (to his slave's misfortune and surprise).

Ithamore sees in stereotypes, vowing to "worship [his master's] nose" (2.3.178) and to bring him a long spoon (since Jews proverbially eat with the devil), and later aligning him with "the devil" (3.3.20). Barabas, in turning himself into a rash enthusiast for murder, fulfills Ithamore's hopes to have in the Jew "the bravest, gravest, secret, subtle, bottle-nos'd knave to my master, that ever gentleman had" (3.3.9–11), and wins his devotion, however transient it turns out to be. Although the Jew underestimates the Turk in his untrustworthiness, Ithamore, preoccupied with a one-dimensional stereotype, underestimates the Jew in his avarice and cunning. The slave capitalizes on the fact that he knows "some secrets of the Jew" (4.2.78) and, under the direction of Pilia-Borza and the spell of Bellamira, extorts payment from Barabas without hesitation, sure that "we'll have money straight" (4.2.83–84). It is difficult to know whether he has believed his master's promises to make him heir, or even to pay him for his services, but here he seems fatally unaware or unconcerned that Barabas's campaign of revenge has been provoked by a comparable act of extortion and almost certainly would not stop at this. While Pilia-Borza anticipates resistance, Ithamore does not and confidently declares, "I know what I know: he's a murderer" (4.4.21–22).

And what he knows does him in. When Barabas comes to the brothel in what seems from his French a transparent disguise, it is literally as well as figuratively Ithamore's inability to see the figure beneath the guise (and the poison within his "posy" [4.4.50]) that leads to his death. For in making the Jew his "fellow" in rashness and murder, he does not see Barabas as a cunning capitalist, who will do anything (among other things) not to lose money.

In contrast, the Jew who appears to Ferneze, who himself sees and rules in terms of capital, is not the murderer but the merchant/usurer, consumed and contained by greed. When Barabas first appears at the Senate house, he plays up his financial tragedy, railing inconsolably about his lost goods and the Christian's "theft," threatening to become a thief (and not a murderer) in order to "compass more" (1.2.130–31). While we have no reason to doubt that he has lost "all" at this point, several lamentations later we learn that he has more than plenty hidden—enough to generate the original sum in less than a month—and that his performance at court has been indeed a performance at court, matching and manipulating the governor's own self-consuming "desire of gold."[51] Yet his posture is effective and convincing. Lamenting the loss of "my goods, my money, and my wealth, / My ships, my store, and all that I enjoy'd," he asks whether Ferneze is not "satisfied," or whether he plans to "bereave my life" as well (1.2.141–47). Instead of taking him up on what would be an expedient move, the governor is, in fact, too satisfied. Treating "covetousness" as the worst of Barabas's "monstrous sin[s]" (1.2.128), he cautions the Jew to be "content" (1.2.156) and naively sets him free.

Both Barabas and Marlowe underscore the governor's naïveté and the Jew's strategy. After continuing his performance in front of the equally gullible Jews, Barabas directs us to

> See the simplicity of these base slaves,
> Who, for the villains have no wit themselves,
> Think me to be a senseless lump of clay,
> That will with every water wash to dirt!
>
> (1.2.219–22)

The "simplicity" we are also to see is that of Ferneze (if not of ourselves as well), who anticipates neither that Barabas has hidden a substantial portion of his wealth nor that he will not be "content" merely to recover his losses. In Act 5, the governor is trapped by his own simplicity once again, when his officer announces that Barabas the Jew is dead. While Del Bosco notices that "this sudden death of his is very strange," Ferneze does not. "Wonder not at it," he commands, offering a facile commonplace ("the heavens are just") which no one here believes and a meaningless explanation ("their deaths were like their lives") (5.1.54–56).[52] Barabas's "death" is more like his life than Ferneze knows—a supreme and supremely manipulative fiction that works through alienation to overcome or overthrow.

That Barabas's fictions are designed to match Ferneze becomes especially clear when the governor actually joins with him in a tenuous alliance. Barabas has overthrown him and it is somewhat unclear whether Ferneze at this point envisions his own subsequent turn against the Jew.[53] Yet if not (and considering his naïveté, it seems likely not), he is again acting on the illusion that the Jew (who intends to "bring confusion" somehow on all) wants only money. Ferneze first promises him "great sums of money" (5.2.89) and then throws in the governorship (which Barabas already possesses) on the side, as if to share power with a (money-hungry) Jew is not to share power. Barabas, who continues to address him as Governor (as if rejecting his own political status), plays along, directing him to "walk about the city" (5.2.93) and make "what money thou canst make" (5.2.95), mimicking Ferneze's own words from Act 1 in bold-faced terms, and though the governor doesn't see the connection, we certainly do. Ferneze ultimately outdoes Barabas (as no one can outdo Tamburlaine), but it is only by pulling his strategies out from under him, in a gesture (to which

I will return) that reinforces the connection and the sense that the Jew Ferneze gets is the Jew he, in effect, constructs.

And so throughout the play does Barabas strategically play the Jew. When he forms an alliance with Calymath, it is neither his greed nor his villainy that he stresses, but his cunning—something the Turk at once expects and shares. Apparently dissatisfied with receiving only the payment of tribute from Malta, the Turks have waited for ten years before demanding their due, conveniently generating an exorbitant national debt that the island, hopefully, cannot meet and thus creating an excuse for war. The Turks have arrived, after all, as the anxious Jews note, in "a fleet of warlike galleys" (1.1.149). Although Calymath grants Ferneze the leniency of a month to collect the money, he is immediately ready, when the end of the month brings no payment, to "batter down" the city's towers and "turn proud Malta to a wilderness" (3.5.25–26) and, after victory, to put the Maltese "under Turkish yokes" and make them "groaning bear the burden of our ire" (5.2.7–8). And even though he eventually places Barabas in charge, it is not without surrounding him with Turkish "Janizaries," ostensibly to "guard [his] person" (5.2.17), figures who, in Hakluyt's accounts of Africa, are presented as having more authority over the region they "guard" than the region's own king.[54]

This ominous sign of constraint notwithstanding, Barabas works his way into a league with the Turks by fashioning his demeanor and desires after Calymath's, laying murder and greed aside and becoming a cunning strategist. Though we hear him ranting against the "accursed town" (5.1.62) of Malta after he has been found dead and tossed outside its walls, when Calymath comes upon the scene, asking "whom have we there? A spy?", his rhetoric changes abruptly and he accordingly becomes "one that can spy a place / Where you may enter, and surprise the town" (5.1.70–72). Now instead of claiming a criminal history as he has done with Ithamore, he, in fact, exonerates himself at Ithamore's expense and accuses the Christians of hiring his slave (whom he, astutely, does not identify as a Turk) "to accuse me of a thousand villainies" (5.1.77). What he emphasizes instead is his uncontainable ingenuity: his ability to deceive his way out of prison (by drinking poppy and mandrake juice and playing dead), to know his way through Malta's "common channels" (5.1.90), and to construct, and even help lead, a two-fold attack. Betraying no other ambitions, Barabas offers to die if his scheme fails, and Calymath believes him, to his own dismay.

Even when Barabas markets himself in religious terms as the Jew, his identity is no more real. Most tellingly, when he is confronted by Friar Barnardine and Friar Jacomo (who is already predisposed to think the Jew has "crucified a child" [3.6.49]) and prompted to confess the murders of Lodowick and Mathias, he first exploits and then dismisses his Jewish identity, offering to turn Christian after becoming an accommodating Jew. When they attempt to incriminate him as a murderer, he continually interrupts and presents himself instead as a usurer and a fornicator. When they attempt to state what he has done ("thou hast———"), he distracts them with what he has ("True, I have money"); and when he is almost accused of being the murderer he is ("Thou art a———"), he confesses only that "I know I am a Jew." They continue to press ("Remember that———"; "Thou hast committed———"), but he diverts attention to lesser crimes of usury and fornication and downplays the latter even further by claiming that "that was in another country, / And besides the wench is dead" (4.1.30–44)—as if any of that matters. When Barnardine finally completes a sentence and directs him to "remember Mathias and Don Lodowick" (4.1.46), he asks if he can turn Christian and reminds them what it means to be a Jew (after admitting that he "must dissemble" [4.1.50]): to be "a covetous wretch," "hard-hearted to the poor" (4.1.55), who in his zealousness has gathered more wealth than "all the Jews in Malta" (4.1.59). If he turns Christian, he promises, his "great sums of money" will go "to some religious house" (4.1.78).

It is appropriate that the climax of his performance here comes as he offers to convert, for in turning Jew he has, in effect, turned Christian, making himself more like the friars than they would like to admit. They have already shown their lust and greed—Barnardine by lamenting that Abigail died a virgin, and both by competing for Barabas's gold. Hoping to share the profits of his sins, they, like Ithamore, Ferneze, and Calymath, naively "make account of him as of their fellow." In efforts to lure him (and his money) into their houses, they wind up dead in his, forgetting to "remember Mathias and Don Lodowick," whose deaths foreshadow their own.

Barabas's career is thus shaped by a series of performances in which he plays the Jew (as Tamburlaine plays the barbarian/hero) his spectators want and need to see, a Jew who ironically tells us more about them than about him. He, in effect, becomes his own capital in a world preoccupied with profit. Yet he remains capital for others too. When we last see him, he is busily constructing

> a dainty gallery,
> The floor whereof, this cable being cut,
> Doth fall asunder, so that it doth sink
> Into a deep pit past recovery.
>
> (5.5.35–38)

His construction here suggests what he has been doing throughout, busily constructing one self after another without the substance beneath, making himself the deceptive and uncertain flooring that leads others to their falls. This time, however, Ferneze undoes him and, before his cue, cuts the cord that holds the device together, using "a Jew's courtesy" (5.5.115) and "the unhallow'd deeds of Jews" (5.5.97) to ultimately disenfranchise the Jew. However successful Barabas's strategies have been before, here they literally fall through, making clear that his fictions can be appropriated—and are—at the cut of a cord.

Once again the Jew becomes the middleman between Malta and the Turks, but this time from a telling position of absence, "past recovery." While Barabas is falling into the pit, the knights are stealing another of his schemes and are massacring the Turkish troops, whom he has lured into a firetrap masquerading as a feast. And it is only by appropriating both of the Jew's anti-Turk devices that Ferneze can demand that Calymath make "good / The ruins done to Malta" (5.5.118–19) and set Malta free. With Ferneze standing above, Barabas's position is suggestive of how he has been defined throughout—as an unknowable figure who takes shape(s) according to the knowing terms of dominating voices, including, of course, his own. Yet the power play does not end here. For despite the governor's insistence that "Malta shall be freed" (5.5.120), Del Bosco stands beside him (as he has through most of the play), the colonizing voice behind the colonizing voice, reminding us that Malta has been circumscribed like the Jew, that Ferneze's Establishment is still anything but established. We are left then with a vision of domination, acted out through five acts and reduced to this suggestive tableau, and left wondering, like Calymath, "what doth this portend" (5.5.95) and whose credit will carry in the custom-house next—in Malta and England too.

Doctor Faustus and *Edward II* bring the discourse of alienation back to Europe, but the leap from Malta (whenever it came chronologically) is not as far as it might seem. For *The Jew of Malta* links imperialism to capitalism, the Jew, the alien abroad, to the merchant, the alien at home.

Ironically and surely not coincidentally, the closer we get to home, the more confused, conflicted, and conflated the discourse on the other becomes, culminating in the figure of the sodomite who could almost be all things (mostly criminal) to all people. Yet Marlowe's disclosure and subversion of this multivalence has been started or stated here, in *The Jew of Malta*, in its complication, triangulation, and breakdown of the self/other opposition, and its insistence that the subject of discrimination is not always its true object. Faustus and Edward II are pressed into their own deep pits past recovery, and though they stand out as European subjects, the Jew of Malta has already set, or will similarly take, the stage.

Part III

The Alien at Home

5. Demonizing Magic: Patterns of Power in *Doctor Faustus*

"Who buzzeth in mine ears I am a spirit?"
(2.3.14)

The European Subject

The prologue to *The Tragicall History of Doctor Faustus* sets the forthcoming material apart from what has come before on the Marlovian stage—from "the pomp of proud audacious deeds," from marches of war and sports of love that "overturn'd" "courts of kings" in Carthage and beyond (Prologue 4–5).[1] Though *Edward II* may be implicated in the latter, the turn marked here is primarily from the broad, cross-cultural landscapes of imperialist competition to "only this" (Prologue 7), the "fortunes" of a man born of "parents base of stock" (Prologue 11), schooled in Germany, and sitting, as the play opens, in his study. While his fortunes include an Icarian rise to things "above his reach" (Prologue 21) and a fall to "devilish exercise" (Prologue 23), they are notably circumscribed, spatially within Europe, temporally within a period of twenty-four years, and textually by a legendary tradition of Faust tales. The center of the drama, too, is not the exterior space of public display but an interior scrutiny of self and soul, of self in terms of soul. Though Faustus, like Barabas, Tamburlaine, and Dido, makes a name for himself by flaunting his unorthodox powers in public, the transgression for which he is called to make account, by us and those onstage, is finally against God, himself, and his eternal fate.

In Marlowe, the division between non-European and European spaces and subjects can only be tenuous; for, as the preceding chapters have argued, the plays insist that the boundaries between "ours" and "theirs" depend upon who is setting the terms, from what place and perspective, and for what purpose. Though the A-text of *Faustus* points primarily inward, to a struggle of soul, the B-text points also outward, to and from a context of imperialism.[2] The fact that the same story can go either way suggests the close connection between "domestic" and "imperialist" concerns. Yet the Faust tale, with its European setting, its Christian framework, and its repeated inscription in legend (which, in the case of the Faustbooks, is canonized as "English" and "German"), announces itself as European, its landscape of devils notwithstanding. Marlowe's version, in either version, does stand out within the corpus of his works because of its unique engagement with Europe and European legend, as with the self, soul, and "mind of man" (1.1.62). Despite the prologue's suggestions to the contrary, *Edward II* stands beside it, with its focus on the English body politic and an English king's body bringing English audiences even closer to home, and with its diminishing landscape pressing the history into an increasingly interior representational space, which is physically inside the king's body.[3] Both plays, like Marlowe's others, vigorously refute the rigid categorization of self and other; yet, in their distinction from the imperialist plays, they expose critical differences not between the alien abroad and the alien at home, but between society's circumscriptions of the alien.

It seems no coincidence that *Faustus* has become the most canonical of Marlowe's plays and appears regularly and singularly in anthologies and course syllabi, despite the fact that, after *The Massacre at Paris*, its text is the least reliable in the Marlovian corpus. The most recent *Norton Anthology of English Literature* singles out the "tremendously successful" *Tamburlaine* to introduce an accomplished and uncontroversial Marlowe, emphasizing the play's innovative use of blank verse and its (implicitly admirable) valorization of human ambition.[4] The play anthologized, however, as more important to an understanding of Marlowe and Elizabethan literature and life is *Faustus*. In order to justify its centrality, the headnote must normalize the play's otherwise alienating elements. Faustus's bargain with the devil and his damnation, we are told, "would have been taken seriously in a time when everyone believed in the reality of devils." While admitting that his inevitable fall disrupts Marlowe's "characteristic" glorification of ambition, the editors diffuse the tension created by this discrepancy by fitting Faustus's "fiendful fortune" (Epilogue 5) seamlessly into a tradition of fortunate falls, of the angels in heaven and humanity in Eden. Ultimately, what is made to argue for the play's importance is that certain scenes (one which occurs in different versions in the A- and B-texts) stand out as the work of "no other Elizabethan," an endorsement that distinguishes Marlowe as an exemplary though unique Elizabethan author.[5]

For Marlowe's contemporaries, *Tamburlaine* was largely the text of choice in incriminations and emulations of the author.[6] Yet, like the Norton editors, modern critics attempting to recover a definitive Marlowe have privileged *Faustus* as pivotal, as if a text that deals directly with "the mind of man" would be more likely to reveal his. Even with Christianity providing the terms of debate, the play's ideology has been produced in radically different ways, as unquestionably transgressive or unquestionably orthodox.[7] Though the conflict has been split between the two existing texts, the question of whether Faustus is damned—generally assigned a subversive answer ("no") in the A-text and a conservative one ("yes") in B—remains as vital and vexing (and misleading, as I will suggest) to these readings as the issue of Hamlet's delay has been to *Hamlet*.[8] Even so, what has prevailed amid and despite all the controversy are interpretations of both play and playwright that discover a largely unconflicted ideological stance. It has been only with the death of the author (and perhaps also of God) and with the growing critical agreement that neither text is an "original Marlowe" that *Faustus*'s indeterminacies have earned a prominent place in the story.[9]

The impulses behind the canonization and clarification of *Faustus* are no doubt varied. In part the privileging of the text and of stable readings of it in the face of glaring textual corruption and critical controversy suggests a desire to find the play distinctively knowable and familiar—a desire that is itself complicit with the kinds of imperialist self-constructions Marlovian drama reacts against. At stake is an assumption crucial to the self/other divide: that "we" are subjects with meaningfully individuated bodies and (Christian) souls, while "they" are objects. Their bodies or, more often, body parts were produced as marvels to and for our gaze, and their souls, when not ignored, provided something to save (to justify colonization) or blame (to justify aggression). When described by the Persians, Tamburlaine becomes a spectacular collection of limbs, joints, postures, eyes, and curls, all promising the divinely ordained destiny his competitors need to see. In Part 2, the Christian king deploys Christian dictates against "the infidel," whether the elusively irreligious Tamburlaine or the Mohammedan Turks, in order to break rather than engender faith, to be aggressively untrue to his vows of peace because "they" are.[10] "Their" souls otherwise do not matter. And though Ferneze castigates Barabas as "the infidel," he is interested in the Jew only as a prop of profit.

Faustus's interior dimensions, however, do claim center stage as the subject of almost everyone's speculation—from the scholars', to the angels', to the devils', to his own, and likewise to ours. In turning at once to

Europe and to a struggle of soul, the play fosters the illusion that Europe is the domain of a uniquely interiorized self. While Tamburlaine may discourse upon "beauty" and "perfect bliss," and the Jew of Malta upon money, murder, and revenge, it is only Faustus who speculates upon the power and possibilities of "that within" (*Hamlet* 1.2.85).

Marlowe's simultaneous evocation and rejection of the morality tradition, in which the saga of soul was played out externally, reminds us that Faustus is not an Everyman; his choices matter not as they impact universally upon a cosmic battle between good and evil, God (who, as critics have often noted, is absent here) and the devil, but as they impact particularly upon him, "the man that in his study sits" (Prologue 28).[11] These are his fortunes, good or bad, and he, his perception, and his self-perception become the determining factors.

At stake also in the canonization and stabilization of the play is the assumption that the European subject is ultimately knowable, unlike non-Europeans whose methods and motives elude "our" grasp. While African or New World natives might attack European visitors erratically, without apparent provocation, European aggression is repeatedly inscribed within a comprehensible pattern of negotiation; while we might wonder about "them," we are given little room to wonder about "us." Faustus is deeply invested in the illusion of knowability, choosing a career path with definitive limits, writing himself into a contract with non-negotiable terms, and ostensibly giving his life "a shape and a certainty that it would otherwise lack."[12] In studying magic and emulating Agrippa (whom, he tells us, "all Europe" [1.1.119] honored), Faustus plans to be "resolve[d] . . . of all ambiguities" (1.1.81) touching the cosmos and his place and power within it.[13] To decide whether the "form of [his] fortunes" and Marlowe's complicity with them is "good or bad" (Prologue 8) is to produce "us" as subjects whose meanings can always be recuperated even (if not especially) from corrupted and controversial texts.

Yet while the play provokes such inscription, it does so only to prompt its spectators to reconsider their assumptions about the superiority and uniqueness of the European subject. In his choice of domestic subjects, Marlowe disrupts the great divide instituted most prominently within imperialist discourse, between Europe as the locus of the self and elsewhere as the locus of the other. For in *Faustus* the European subject on display is a notorious other, a black magician whose practice was not neutralized in early modern social discourses into a comforting pattern of fortunate falls. To the contrary, black magic was set repeatedly against white or "natural" magic and orthodox religion as "an execrable and monstrous thing" that "consist[ed] wholly in the operations and powers of demons."[14] In *Edward II* and *The Massacre at Paris*, too, the "heroes"—Edward, the "homosexual" king, and the Machiavellian Duke of Guise—are comparably other. More than Dido, Tamburlaine, or Barabas, these subjects, because they are European, bring home the point—and for imperialist discourses, the problem—that otherness resides not only abroad but also, more immediately, at home.

And not just within the confines of Europe—the play points us also to an otherness within the self. Though Faustus is given a unique interiority, it is a source and center of crisis. Despite imperialist discourses that seemed to suggest otherwise, the self was a radically unstable site of knowledge.[15] Hamlet, arguably the most introspective of Shakespeare's characters, if not also on the Elizabethan stage, is also the most elusive, appearing most definable when he is taking his passion and cue from others and least when he articulates what it means for him to be or not to be.[16] Even as he attempts to look inward, in his famous set piece, to determine what it means to be, he returns to externals, to the wearying "fardels" (*Hamlet* 3.1.75) of the world which in his view circumscribe existence, and displaces his anxiety about what or whether being means onto the "undiscover'd country" (3.1.78) of the afterlife. Ultimately he can only garner identity from men who act (the Ghost, the player, Fortinbras's men, and Laertes), modeling his behavior on theirs, however fleetingly. As he does so, interiority gives way to action, which proves finally more able to be suited to the word and to tragic form and meanings than whatever lies within.

In asking the quintessential question, "Why does Hamlet delay?," critics have recast his internal dilemma in terms of action. Yet the question is misleading, for in giving a definitive effect, it presupposes a definitive cause rooted knowably within a knowable self. In the play's opening line, Shakespeare poses another question—"Who's there?" (1.1.1)—that defies answer both within the initial scene and throughout: just as the guards, wrapped in a fog of unknowing, have no immediate answer, neither does the play. Though Lear, in madness, fixates on an image of humanity that will tell him who he is, neither Hamlet nor his play proffers a stable image of "unaccommodated man" (*King Lear* 3.4.106–7) that works in reason.

In *Faustus* as well, interiority complicates rather than clarifies identity. Though Faustus seems sure of his ability to know himself and his fate, we are not, especially when alternative texts ("*Homo fuge!*" [2.1.77]) appear and disappear on his arm and alternative voices continually interrupt his resolve. In constantly reiterating his resolve to be resolved, Faustus himself casts doubt on what he is doing and what he knows about what he is doing. Like Barabas, the more he talks about his motives and ambitions, the less clear they become, even though he, unlike Barabas, charts his journey in terms of soul. Just as Barabas voices desires for profit, revenge, and power, but achieving all, is satisfied with none, so similarly does Faustus contemplate taking command of "a world of profit and delight / Of power, of honor, of omnipotence" (1.1.54–55), only to carry through with the most menial tricks, as critics have often complained, his bargain with the devil notwithstanding.[17]

While it is tempting given the interior terms of the drama to locate a singular motive behind his actions—to see him trying, as Dollimore has argued, to "escape agonised irresolution" and "an *impasse* of despair" or, as Greenblatt contends, "to give his life a clear fixed shape"—Faustus's almost haphazard articulations of purpose argue against such clarity.[18] Though we know that there is "nothing so sweet as magic is to him" (Prologue 26), because he gives such different reasons for his choice we do not know exactly why. We cannot be sure whether his point is to "settle" (1.1.1) his studies, the shape of his life, or the fate of his soul, to "be great emperor of the world" (1.3.104) and to command "all things that move between the quiet poles" (1.1.57), to be "as cunning as Agrippa was" (1.1.118) and garner comparable fame, to gain a wife or lover (as suggested in his initial and final requests), all of the above or none.

Instead of assigning Faustus a governing interiority that gives his fortunes a definitive and meaningful shape, Marlowe positions that interiority as a manipulable construct (like Barabas's status as Jew or Tamburlaine's barbarity). Like Barabas and Tamburlaine, Faustus emerges as the subject of a discourse dictated from without by those who have more of a stake in his soul than he, a subject whose fortunes are framed by and within the self-authorizing displays of the devil. Though he attempts to create and sustain the illusion that he is writing himself into a knowable position of knowledge and power, it is not he but Lucifer's agent Mephastophilis who acts "of [his] own accord" (1.3.44), who invests Faustus's choice with meaning and hands him the dagger of his own undoing, and who in the B-text turns the pages to lead Faustus's eye toward damnation. And it is not he who demonstrates his power by transgressing, but Lucifer and Mephastophilis who demonstrate theirs by coercing him into a position of transgression, appropriating him as a convenient and necessary other.

As I have argued, the imperialist plays dramatize similar manipulations. Yet what is significantly different here (as in *Edward II*) is that the appropriation is played out in terms of interiority. In Marlowe's Europe, thoughts *are* subjects, and the discrimination that he locates there is one that reaches into the self, into the soul and "mind of man."

The Renaissance Magician

The Renaissance magician in general and the figure of Faust in particular provided the perfect subject for this self-scrutiny, for across Europe they were among the most visible targets of demonization within the domestic discourse of the early modern period. During the medieval period, the magician emerged prominently within literary texts as a kind of Vice figure whose tricks catalyzed the more important fates and actions of others.[19] In the Renaissance, however, the magician's, especially the black magician's, fortunes were more centrally and significantly on display. With the eruption of the witch craze in the 1550s came an outbreak of texts demonizing magic, such as Jean Bodin's *De la demonomanie des sorciers* (1580), Francis Coxe's *A short treatise declaring the detestable wickedness of magical sciences* (1561), and of course, James I's prominent *Daemonologie* (1597).[20]

In the early sixteenth century, Faust became a sort of cult figure, the story of his pact with the devil told and retold across Europe on all levels of society, in ballads, books, and plays. Almost immediately after the historical Faust's death in the late 1530s, the legend arose, and before the emergence of the seminal German Faustbook (*Historia von D. Johann Fausten*), published in 1587 and heavily influenced by Martin Luther's writings, at least two other German collections of tales existed in manuscript alongside oral counterparts.[21] The German Faustbook was translated into English sometime during or before 1592, and Marlowe brought its material to the stage shortly and spectacularly thereafter.[22] The subject was sure to sell seats in the theater (and perhaps to vacate a few, as the actor playing Faustus, on one by now well-known occasion, allegedly conjured up a real devil and sent audiences running).[23] On the stage too during the period was an unusually large number of magician plays—such as Robert Greene's *Friar Bacon and Friar Bungay*, Anthony Munday's *John a Kent and John a Cumber*, Shakespeare's *The Tempest*, and Jonson's *The Alchemist*—which, though their magicians were not as black, nonetheless problematized the magician's place and power.[24]

Ironically—and, I would argue, not coincidentally—while the Renaissance magician was such a prominent subject, he was also one of the least well-defined (along with the sodomite, to whom I will return). Not only was magic separated into black and white; it was also divided into learned and unlearned practice.[25] On the one hand, figures such as Marsilio Ficino, Giovanni Pico della Mirandola, and Cornelius Agrippa were promoting occult philosophy that, in adding knowledge of divine mysteries to natural philosophy, could lead the mind intimately close to God's.[26] On the other hand, in less learned circles, the village "cunning men" and "wise women" were curing everything from headaches and toothaches, to dog or scorpion bites, to "the falling evill," to demonic possession, and were detecting treasures, thieves, witches, stolen goods, and good matches.[27]

These distinctions, however, were not as absolute as they might seem. While Agrippa embraced magic as a means to spiritual enlightenment in his influential *De Occulta Philosophia Libri Tres* (1533), he also saw it in more earthly terms as giving access to power, profit, love, revenge, and advantage in disputes.[28] And what made the social space of these practices even less distinct was that it bordered on that of other traditionally legitimate fields of knowledge, such as religion, humanism, medicine, science, and law.[29]

Yet despite, if not because of, the slippery liminality and legitimacy of "white" and popular practices, magic was given its clearest and most prominent form as it was demonized and criminalized, especially during the mid-sixteenth to late seventeenth centuries, the period of the witch craze. Black magicians and witches, distinguished inconsistently (if at all) from each other, were repeatedly invoked as the dark side of safe practices, which therefore seemed destined to go astray. Bodin's *De la demonomanie des sorciers* and James's *Daemonologie* allowed occult philosophers no other fate than joining pridefully in league with the devil and accused both Pico della Mirandola and Agrippa of witchcraft. Others also condemned Agrippa as "the blackest of black magicians," and one of his followers, John Dee, once in high favor at Elizabeth's court, was ultimately forced to defend himself against charges of being a conjurer.[30] The cunning men and wise women faced less prominent fates, but their activities were outlawed nonetheless as felonies.[31] Yet while these incriminations treated magic as if it were a matter of black and white, they simultaneously reinforced the slipperiness of its legitimacy, making clear that at any moment natural magic could become unnatural, divine pursuits become demonism, and white become black.

The witch craze and the demonization of magic more generally no doubt served a number of political, social, and psychological purposes, as Keith Thomas, among others, has argued.[32] Wherever there was uncertainty, the black magician and his alleged ally, the devil, offered certainty; wherever uncontrolled desire, an impetus for repression; wherever dissent, a sure excuse for suppression. Their malign presence could explain away otherwise ordinary but perplexing problems: "greefe, sicknesse, losse of children, corn, cattell or libertie," unexpected success, unmotivated crime, and even erotic fantasies and wet dreams.[33]

Yet importantly, the demonization of magic allowed both church and state an important image of their control over the self, over the interior dimensions of mind and soul. Because the practice of magic was so inclusive, extending from the unlearned to the learned and touching the most mundane as well as the most ethereal aspects of existence, the figure of the magician was a sort of "everyman," invested in some way in knowledge or self-knowledge. To send him or her to hell for a career of vaguely defined "transgressions" was to mystify the boundaries of the law, to criminalize knowing and self-knowing, and to monopolize the right and ability to distinguish self from other, the saved from the damned. It was also to universalize transgression, to put all in danger of unwittingly selling their souls to the devil and all in need of regulating structures that would in some way save them—providing, of course, they could be saved, which in the case of Calvinism, with its doctrine of election, was not always possible.[34] Still for Calvinists, too, the demonization of the magician was an especially potent reminder that the fate of self and soul was in the hands of a higher authority, whose decision one could decipher (as much as one could) only by following church doctrine. In any case, the example of the magician put the self in a dangerous place of unknowing beneath the authority of an omniscient church or state.

The legend of Faust, a particular favorite of Protestant reformers, brought the lesson emphatically down to earth, perhaps more than any other example. Historically, the picture of the "real" Faust is sketchy at best. Although he seems to have been making a name for himself in Germany during the first half of the sixteenth century, that name itself, ironically, was obscured. The original Faust, Georgius of Helmstadt (or Jorio or Jeorius and the like), a "doctor" of some sort and, for a short term, a schoolmaster, became confused with Johannes, an astrologer.[35] Georgius was known above all as a showman, at once embraced and alienated within learned circles. Although patronized by the Catholic middle classes, he was ostracized by civic authorities and was banned from Ingolstadt in 1528 and Nuremberg in 1532.

Precisely what he showed is unclear, but whatever it was, it earned him the reputation of being "a vagabond, an empty babbler and a knave: worthy to be whipped," "a shit-house full of devils," and "the Devil's brother-in-law" (a title he allegedly claimed for himself).[36] He was also, almost inevitably, accused of sodomizing his schoolboys—a charge that is not surprising, given the ease with which sodomy was applied across the board to all sorts of "others."[37] Though the historical material suggests that he was at worst (if not also at best) a bombastic fraud, after his death he was turned into a notorious black magician doomed to an afterlife in hell. The Protestant reformer Johannes Gast (under the influence of Luther) initiated the transformation in 1548 and reported that Faust had sold his soul to the devil and had been fetched, supplying his broken neck, "the classic retribution for those who sell their souls" thus, as the ocular proof.[38] And it was this demonic side of the story that prevailed.

While the legend emphatically inscribes the end of Faustus's life and practices as extraordinarily transgressive, it also presents his earlier exploits as notably ordinary. The author of the English Faustbook, an unidentifiable P. F., Gent., describes him as "a worldly man" who "named himselfe an Astrologian, and a Mathematician, and for a shadow sometimes a Phisitian, and did great cures; namely, with hearbs, rootes, waters, drinks, receipts, and clisters."[39] Armed with magic, the English Faustbook's Faustus becomes a sort of Epicurean cunning man and spends his time traveling about the universe, visiting the Great Cham (who allegedly gave Barabas a hat), a Turkish Emperor, and a harem of Turkish concubines, and writing home about it; feasting with students, consorting with "Doctors and Masters" (p. 89), and producing such "strange sights" as fruit in winter (p. 111); cozening a Jew out of money, making a match between lovers, and marrying—and having a son by—Helen of Troy!

In other accounts, he appears as a "brilliant heretic among stuffy academicians," who delved into "forbidden knowledge" but whose crimes were similarly innocuous, the worst consisting of frightful conjurations— of the Cyclops "with Greeks dangling from his teeth," for example—which (like Marlowe's play) terrorized audiences, and the best, of stealing food and drink from the King of England to serve to his own guests.[40] Despite the triviality of his deeds, he was nonetheless assumed to be a black magician, infernally in league with the devil. Though P. F. praises "the excellency of his wisdome" in divinity, he centers on Faustus's "very ungodly life" (p. 2), emphasizing how "the wicked wretch," "in-flamed" by his power over Mephostophiles and fully "resolved in himselfe" "to doe whatsoever the Spirit and his Lord [Lucifer] should condition upon" (p. 7), "forgot the Lord his maker, and Christ his redeemer, [and] became an enemy unto all man-kinde" (p. 10).

The legend served, of course, as evidence of the reality of the devil, providing Protestantism and its daily scrutiny of self and soul a useful impetus and "ally."[41] The publisher of the German Faustbook, Johann Spies, introduces the tale as "a fearful example of the Devil's deception and of his murder of body and soul, so that it might be a warning to all Chris-tians."[42] The story also usefully implicated Catholicism (as does Marlowe), displaying the fate of one who "went to Hell for the same reasons that all good Catholics were going there: . . . for the vain presumption that he might try to *deserve* redemption."[43] Yet that "vain presumption" was not isolated in Catholics nor the message directed primarily toward them. For it was the Protestant populace that was to see the disastrous fruits of "for-bidden knowledge," to witness the violent demonization of one who started off pursuing a fairly "normal" career.

P. F., Gent., who seems heavily invested in the Protestant cause, offers the story as a lesson for "the stiffe-necked and high minded," cautioning them "to feare God, and to be careful of their vocation, and to be at defi-ance with all divelish workes." It is unclear here who qualify as the "stiffe-necked and high minded" and what constitutes "divelish workes." Yet instead of obscuring the message, this lack of clarity amplifies it by bring-ing us all into the picture, cautioning all to "take God alwaies before our eies, to call alone upon him, and to honour him all the dayes of our life, with heart and hearty prayer" (pp. 128–29). If we do not, we too risk falling to a "frightful end" and finally and fatally becoming (or proving ourselves already) "they."

Noticeably on the Renaissance stage, where hegemonic forms of power were more likely to be questioned than affirmed, magicians (at least the ones we know of) faced less serious consequences, even when devils were involved. Friar Bacon, Faustus's ancestor or heir, admits to having "dived into hell / and sought the darkest palaces of fiends," but his prize possession and preoccupation is an outrageous "brazen head," allegedly able to "unfold strange doubts and aphorisms / And read a lecture in phi-losophy" (*Friar Bacon and Friar Bungay* 2.25–28).[44] When he sleeps through the head's great moment of revelation, he vows that he will break his crystal and repent, which he does. It is not he but his attendant Miles (a descendant of the Vice) who rides to hell on the devil's back, but even his fate is produced as comic. Meanwhile, Friar Bacon survives to become a prophet for England's glorious future, and as his necromancy gives way to national politics, his magical arts are redeemed as part—an innocuous part—of the status quo. This ending is a far cry from the final image of the English Faustbook's Faustus, whose soul is sent to hell and, as if that is not enough, whose brains are left clinging to his chamber wall, his teeth scattered into its several corners, and the rest of his body ripped apart and thrown outside on a pile of horse dung.

The magicians who follow are increasingly identified with power plays that set them in the mainstream of social and political negotiations and neutralize the otherness of their magic. Colonialist readings of *The Tempest* treat Prospero as the consummate colonizer, working his way back into a position of authority by imposing a legitimating narrative of his mastery upon a "brave, new" island "world" and upon those who come or live there.[45] Though these interpretations bring out an important and, in earlier criticism, generally suppressed political edge vital to Prospero's and Shakespeare's dramas, they are limited by a singularity of focus like that marking earlier studies. Whereas before we were given a magician—and usually a good, white magician—and not a colonizer, now we are given a colonizer rather than a magician.

Yet Prospero is clearly both; his magic is integrated into, and not subsumed beneath, his political purposes. Part of what is at stake here, in addition to colonialism, is the magician's social place. Colonialist critiques take issue with Caliban's identity as a "thing of darkness" (*The Tempest* 5.1.275); yet Prospero's pursuit of "secret studies" (1.2.76–77) marks him also as an other, forcing him into a literal position of alienation. While the play does not finally redeem him, it does normalize his magic. Magic becomes a not-so-extraordinary means to political power, allowing Prospero to reclaim a place, however good or bad, within the society of Milan. At the end of the play, Alonso declares "this business" "as strange a maze as e'er men trod" (5.1.242–43), but Prospero assures him and us in his monolithic way:

> I'll resolve you
> (Which to you shall seem probable) of every
> These happen'd accidents.
>
> (5.1.248–50)

As we wait for his next self-authorizing narrative, we are not to "infest" our minds "with beating on / The strangeness of this business" (5.1.246–47), and as the wheel comes full circle, initiating a new chain of events and narratives in Milan, the strange business of magic seems little different from the strange business of state. When Jonson picks magic up in *The Alchemist*, it becomes just one of many "natural follies" (Prologue 23) fit for gulls and gulling, one more means of fraud within a community of metaphoric "fiend[s]" (5.4.138) all out for worldly, not otherworldly, gains.

The normalization of magic on the stage stands in striking contrast to the demonization advanced so prominently by Protestant propagandists. Though the magicians produced onstage are incriminated for foolishness, colonialism, and fraud, they are not damned or even, finally, arrested. Their practices stand as a part of, and not apart from, the sometimes unsavory routines of social and political negotiation. Yet while the plays do not participate in the kind of demonization effected by church and state, neither do they directly address or subvert it. For in taking the magician out of the hands of the devil, they take him or her also out of the context of religion and contest of soul—out of the cultural register, that is, in which magic was so visibly and coercively inscribed. The exploitation that these plays display is one assigned for the most part to the magician, who, instead of being dominated, coerced, or deceived, uses knowledge and art to dominate, coerce, or deceive. And what results is another kind of appropriation—this time without the demons—one that incriminates magic as a conforming rather than transgressive part of society's standard operating procedures.

Yet there were two prominent texts circulating in the early modern period that did directly address and subvert the demonization of magic: the one, Reginald Scot's remarkable *The discoverie of witchcraft* (published in 1584) and the other, Marlowe's *Doctor Faustus* (to which I will return). Like no other author of the era, Scot protested against "Bodins bables" and exposed the witch craze for what it was: a manipulation of the powerless by the powerful.[46] In *The discoverie*, he makes a significant distinction between "naturall magicke" and what was being designated as witchcraft and, aligning himself with Agrippa at several points, describes the former as a divine art "wherein a man may learn the properties, qualities, and knowledge of all nature" and "set forth the glorie of God, and be many waies beneficiall to the commonwealth" (p. 290). At the same time, he presents its sinister counterpart not as a malignant extension or inevitable abuse of these pursuits, but as a product of "nothing else but knaverie, cousenage, and old wives fables."[47]

Setting himself up as an advocate for the poor (among whom he counts himself) and enlisting the aid of Sir Roger Manwood, their "verie father," Scot accuses witchmongers, whose "names give more credit to this cause than their writings," of "pursu[ing] the poore, . . . accus[ing] the simple, and . . . kill[ing] the innocent; supplieng in rigor and malice towards others, that which they themselves want in proofe and discretion, or the other in offense or occasion."[48] The most vulnerable and common targets of this malice are those "least sufficient of all other persons to speake for themselves,"[49] particularly "women which be commonly old, lame, bleare-eied, pale, fowle, and full of wrinkles: [the] poore, sullen, superstitious, and papists; or such as knowe no religion" (p. 7), or those who have "leprosie, apoplexie, or anie other strange disease" (p. 23). Scot declares their alleged offenses (giving themselves or their children to the devil, boiling infants, and being cannibals, for example) "untrue, incredible, and impossible" (p. 32). "If more ridiculous or abhominable crimes could have beene invented," he adds, "these poore women (whose cheefe fault is that they are scolds) should have beene charged with them" (p. 34). At one point his frustration with these fictions erupts and he "exclaims" in unusually large type: "Good Lord! how light of credit is the wavering mind of man! How unto tales and lies his eares attentive all they can?" (p. 96).

The text is clearly not without its biases; the skepticism with which it treats the demonization of the underclasses does not extend completely across gender, national, or racial bounds. For though Scot insists that witches are not "real," he implies that "scolds"—some of the stuff on which witches are made—are. And while he doubts that any "honest man in England [or] in France" has seen a witch eat another human being, he acknowledges that "Anthropophagie and Canibals" (p. 33) do exist elsewhere. Later, he admits being suspicious of rumors (reported by "manie great and grave authors") that "certeine families in Aphrica" "bewitch whatsoever they praise" and so cause it to wither, decay, and die. Still, he discredits absolutely *only* the "superstitious fooles" who assign this "mysterie" to witches "here in Europa" (p. 484). And while he doubts that witches sacrifice their children, he is sure that Jews do.[50]

Despite these biases, however, his "discovery" offers a strong voice against the exploitation of vulnerable factions of the populace—the poor, the aged, the ill, the ugly, or the religiously or socially incorrect. In his text it is the witchmonger and not the witch who challenges the authority of

God, blaming divine acts on witches (whom, he reminds us, Christ, Moses, and Job never mentioned) and audaciously presuming to be omniscient judges.[51] Scot himself seems to have been in sympathy with Protestant, if not Calvinist, reform. Yet the witchmongers he attacks, though not identified explicitly as Protestant, are condemned for tactics deployed vigorously by Protestantism. He mentions, for example, that they conjure up witches when they are confronted by "any adversitie" or "the hand and correction of God" (p. 1). He notices, too, that since "the springing up of Luthers sect, . . . priests have tended more diligentlie upon the execution of them; bicause more wealth"—for some unexplained reason—"is to be caught from them" (p. 16). Because he is more preoccupied with how this process happens than with why, his incriminations do not go as far as they might. Still, *The discoverie* at once separates magic and religion and shows how they were being brought coercively together in the service of church and state. Despite its radicality, the text incited only limited and fairly neutral contemporary comment; yet tellingly, King James not only banned it but also directed his own *Daemonologie* specifically against the German Johann Weyer, who "defended" witches by declaring them deluded and melancholic, and against "one called Scot an Englishman."[52]

Doctor Faustus or Mr. Hyde

It was not until Francis Bacon began reforming traditional conceptions of what qualified as legitimate knowledge that the place ascribed to magic came seriously and directly under fire. On the stage, however, Marlowe brought religion and magic together even more pointedly than did Scot and opened up the subject's relevance to a greater portion of the populace, insisting that the damned are not born but made. Ironically, the transformation of Faust resembles the demonization of Marlowe himself, who, with the help of his "monstrous opinions" and unorthodox dramatic art, was metamorphosed into a notorious atheist (as I have suggested in Chapter 1). His Christian contemporaries pressed the elusive "facts" of his life into a singular and singularly reprehensible trajectory, assigning it a clear-cut meaning and universal relevance and using it to warn "all Atheists" "in all the world" "to forsake their horrible impiety."[53] It is precisely that kind of strategic shaping, and how it was played out upon the magician and extended to implicate all, that his play undertakes and undermines.

In an important treatment of the play, Jonathan Dollimore has argued that Faustus is finally bound by the "limiting structures" of Protestantism, which elevated the self by placing him/her newly within an unmediated relation to God while at the same time subjugating him/her by still demanding total submission to that God.[54] This framework, especially in its most radical, Calvinist form, "holds the individual subject terrifyingly responsible for the fallen human condition while disallowing him or her any subjective power of redemption." What this dilemma produces, Dollimore contends, is despair and defiance, and with them a "mode of transgression identifiably protestant in origin."[55] It is this mode, according to the argument, that Faustus embraces, defying the limitations that constitute him and provoke his revolt.

I would argue, however, that while the play certainly critiques Protestantism's catch-22, it does so not by exposing how Protestant ideology engenders trangression within the individual subject but, more subversively, by showing how it imposes a transgressive identity on that subject from without. For even though Faustus indulges in "unlawful things" (Epilogue 6), the play does not define him as a willful and defiant trangressor. Rather, it presents him as the subject of Lucifer's manipulations, unwittingly coerced into a transgressive position to provide the necessary ocular proof of the devil's (and with it, ironically, Protestantism's) power.

Lucifer is an imperialist, wanting Faustus's "soul" in order to "enlarge his kingdom" (2.1.39–40). Importantly, although Faustus is the subject of choice for this self-authorizing "enlargement," he is not the only subject available. There is also the ostler Robin, for example, who steals one of Faustus's books and who, in attempting to conjure up naked maidens, free wine, and other such "spirits," necessarily conjures up spirits of the other sort. The often-noted parallels between Faustus's activities and those of the tavern folk show us, however, not only that the difference between their learned and unlearned pursuits is not in itself great, but also that the difference between their value as learned and unlearned subjects is. The tavern figures exist on the margins of their society, where their licentiousness is licensed and its threat neutralized, where their names blur into a category of class and distinguish status more than selves. Faustus, in contrast, is embedded and renowned in mainstream culture, a figure of learning, "grac'd with doctor's name" (Prologue 17), "that was wont to make [the] schools ring with *sic probo*" (1.2.1–2), who is watched and followed by a fan club of scholars, and who could sign his name in blood if only his blood would cooperate—a figure, that is, of sound and significant mind and soul whose radical transformation would mean. To provoke and contain his transgression would be to create an unforgettable spectacle of power. And that is precisely what Lucifer does.

In Marlowe's play as in other inscriptions of the Faust legend, the representation of Faustus (like that of Tamburlaine) is significantly conflicted, producing a disruptive gap between his fairly innocuous existence as a sort of carnivalesque showman and his increasingly ominous career as a conjurer. On the one hand, he produces grapes out of season for the Duchess of Vanholt, conjures up "such spirits as can lively resemble Alexander and his paramour" (4.1.50–51) and tricks and plagues a pope, a knight, a horse-courser, and various other commoners. On the other, he embraces Mephastophilis, makes a pact with the devil, and signs with his own blood. Though in the source material the latter seems to evolve almost causally from the former, Marlowe's constant vacillation between Faustus's public antics and his soul-searching interactions with the devils amplifies the difference between them. In the process, it diminishes our sense of Faustus's sense of purpose, making his actions seem not only trivial but also arbitrary, as if he is following rather than leading the way to "settle" his studies and his soul.

Even if we set these discrepancies aside and look only at the darker necromantic side of Faustus's life, which in the sources is inscribed as willfully and knowingly transgressive, we find that it too is conflicted on Marlowe's stage. The prologue, while ostensibly leaving it up to us to decide whether the "form of Faustus' fortunes" is "good or bad," nonetheless explains his fall as that of an occult philosopher turned black magician who, "swoll'n with cunning of a self-conceit," "did mount above his reach" (Prologue 20–21). It suggests also that the "heavens conspir'd his overthrow" (Prologue 23), evoking the Protestant dilemma that Dollimore places at the center of the text.[56] Yet, like Machevill's opening speech in *The Jew of Malta*, its terms do not adequately define the figure or the fortunes we are about to see. Barabas may follow to some degree in Machevill's footsteps, but neither he nor his drama is defined exclusively or primarily in the terms of Machiavellianism that Machevill, hoping to reclaim his dominance, leads us to expect.

Though not a personality per se, the Chorus in *Faustus* seems to have its own agenda too and, like the Good and Bad Angels, the scholars, and the Old Man, to be determined to impose a moral on the tale. Yet just as Marlowe flaunts and denies the morality tradition, turning its voices into a sort of background noise that is often not heard and when heard, of negligible impact, so also does he undermine the Chorus, proving its terms inadequate to the task.[57] For despite its omniscience, the Chorus's terms are notably abstract and (like the Norton headnote) transform the wavering circumstances of Faustus's resolve and the questionable circumspection of his "cunning" into a neat and clearly sighted Icarian pattern of rise and fall.

The choric prefaces to Acts 3 and 4 are less problematic because they record rather than interpret the events that occur between the acts. Yet when the Chorus returns to speak the epilogue, it frames the tale with the kind of reductive aphorisms that Faustus has long been criticized for relying on and underscores, by amplifying, the "sins" of the prologue. For the Chorus, the moral is simple: we are to "regard" the "hellish fall" of a "learned man," a "branch that might have grown full straight" and, if we count ourselves among "the wise," "only to wonder at unlawful things" (Epilogue 1–6). Once again, Faustus's tale is obscured by abstraction, and the Chorus leaves its substance vague, giving only a beginning and an end and omitting all the complicating factors in between which preoccupy the play. Here indeed, "Faustus is gone" (Epilogue 4)—the play as well as the figure.

Within the frame, as if in defiance of such moral packaging, Marlowe presents an alternative text and an alternative vision of Faustus as an impatient if not sometimes careless scholar, taking a course of action whose consequences he does not fully see. When he appears to settle his studies, he fixates on precisely the kind of "finite, static irreducibles" he pretends to abjure, missing the real point of these disciplines as of intellectual pursuits more generally and looking for a kind of immediate use-value such studies generally resist.[58]

Critics continue to load his turn from divinity to necromancy with transgression, but it is Faustus and not Marlowe who presents it as a radical departure. For although Faustus embraces magic, passionately, as a ravishing art more powerful and less limiting than others, he has clearly been searching for a "miracle" (1.1.9) all along, hoping to "make men to live eternally" (1.1.24) or raise them from the dead, to "be eterniz'd for some wondrous cure" (1.1.15) and so on. His choice is part of a series of choices for and against studies—law, medicine, logic, divinity—which are legitimate and legal. The roulette wheel could have stopped at almost any point, and Faustus seems to stop it here, almost arbitrarily, because after he surveys "the end of every art" (1.1.4) there seems to be nothing else left.

It is clear very quickly, of course—as Faustus turns to "necromantic books" and then summons Valdes and Cornelius, who are "infamous through the world" for "that damned art" (1.2.30−31), to teach him "concealed arts" (1.1.103)—that Faustus has undertaken black and not white magic. What is not clear, however, is that he understands the implications of his choice. In the first place, he does not present his turn to magic as a turn against divinity per se. Divinity is the last study he casts aside but not the only one, and its position seems more coincidental than consequential. In fact, as he begins his necromantic pursuits, he brings divinity into them, suggestively (even if accidentally) ignoring their incompatibility. His initial conjuring circle is filled with "Jehovah's name, / Forward and backward anagrammatiz'd" in otherwise safe cabalistic fashion, as with

> The breviated names of holy saints,
> Figures of every adjunct to the heavens,
> And characters of signs and erring stars
> By which the spirits are enforc'd to rise.[59]
>   (1.3.8−14)

In addition, he makes Mephastophilis dress as "an old Franciscan friar" (1.3.25) and declares his own words "heavenly" (1.3.27). His only direct rejection of "the threefold divinity of Jehovah" (1.3.16−17) comes in Latin, in a prefabricated conjuring ritual presumably not of his own making, and one that the illiterate portion of the audience would not have understood. Until Mephastophilis explains that he always comes "when we hear one rack the name of God, / Abjure the Scriptures and his savior Christ" (1.3.47−48), Faustus does not make the connection.

It is not until Act 2, after Mephastophilis has introduced the idea of damnation, that Faustus begins to think in terms of his soul. In the English Faustbook, before finalizing his pact with Lucifer, Faustus ponders "how he might obtaine his request of the divel without losse of his soule" (p. 7) and then conveniently forgets "Divinitie or the immortalitie of his soule" (p. 15) when he finds no way to avoid that loss. Marlowe's Faustus, in contrast, initially discounts the matter of soul. In rejecting divinity he admits and regrets that we "must die, an everlasting death" (1.1.47), but he never specifies quite what that "everlasting death" is. Although he knows he is dealing with devils, at first he is too "glutted with conceit" (1.1.79) of his worldly powers to consider otherworldly consequences. He treats the soul nonchalantly as a "vain trifle" and "damnation" as a word which "terrifies not him," and gives his "ghost" to "the old philosophers" (1.3.60−63)

who do not believe in eternal punishment or reward. And he continues to
believe that "hell's a fable" even after Mephastophilis offers himself as "an
instance to prove the contrary" (2.1.137). Ironically, Faustus even uses hell
as a positive image, rather than the ultimate negative reality, to represent
his glowing past, boasting that he

> made the flowering pride of Wittenberg
> Swarm to my problems as the infernal spirits
> On sweet Musaeus when he came to hell,
>
> (1.1.115–18)

treating the infernal afterworld as a place of fame. And when he sets up
Agrippa as his role model, he thinks only of the honor, and not the potential hazards, Agrippa's conjured "shadows" (1.1.119) brought.

Significantly, too, Faustus discounts not only hell but also heaven. He
scoffs, for example, when Mephastophilis becomes "so passionate / For
being deprived of the joys of heaven" (1.3.83–84). Rejecting the idea that
"after this life there is any pain" (2.1.135), he ignores the possibility that
there is any immortal pleasure either. By the end of the play, however,
Faustus does believe that his soul is at stake in his bargain with the devil
and calls desperately to God, acknowledges that Christ's blood "hath ransom'd me" (5.2.92), curses Lucifer, and vows to burn his books. Ironically,
it is Mephastophilis, his infernal tutor, who has taught him to believe, to
understand and desire "heavenly joys" and, in believing himself deprived
of them, to understand and resist damnation—Mephastophilis, that is,
who leads Faustus to heaven in order to send him to hell.

From the outset the infernal spirit is clearly in charge of the show.
His predecessor in the English Faustbook initially refuses to reappear
at the time Faustus appoints, but Marlowe's devil behaves like a "pliant"
(1.3.29) spirit, ready to change costumes at Faustus's command and to
come and go as he orders. Yet while Faustus takes credit for his "obedience and humility" (1.3.30), Mephastophilis emphasizes that he has come
of his "own accord," ostensibly to persuade Faustus to sign away his
soul. Almost immediately, Faustus is already pledging allegiance to the
principle that "there is no chief but only Belzebub, / To whom Faustus
doth dedicate himself" (1.3.57–58), and while part of their agreement is
that Mephastophilis remain at his beck and call, the fact that the spirit
engages him in a sustained and instructive discourse suggests a darker purpose, more devious and more subtle: to teach Faustus to read the conse-

quences of his choice as damnation and to resist. For it is only when Faustus believes in salvation and fears its loss that he will rebel against Lucifer, and it is only when he rebels against Lucifer (not God) that he provides a fitting subject for a display of the devil's power to contain and destroy.

Notably, instead of covering up the torments of hell (as we might expect from one trying to sell damnation), Mephastophilis continually brings them into view. Granted, he periodically conjures up spirits "to delight [Faustus's] mind" (2.1.82), to enforce the reality of hell in non-threatening if not desirable terms, making devils dance before him and bring him "crowns and rich apparel" (stage direction) or displaying a comic array of easily subjugated Deadly Sins. Yet he also produces a darker, more immediate, and more sustained vision of damnation, presenting hell as a state of absolute and limitless negation. Though Faustus thinks of hell as a remote if not fictional place, Mephastophilis insists, in a well-known passage, that

> Hell hath no limits, nor is circumscrib'd
> In one self place, but where we are is hell,
> And where hell is there must we ever be;
> And to be short, when all the world dissolves
> And every creature shall be purify'd,
> All places shall be hell that is not heaven.
>
> (2.1.122–27)

Hell is a place of limitless limitation, for "ever" boundlessly bounded by the knowledge of what it is not. Lest Faustus take refuge in the pleasure of the world, as he does throughout, Mephastophilis makes clear that the world itself will dissolve, leaving only two undeniable options, heaven and hell.

In the process, in another move that would seem to undermine the devil's purposes, Mephastophilis presents heaven as the ultimate object of desire. Earlier, in an equally famous passage, and in response to Faustus's skepticism about the reality of hell (and how the devil can be out of it if he is damned), he retorts:

> Why this is hell, nor am I out of it:
> Think'st thou that I who saw the face of God
> And tasted the eternal joys of heaven

> Am not tormented with ten thousand hells
> In being depriv'd of everlasting bliss?
>
> (1.3.76–80)

Heaven becomes the place of "everlasting bliss," equal in "joys" to the horror of "ten thousand hells," where what Faustus most enjoys, worldly sensation (seeing and tasting), has a place. In posing the description as a rhetorical question, Mephastophilis prompts Faustus to participate in the answer (a resounding "no"), to "think" about the kind of deprivation that "is hell." He then warns Faustus to "leave these *frivolous demands*, / Which strike a terror to my fainting soul" (1.3.81–82; emphasis added), and though he means Faustus's endless questions, the warning resonates more broadly, encouraging Faustus to fear his more dangerous pursuits which might indeed "strike a terror" to a "fainting soul."

Lucifer also participates in the process, offering similar kinds of subliminal suggestions of heavenly joys. Hearing Faustus call on Christ, the devil appears to voice a heretofore unstated part of the bargain: that Faustus not talk of Christ or God (though ironically it was his talk of Christ, we are told, that elicited infernal attention in the first place). Significantly, this warning parallels Faustus's own warning to the horse-courser, to whom he sells a horse: "ride him [the horse] not into the water at any hand" (4.2.21). Both stand as conditions that beg to be broken, limits that beg to be crossed, and both produce the transgression they seek. The horse-courser, sure that his new horse had "some rare quality" that Faustus, in prohibiting water rides, "would not have had [him] know" (4.2.44), inevitably rides into the water, only to find his horse devolving into hay. Faustus, being told that he "should'st not think of God" (2.3.93), thinks automatically of God and vows "never to look to heaven, / Never to name God" (2.3.96–97) while doing both. Though the fate of the horse-courser teaches him nothing, it tells us a lot. We are ready to see Faustus fall, not from grace but into it, and into the devils' hands.

Helen and Hell

After his and Mephastophilis's first disputation on hell, Faustus begins to consider the possibility of damnation, sporadically but with increasing perturbation. At the beginning of Act 2, he dismisses thoughts of God as futile, ignores or does not hear the Good Angel's plea to "think of heaven and heavenly things" (2.1.20), and casually takes damnation as a given without further thought of what that means. After the second conversation, he is ready to "repent and curse" the "wicked Mephastophilis" for depriving him of heaven's "joys" (2.3.1–3). Mephastophilis urges him along by giving heaven a worldly shape, insisting that it was "made for man" while ostensibly arguing that man is "more excellent" (2.3.8–9). Yet although Faustus momentarily decides it was then "made for me" (2.3.10), he automatically breaks into debate on "divine astrology" (2.3.34) and speaks of the heavens as a physical and not metaphysical space. The next time he repents, he does so in a sort of childish anger, because Mephastophilis refuses to tell him who made the world, and his resistance there, as before and thereafter, is as short-lived as it is shortsighted.[60]

It is with the vision of Helen, however, that his course takes a definitive turn, that his vacillation ceases and his calls to heaven become more sustained and sincere, that he becomes the other the devils have contracted. Critics have often singled out this moment as the point of no return, at which his damnation is finally sealed—either because he makes physical contact with a succubus, or because he gives in, or feels guilty for giving in, to sexual desire, or because he transgresses in some other definitive way.[61] Yet such interpretations implicate Helen as a taboo in a way that Marlowe does not, presenting the union as an unforgivable violation of established religious, social, or psychological laws. As the variations between these readings (and between them and others that do not treat this as a pivotal event) suggest, Renaissance rules of demonology and behavior were anything but clear. (Even if they were, they would be sure to meet some turbulence on Marlowe's stage.)

Rather than transgression, what this moment signals is a change of heart and mind, a recognition and not a defiance of "heavenly joys," a desire for and not against heavenly immortality. For in seeing Helen, Faustus also sees the possibility of "eternal bliss" written out in (worldly not otherworldly) terms that he can comprehend. And what comes with that knowledge and the desire it generates is an experience of deprivation that at once puts Faustus in the kind of hell Mephastophilis describes and, by inspiring resistance, gives the devil a defiant and unwilling subject to control and contain.

Marlowe situates the episode as part of a frame that marks the beginning and end of Faustus's contracted career and of Mephastophilis's strategic efforts to "delight his mind." Immediately after signing away his soul, Faustus sets the terms of his desire by declaring himself "wanton and lascivious" and in need of a wife, preferably "the fairest maid in Germany" (2.1.141–42). The play underscores his focus in the tavern sequence, in which Robin anticipates using the powers in Faustus's magic book to make "all the maidens in [his] parish dance . . . stark naked before [him]" (2.2.3–4), and to make Nan Spit, the kitchen maid, give in to Rafe's sexual desires. Though Mephastophilis first scoffs and produces only "a devil dressed like a woman, with fireworks" (stage direction), whom Faustus rejects as "a hot whore," he then immediately encourages those desires by offering to bring "the fairest courtesans" "every morning to [Faustus's] bed" (2.1.153–53). "She whom thine eye shall like," he promises,

> thy heart shall have,
> Be she as chaste as was Penelope,
> As wise as Saba, or as beautiful
> As was bright Lucifer before his fall.
> (2.1.155–58)

Significantly, he not only compares the courtesans with women like Helen, prominently idealized in myth, with the long-suffering but ever-faithful Penelope and with "Saba," the wise Queen of Sheba.[62] He also allies Lucifer with these figures, betraying the catalog's ominous elision of fallen and unfallen states, of the purest of women and the hottest of whores, suggesting that there is dangerously more to his enticements than meets the eye.

This exchange sets us up for, and renders us suspect of, the conjuration of Helen that completes the frame four acts later, and that emerges as the last of Mephastophilis's attempts to delight and deceive Faustus. Importantly, despite the devil's promises, we neither see nor hear further of the courtesans. To the contrary, Mephastophilis puts Faustus's erotic desires on hold, immediately diverting his attention from carnal to "scientific" knowledge and giving him books on almost everything else in the physical universe, from plants to planets. In the German and English Faustbooks, there is no such occlusion; part of Faustus's infernal tour around the universe lands him in a harem at the court of a Turkish sultan, where he can and does indulge his sexual longings.[63] In excluding the harem episode, the play confines the issue of desire within the frame, allowing Mephastophilis a pivotal site of and for resistance, a carrot to dangle before the conjurer's eyes at precisely the right moment to effect his fall.

That moment comes with the conjuration of Helen. No longer using Faustus's will to knowledge to distract him from desire, Mephastophilis now brings the two together, using eroticism to incite a new kind of knowing—of unreachable pleasures beyond though embedded in worldly experience. In this case as before, Faustus initiates the event, this time by requesting that Mephastophilis "glut the longing of [his] heart's desire" and let him "have unto my paramour / that heavenly Helen" (5.1.83–85). Accordingly, Mephastophilis, with the ostensible compliance he has shown throughout, "performs" the conjuration with the ominous "twinkling of an eye" (5.1.90).

In looking upon Helen, upon "the face that launch'd a thousand ships," Faustus is able to see a "heaven in her lips" and, for the first time, wants to be made "immortal with a kiss." "Her lips suck forth my soul," he tells us,

> see where it flies!
> Come Helen, come, give me my soul again.
> Here will I dwell, for heaven be in these lips,
> And all is dross that is not Helena.
>
> (5.1.91–97)

What she offers that the abstractions of divinity do not is transcendence translated into physical terms that answer "the longing of [Faustus's] heart's desire." In kissing her, giving her his "soul" and taking it back again, he has a sort of out-of-body experience, paradoxically grounded in the body and producing a highly desirable experience that he can see, touch, and taste. Now and only now does he recognize and hope to transcend the temporal and spatial limits of earthly existence, to "dwell" eternally in a world, and body, beyond his own.[64]

In the sources this scene becomes yet another of his worldly exploits; he and Helen get married and have a son, as mentioned earlier. When Faustus dies, these figures simply dissolve, and their significance fades likewise into the text's margins. In the play, however, it becomes a critical moment of knowing that he and Marlowe translate into Christian terms. In the next scene Faustus turns his desires from the heavenly Helen to a Christian heaven and for the first time tries desperately to "leap up" to God (5.2.70), whom he sees (or thinks he sees) "stretch[ing] out his arm" and "bend[ing] his ireful brows" (5.2.76–77). For the first time too, he sees, or thinks he sees, "Christ's blood stream[ing] in the firmament" and asserts that "one drop," or even "half a drop," "would save my soul" (5.2.71–72). Even if he must serve a thousand or a hundred thousand years in hell, he thinks he should be saved, since Christ's "blood hath ransom'd [him]" (5.2.92).[65] The point is not that Faustus now realizes the truth of heaven, but that he constructs a truth, a heaven, from the vision of Helen based on his desires—a seeable and touchable heaven whose physicality offers a comforting physical eternity for the soul.

Significantly, Marlowe prefaces the event with another conjuration of Helen, this time comic, that calls attention to the "shaping fantasies" at work here and at issue throughout the play. Shortly before calling for Helen himself, Faustus presents her to a group of adoring scholars who have held a "conference about fair ladies" and have decided that Helen "was the beautiful'st in all the world" and "the admirablest lady that ever lived" (5.1.9–12). As he brings her forth, what stands out is not her heavenly beauty or majesty which the scholars so long to see, but the ineptitude of their language, as they, with excessive superlatives ("admirablest," "beautiful'st"), transform a potentially erotic moment into comedy. When Helen passes across the stage, the Second Scholar admits, "Too simple is my wit to tell her worth / Whom all the world admires for majesty" (5.1.25–26), and we are inclined to agree, especially since his final phrase ("whom all the world admires for majesty") repeats exactly what the First Scholar has said only a few moments before. For them the vision shows "the pride of nature's works" (5.1.30), for us, their inability to see or appreciate even that. But when Faustus replays the spectacle, he invests it with a meaning beyond what they and we have seen.

Yet his own production of meaning is itself produced, framed by and within Mephastophilis's coercive manipulations, and is poised on the brink of Faustus's fall into a self-abnegating self-awareness. The image of Helen points back to Mephastophilis's catalog of courtesans, for like them, she is caught between the ideal and the corrupt, in some texts worshiped as a paragon of beauty and in others demonized as a whore, an object to desire and a subject to fear.[66] In Marlowe's play the image is comparably double-edged. For to know Helen is to know not only alluring possibilities but also deprivation and lack, to know and desire what is ultimately and eternally unreachable. It is no coincidence that Faustus's famous question, "Was this the face that launch'd a thousand ships . . . ?" (5.1.91), recalls Mephastophilis's own rhetorical query, "Think'st thou that I who saw the face of God . . ." (1.3.77), or that his assertion that "all is dross that is not Helena" (5.1.97) matches the devil's warning that "all places shall be hell that is not heaven" (2.1.127). In fetishizing Helen as Mephastophilis has been fetishizing God, Faustus follows the devil's dangerous cues right into the experience of deprivation that the devil has described as hell. Immediately after he claims her as his only "paramour," she leaves and is replaced by the Old Man, who defines him in terms of exclusion, as one who "exclud'st," and so is excluded from, "the grace of heaven" (5.1.112). And this time, unlike before, the warning has a meaning—and what it means is hell.

It is at this point, as Faustus, led on by Mephastophilis, constructs an otherworld of desire and deprivation, that he becomes willfully defiant—not (as Dollimore suggests) against God, but against the devil. Calling out "my God, my God" (5.2.112), Faustus curses Lucifer "that hath deprived [him] of the joys of heaven" (5.2.107) and then, as devils enter, directs hell to "gape not" and Lucifer to "come not" (5.2.114). In a final gesture of resistance, he casts all infernal authorities aside, proclaiming, "I'll burn my books. Ah Mephastophilis!" (5.2.115), as if in recognition that he has been betrayed, as indeed he has. As he stands finally firm in his resolve, the devils "exeunt with him" (stage direction), producing an unforgettable spectacle that we are to watch and wonder at, a spectacle of a "fiendful fortune" and a "hellish fall" that instantiates not, as the Chorus would wish, "heavenly power" (Epilogue 4–5), but Lucifer's. The prologue's conspiracy theory is right; someone did "conspire" Faustus's overthrow, but it was not God.

At stake here finally is not Faustus's soul, but the ways in which his perception of his soul, his interiorizing self-awareness, is fashioned and framed in the service of another's power. Whether or not there is "any pain" for him "after this life," he is "damned" by the devils who claim him as their subject—but only by the devils, for, tellingly, God has not said a word. Milton's Satan will reiterate the lesson that Mephastophilis teaches: "The mind is its own place, and in itself / Can make a Heav'n of Hell, a Hell of Heav'n" (*Paradise Lost* 1.254–55). Yet it is a lesson as misleading in *Doctor Faustus* as it is in *Paradise Lost*, whose sinners seem to be in the hands of an angry God intent on setting the bounds of heaven and hell. Marlowe's devils encourage Faustus to believe that he is finally responsible for his fortunes, that his soul gives ultimate meaning to his self, and that he determines its fate. Yet all the while, they—like Protestantism itself—are setting the terms and determining the form of those fortunes, turning the tale of a magician into a Christian moral drama that, by producing the soul as a site of struggle, can only affirm their power.

Like Protestantism itself—which is here dressed in devils' robes and damned. In a radically subversive move, Marlowe reverses Protestant attempts to put the devil in the center of its authorizing narratives by putting those narratives in the hands of the devil. For Marlowe, the dilemma that Protestantism poses as it imposes a limited subjectivity is not that it cuts the individual off from redemption and so produces transgression, but that it defines the individual in terms of redemption and itself in terms of his or her transgression—in terms, that is, that deny the mind its own place outside of heaven or hell. Ironically, though the European other is doomed on the basis of a signifying interiority, she/he, like non-European counterparts, is necessarily deprived of it, of a self that constitutes itself in alternative terms. Faustus, indeed, is gone.

Imperialist Revisions

The text of *Faustus* ends uniquely with the tag, "The hour ends the day, the author ends the play" ("*Terminat hora diem, terminat Author opus*"). This claim to authorial agency can only be ironic for us, who are faced with two competing and unreliable versions of the play. As Leah Marcus has argued seminally, the two texts present us not with Marlowe but with a "Marlowe effect," attempts by others to make Marlovian drama Marlovian, "to keep the play, amidst shifting conditions in church and state, on the same 'ravishing' razor edge between exaltation and transgression" that was identified with Marlowe.[67] While the A-text plays into a context of Protestant reform, Marcus argues, the B-text came later, as England's anxieties were redirected toward international relations, and speaks to issues of imperialism. As I have noted above, that Faustus's story could be reappropriated thus suggests a close connection between imperialist and domestic constructions of the other, a connection that is itself a significant "Marlowe effect." In reinscribing the form of Faustus's fortunes, the B-text underscores the pattern of appropriation evident in the central episodes (Faustus's interactions with the devil) by reproducing that pattern in its secondary sequences. Juxtaposed to the A-text and standing alone, the later version shows that resistance is continually produced as proof of irresistible power not just in the otherworld (whether spiritually or spatially defined) but in the world. In the process, it bridges the gap between the worlds and otherworlds of Marlowe's domestic and imperialist plays and, subversively, allies the separation of self from other with the separation of self from self.

Critical interrogations of the differences between the two texts have generally been most interested in the final sequence, when the Old Man gives his—in the A-text, disparaging and in the B-text, hopeful—warning for Faustus to make a mid-course correction, and when Faustus, unable or unwilling to do so, confronts his fate and is escorted offstage by devils in the A-text and in the B-text also sees hell and is ripped limb from limb and left for the scholars to lament and collect.[68] Yet the differences between the representations of the central events are not the only ones that make a difference to the ways we read those negotiations. The B-text includes two comic sequences—the one at the papal court and the other at the court of the German emperor—which are extensions of the shorter sequences in A. Each creates a display of authority organized around the transgression and containment of an other, who is sometimes appropriated, sometimes provoked, and sometimes invented, and provides an ominous though comic shadow of what is happening, disastrously, to Faustus.

In the first, in the scenes at Rome, the pope attempts to define and confirm his authority by keeping a manageable contender always underfoot. When he first appears, he immediately orders Bruno, his prisoner and rival for the papacy, to "crouch before the papal dignity" as a footstool, so that "Saint Peter's heir / From Bruno's back [can ascend] Saint Peter's chair" (3.1.93–95). The pope adopts this image as his inherited sign of power and aligns himself with Pope Alexander, who

> trod on the neck of German Frederick,
> Adding this golden sentence to our praise,
> "That Peter's heirs should tread on emperors."
> (3.1.134–36)

His action also has a precedent in *Tamburlaine*, as Tamburlaine, his "sights of power" showing, demands that Bajazeth

> Fall prostrate on the low disdainful earth,
> And be the footstool of great Tamburlaine,
> That I may rise into my royal throne.
> (*Tamburlaine* 4.2.13–15)

The pope's imperialist ambitions are more narrow than Tamburlaine's; he hopes only to impose his "authority apostolical" (*Faustus* 3.1.141) over the

German emperor's realm. Yet so are his resources; all the pope can do is "bind or loose, lock fast, condemn, or judge, / Resign or seal" (3.1.153–54) and voice a "dreadful curse / To light as heavy as the pains of hell" (3.1.156–57), ironically evoked as Mephastophilis stands by, watching. And that is precisely what he does to Bruno, who provides the perfect occasion and object for these displays, until, of course, Mephastophilis and Faustus intervene.[69]

Yet when they do, when they take his prisoner and steal his meat and drink as he sits at a state dinner, because their ploys (like the emperor's power) are beyond his reach, he responds to both by inventing a punishable other. In the first case, with no evidence he indicts two innocent cardinals for freeing Bruno and, calling on all of his powers, condemns them to prison, torture, and "hellish misery" (3.2.54). In the face of his disappearing feast (which obviously mocks communion ritual), he leaps upon the archbishop's suggestion that the culprit is "some ghost crept out of purgatory" "come unto your Holiness for his pardon" (3.2.79–80), a suggestion that puts the pope in a place of power over a submissive "ghost." Imposing a show of control in a situation out of control, he directs his priests to sing an ameliorating dirge, damning the ghost's soul on his way out.

Obviously neither response (to the cardinals or the ghost) speaks well for the Catholic church, betraying the papacy as a power-mongering institution organized around self-serving fictions of the sort Lucifer himself deploys. In addition to condemning Catholicism, however, this sequence highlights the means and ends of the appropriation of an other which are cloaked behind devious subtlety in the devil's case and which, embodied thus in comic form, stand out clearly for incrimination.

Faustus exercises similar strategies to display his powers and likewise comically underscores what is happening, tragically, to him. Just as the pope appropriates Bruno's resistance, so too, though more successfully, does Faustus exploit the skepticism of Benvolio, a member of his audience at the German court, to enforce the compelling force of his conjurations—not coincidentally, while Bruno, now pope (thanks to Faustus), looks on, his presence creating a significant link between this sequence and the other. As others gather to see Faustus "perform such rare exploits . . . / As never yet was seen in Germany" (4.1.31–33), Benvolio scoffs from afar, insisting that though Faustus "speaks terribly," "for all that, I do not greatly believe him" (4.1.71–72). Challenging Faustus publicly, he protests that he "could eat my self for anger to think I have been such an ass all this while, to stand gaping after the devil's governor, and can see nothing" (4.1.86–88), and then insists that he will turn himself into a stag if Faustus conjures up what is promised. Faustus takes advantage of this resisting voice and turns Benvolio's words against him, putting horns on his head and directing him to hide and to "let not all the world wonder at you" (4.1.133–34). Yet the spectacle functions to do just that, to let all the world wonder at the immediate and punishing effects of Faustus's magic. Significantly, the display translates directly into power (as the pope's does not): the German emperor, impressed by the show, offers Faustus command of all Germany, "in recompense of this thy high desert" (4.1.164).

Though Faustus is not interested in political rule, the play reiterates his investment in such shows by bringing Benvolio and his friends back to seek revenge, only to find themselves the objects of another shaming ritual that Faustus again constructs around resistance. After their failed attempts to chop off his head and sell or recycle its parts, Faustus first commands his devils to fly them to heaven and pitch them into hell. Yet because he wants "the world [to] see their misery" (4.2.82) and his power, he changes his mind and orders a visible, worldly fate: one offender is to be hurled into a lake of mud, another dragged through thorns and briars, another thrown from a "steepy rock" (4.2.89). When the revengers reappear, they bear the visible imprint of their punishment and are not only covered in mud and briars, but are also topped by horns, recalling Benvolio's original crime, reliving his original punishment, and reinforcing Faustus's continued control over all. Fearing that they will become "laughing stocks to all the world" (as they probably already are to the audience), they retire to the woods to "live obscure" since "black disgrace hath thus eclips'd [their] fame" (4.3.20–25). Yet their fates are not obscure in Marlowe's play, but stand before "all the world" as a comic but consequential sign of Faustus's cunning.

Significantly, these episodes not only underline what we see in the central negotiations; they also open the possibility of coercion to "all the world." It is not just the magician who can be forced into a position of alienation in the service of another's power, but also figures on many levels of the social scale, from the highest circles of church and state to the lowest. Though the play's focus remains in and on Europe, its implications reach also to the ways that Europe was making a name for itself throughout the world, constructing and containing others in order to construct and distinguish the self.

Yet there is a significant difference that sets domestic apart from im-

perialist appropriations, a difference made apparent by the difference between the domestic-centered A-text and the more imperialist B-text, and
in the B-text between the serious stage business and the comic episodes
that give the play its imperialist edge: the exploitation of the domestic
subject takes place in an interior register, at the level of mind and soul.
The pope is decidedly (and for a spiritual leader, oddly) not interested in
Bruno's soul and ignores it, turning his prisoner into an object and enlisting the "pains of hell" and "hellish misery" only metaphorically, to give
force and fury to his threats. And though Faustus is provoked by Benvolio's mind, he directs his punishments against the skeptic's body, opting
against sending him to hell in order to make a better spectacle of him on
earth. In the domestic sequences, however, Lucifer targets the interior
spaces of Faustus's self and soul. And what becomes subversively clear in
the process is that the very space that cross-cultural representations use to
distinguish self from other (usually by denying it to the other) itself becomes, in domestic discourse, a site of coercion and containment incriminating the self *as* other.

6. The Show of Sodomy: Minions and Dominions in *Edward II*

> "By indirections find directions out."
> (*Hamlet* 2.1.63)

Renaissance "Homosexuality"

Perhaps the most spectacular and disturbing moment of Edward II's career, at least as it was handed down by historians to the Renaissance, was his death. As Holinshed records it, two murderers

> came suddenlie one night into the chamber where he laie in bed fast asléepe, and with heavie featherbeds or a table (as some write) being cast upon him, they kept him down and withall put into his fundament an horne, and through the same they thrust up into his bodie an hot spit, or (as others have) through the pipe of a trumpet a plumbers instrument of iron made verie hot, the which passing up into his intrailes, and being rolled to and fro, burnt the same, but so as no appearance of any wound or hurt outwardlie might be once perceived.[1]

On display here is, paradoxically, a vivid symbolic recreation of a crime, sodomy, that was not to be seen, a punishment that flagrantly reveals and carefully conceals its subject. The distinguishing mark of the method is that it leaves no trace of itself or what it represents. Indeed, the regicide takes place in a prison chamber, closed off from the public gaze, unseen even by the king, who "laie in bed fast asléepe" and who was immediately covered up by "heavie featherbeds or a table." Only after describing the murder does Holinshed add that "as the tormentors were about to murther" him, he "utter[ed] a wailefull noise" and disturbed "manie" in the castle and town, who "understood by his crie what the matter ment" (p. 587).

Renaissance executions (especially of monarchs) were carefully or-

chestrated public spectacles, their verbal and visual statements tightly regu-
lated to impose an unmistakable moral on the tale of crime and to produce
an unquestionable idea of order.[2] Though Edward is murdered and not
executed by legally sanctioned means, the event is nonetheless positioned
in the chronicle as the crowning moment of the deposed king's career, as
a fitting conclusion that gives meaningful closure to Edward's life and
death, incriminating the king and not the kingship, implicating the body
in its innermost recesses and not the body politic as the site of subversion.[3]

Yet like the punishment itself, the account makes its point by con-
cealing what is so obviously revealed, displaying an event that has sodomy
written all over it while refusing to say the word.[4] Instead of correlating
the punishment to the crime, Holinshed presents the method as an almost
arbitrary last resort of Edward's captors, who had tried poison but failed
because Edward, "a man of a tough nature," had repeatedly "purg[ed]
either up or downe" (pp. 586–87). Since he was, "as it séemed," "verie like
to escape that danger" (p. 587), the murderers found other, more expedient
means to destroy his entrails. Holinshed also retreats from narrative authority and produces the symbolically loaded details as controversial, offering competing "facts" about the method and deferring to what "some
write" and "others have."

At the same time, however, he places this unseen spectacle in the
sphere of public discourse, making whether Edward was held down by
featherbeds or a table and whether he was raped by a hot spit or a plumb-
er's instrument a matter of public debate. The details in either case serve
the same symbolic (not to mention literal) end and, without authorial
intervention, effectively spell out the word that is so obviously unspoken
here by Holinshed as by "some" and "others" too. Just as Holinshed, in
recording public reaction to Edward's resulting "wailefull noise," tells us
without telling us "what the matter ment," so too does his description of
the murder. Here, as within the cultural discourse more generally, sodomy
emerges as an offense that can be neither seen nor spoken (at least in the
polite company of historians) but nonetheless can mean. And what it
means is made clear, paradoxically, by its obfuscation: unseen, sodomy
becomes unseeable; unspoken, unspeakable.

Marlowe brings homoeroticism to center stage, not only (though
most blatantly) in *Edward II*, but also in *Dido*, which opens upon Jupiter
and Ganymede exchanging tokens and promises of love, and in *Tamburlaine*, whose Persian king gives his voice and affections publicly to Meander.[5] Even Faustus is ready to give "as many souls as there be stars"

(*Faustus* 1.3.102) for love of Mephastophilis, whom he affectionately claims as "my Mephastophilis" (2.3.30).[6] And in *The Massacre at Paris*, Henry III of France is surrounded and defined by "minions" (3.2.16) and charges of being "wanton" (5.2.55).

Marlowe's own alleged sodomitical inclinations, whether a reality or an attempt to fit himself into the subversive space society had opened for him, probably had something to do with homoeroticism's many appearances on his stage. Yet the prominence of the sodomitical here, in plays about constructions of the other, reflects its crucial importance to those constructions in both cultural and cross-cultural discourses—but with one important difference. Outside Marlowe, sodomy finds its most bold-faced expression in descriptions of other worlds (especially the "New World"), in texts such as Las Casas's.[7] At home, in Holinshed, for example, it is discovered with more reserve. Marlowe, however, turns the tables, giving sodomy its most prominent place in the domestic plays and the domestic spaces of England and France, locating this spectacle of strangeness where it belonged, intimately close to home. For it was on the home front, for the benefit and regulation of the self, that sodomy was being deployed as the consummate sign of otherness and both pressed beyond and deeply imbricated in the registers of language and spectacle. In Marlowe sodomy is finally neither unseeable nor unspeakable. Rather it is exposed as a subject obscured and displayed as beyond display by those who would maintain a hegemonic hold over "what the matter ment."

Before turning to Marlowe, I want to consider how sodomy figured within the social discourses of the early modern period.[8] Studies of Renaissance society and sexuality differ on to what extent what we call "homosexuality" was recognized and tolerated.[9] Yet what is commonly acknowledged as a major impediment to our, and the early modern, understanding of it is the vagueness and inconsistency through which acts of sodomy were delineated. As historians have aptly detailed, sodomy included almost anything from intercourse between males, to heterosexual intercourse in "unnatural" positions or "outside of the fit vessell," to sexual acts between men or women with "beasts," and was conflated if not confused with other forms of "debauchery," such as gluttony, drunkenness, idleness, witchcraft, usury, heresy, and so on.[10] To make matters worse, its relation to orthodox behaviors was also unclear. Alan Bray has argued that while sodomitical bonds were set in direct and absolute opposition to male friendship, the signs that distinguished the two often collapsed.[11] The figure of Ganymede, one of the most prominent images of the sodomite, for example, appears in early modern texts as both the chaste friend and the illicit sexual partner or male prostitute, sometimes alternately and sometimes ambiguously at the same time.[12] What is clear, however, as Gregory Bredbeck has suggested, is that sodomy took meaning *through* and not despite the multivalence that surrounded its inscription.[13]

It is impossible to know absolutely how consciously the various terms were deployed, whether they reflect a genuine abstractness in the cultural understanding or a sort of willfull ignorance and denial (as we have faced during the Reagan/Bush era, in the case of AIDS), or whether they express some darker purpose. Yet I would argue that the multivalence within this discourse (as in the case of magic) was not merely an effect but also a cause, that it served a strategic purpose and was the point as much as the problem of its inscription. It wasn't that the terms were not there. Indeed, though classical representations of the sodomite may have created their own conflicts, they were remarkably direct about the act itself.[14] Bruce Smith has noted that Greek romances, which "portray homoerotic desire with undisguised directness," were vigorously translated and published during the early modern period. What made them safe, according to Smith, was that they were in fact romances, presenting "a time and a place apart" "where free reign [could] be given to desires that normally [were] held in check."[15] Nonetheless, as the models were incorporated into early modern texts, and even into early modern romances, into a society much less tolerant of homoeroticism, their explicitness (except in translation) was mostly lost.

That loss, however, produced important gains. Just as the uncertain delineation of the magician's activities widened the threshold of transgression, so too did the obfuscation of sodomy. But even more so—for while the black magician was given a definitive shape as his vague and relatively innocuous career was turned into damnation, the sodomite, even and especially as he was criminalized out of chaste friendship, was not. While the adverse consequences of the magician's subversive actions were limited primarily to the spiritual and made to impact almost exclusively upon him, the sodomite was made culpable of enacting and effecting a widespread corruption, as apparently limitless as it was amorphous, touching and transgressing almost every aspect of the social and political order and categorized alongside almost every disorder. Concealed and abstracted within an all-inclusive discourse, the display of sodomy provided a means of specifying and amplifying the criminality of a wide range of—in some cases, hard to criminalize—offenses, including sodomy itself. Because its parameters were never clear and never allowed to be clear, it could turn those offenses into unspeakable transgression.[16]

At stake and at risk with it was the idea of the private, for the inscription of sodomy as unseeable created a separate space for the private, albeit private transgression and one that was continually forced into the public sphere. The criminalization of sodomy differed from the demonization of magic in that the ostensible subject of the former was the body, the individual, sexual body. To claim control over it, as over the soul, was to assign and deny the self a meaningful individuality. Yet the tension between these two impulses was even greater in the case of the body, whose sexual acts required and acquired a private space in a way that spiritual acts, which needed to be seen, did not. To produce and criminalize sodomy as unseeable and unspeakable was to produce and criminalize privacy, to disallow distinctions between the public and the private that the inscription of sodomy simultaneously created, to press the private visibly and incriminatingly into the public as taboo. It was also to occlude the recognition of "homosexuality" which, I would argue, was beginning to have a place, however nameless, formless, and faint, in Renaissance discourse.[17]

Holinshed and the "everlasting marke of infamie"

These strategies are perhaps most striking in Holinshed, where sodomy becomes an unspeakable matter of public record, at once displayed and concealed, and concealed as a means of display.[18] Clearly Holinshed was invested in upholding the sanctity of the kingship. In the case of Edward II, however, whose reign was one of the most unstable in the history of the English monarchy and whose pastimes were known to include sodomy, such an agenda could only be deeply vexed. The politics were problematic enough, all sodomy aside, for during Edward's time, the authority of the king (who was elected) had not yet been clearly established.[19] Edward faced continual opposition from the baronage, who "proclaimed that the rights of the crown must be integrally maintained" but were "ready to resort to violence and rebellion," and even civil war, when their own competing rights and claims to land were threatened.[20] Instead of placing the power of the kingship at issue, the nobility (and historians siding with them) justified what might otherwise be labeled treason, the uncertainties in the power structure notwithstanding, "by claiming that they were attacking not the king's proper authority but one perverted by the counsel of evil favorites."[21] Recountings of the reign that bring in the issue of sodomy follow suit and, as Bredbeck has argued, "typically shift the focus from political errors (the body politic) to fleshly homoeroticism (the temporal body)," removing Edward's weakness from the realm of the political and "ultimately solidif[ying] monarchical right."[22]

Holinshed deploys a similar strategy, blaming Edward for surrounding himself with "flattering parasites" (p. 547), especially those who were "not worthie of those places which they occupied" (p. 562), and "sodomizing" that flattery in order to condemn the king without condemning the kingship. Yet in Holinshed the negotiation between the politic and the temporal is more complicated. For the text not only separates but also collapses the two categories, using the sexual to incriminate the political and, reciprocally, the political, the sexual. While on the one hand Holinshed asserts the difference between them to take the pressure off the kingship, on the other hand he denies that difference to put pressure on the king. Though the kingship remains relatively unscathed, the account blurs sodomy into politics and condemns the king for both personal and political transgression, loading Edward's speakable public offenses with unspeakable consequences and his unspeakable private offenses with speakable public consequences.[23] What is strategically gained in the process is a double level of incrimination, and what is strategically lost is the idea of sodomy and the recognition of homosexuality itself.

Though Holinshed seems to switch allegiance several times from the king to the barons to the king, he supports the absolute power of the monarchy. At the end of the account, after presenting Edward's murder, he accuses the king for "want[ing] judgement and prudent discretion to make choise of sage and discréet councellors, receiving those into his favour, that abused the same to their private gaine and advantage" (p. 587). Yet the accusation turns quickly from the king, first to the abusing favorites, then to "the common people & nobilitie" who, thanks to the "covetous rapine, spoile, and immoderate ambition" of the favored, "were quite estranged from the dutifull love and obedience which they *ought* to have shewed to theire sovereigne" (p. 587; emphasis added).

Holinshed directly accuses the lords of "tyrannie" (p. 587) and elsewhere criticizes them harshly for indiscriminately pillaging and destroying the property of the allies of two key favorites, the Spensers, "the innocent with the nocent, the guiltlesse with the guiltie" (p. 561). And as he describes Edward's deposition and his admission that "he was fallen into this miserie through his owne offenses," he closes the event by breaking his own facade of objectivity, exclaiming: "Ah lamentable ruine from roialtie to miserable calamitie, procured by them chéefelie that should have beene the pillers of the kings estate, and not the hooked engins to pull him downe from his throne!" (p. 585). The deposition becomes a "lamentable ruine," brought about by those who "ought" to have showed their sovereign "dutifull love and obedience." Its only benefit is that it secures the line, the nobles otherwise threatening to bar Edward's son from the throne, insisting that "the people" "in respect of the[ir] evill will" (thus incriminated) "would not faile but procéed to the election of some other that should happilie not touch him in linage" (p. 585). The supremacy of the monarch prevails, and the center of power remains secure.

The kingship, secured thus within a political register, is to some degree decentered. The source of corruption is located outside both the body politic and the king's body and is displaced initially onto the figure of Edward's first and most intimate favorite, the infamous (and infamous sodomite) Piers de Gaveston. We are prepared for the trouble in the account of Edward I, which mentions that the prince, led on by this "lewd and wanton person," had "riotouslie broken the parke" of the future Bishop of Coventry (p. 539). The prince was imprisoned and Gaveston was banished, Holinshed explains, "least the prince, who delighted much in his companie, might by his evill and wanton counsell fall to evill and naughtie rule" (p. 539). In the account of Edward II, Holinshed amplifies Gaveston's corrupting influence (and the king's innocence) by skewing chronology and placing him in England and in control sooner than he was. The chronicle begins with Edward's first official act, mentioning that he recalled the banishment, imprisoned the Bishop of Coventry, and handed him and his "mooveables" over to Gaveston (p. 547). Later it becomes clear that the king seized the bishop before Gaveston's return and reassigned the properties some time after, but because these events are compressed in the narration, it seems at first as if they occured in rapid succession, with Gaveston on hand throughout to deflect blame from the king.

Though introduced in the previous account as a political threat, here Gaveston's offenses appear as a matter outside, though impeding, politics. The problem is that he distracted the king from his duties and

> furnished his court with companies of jesters, ruffians, flattering parasites, musicians, and other vile and naughtie ribalds, that the king might spend

both daies and nights in jesting, plaieng, blanketing, and in such other filthie
and dishonorable exercises. (p. 547)

What makes these implicitly (if not exclusively) sodomitical "exercises"
relevant to the body politic is that they make the king "forget himselfe,"
"have his nobles in no regard," and "take small héed unto the good governement of the commonwealth" (p. 547). Rather than figuring as a crime
unto themselves, they are contemptible because they occlude something
else, "good governement," which is otherwise arbitrarily related. Because
the link is more circumstantial than essential, it is not what can or does
impugn the sexual offense. Instead sodomy is blurred into abstraction, as
what "vile and naughtie ribalds" do and as part of the "filthie and dishonorable exercises," and is rendered unspeakable.

The passage is structured around two categories, one of offenders and
the other of offenses; yet each inscribes a more important unspoken difference, between the speakable and the unspeakable, the tolerable and the
execrable. Jesters, ruffians, parasites, and musicians are categorized as, but
nonetheless set off from, "other vile and naughtie ribalds," and jesting,
playing, and blanketing, from "other filthie and dishonorable exercises."
The sexual offenders and offenses are doubly implicated, explicitly as part
of an abstract but inclusive category of ("vile," "naughtie," "filthie," and
"dishonorable") corruption, and implicitly as a distinct but unspeakable
(because unspoken) kind of corruption.

By defining sodomy through such abstraction, Holinshed not only
obscures the indirectness of its link to politics; he also, ironically, assigns
it more precise and punishable political consequences. The abstract quali-
fiers carry across to and associate sodomy with other, public transgressions
whose criminality is unquestionable. For example, in an odd but telling
turn of narrative, Holinshed writes of a "*naughtie* fellow called John Poidras" who "thrust himselfe into the kings hall" and "gave foorth that he was
sonne and right heire of king Edward the first" (p. 557; emphasis added).
Though his claim, based on a changeling story, posed no real threat to the
king's legitimacy, it was important enough that he was publicly "drawne,
hanged, and as a traitour bowelled" (p. 557).[24] If Karen Cunningham is
right that convicts' last words were regularly coerced and constrained, he
was probably also forced to neutralize his original charge by confessing
what he allegedly confessed, that he was assured of the kingship by "a
spirit in likenesse of a cat" (p. 557).[25] This event, obviously, has little to do
with sodomy. Yet Gaveston and his "naughtie ribalds," with their unspeci-

fied and unpunishable offenses, and the "naughtie" Poidras, with his specified and punished offense (treason, not to mention witchcraft), are subsumed beneath and linked within the category of the "naughtie."

The abstractness with which Gaveston's vices are inscribed also allows them to be slipped into and amplified through a political register and the inconsistencies evoked with that move masked. Gaveston first emerges as a sort of early modern playboy, distracting Edward from the outside, from the more serious business of state. At the end of the account, however, he is placed on the inside, ambitiously between the king and the nobles, as a part of and not apart from the power play. No longer sexual, his offenses and their consequences are described (not coincidentally) in notable detail. Returning from a second exile, Gaveston, we are told,

> being nothing at all amended of those his evill manners, rather demeaned himselfe woorse than before he had donne, namelie towards the lords, against whom using reprochfull speech, he called the earle of Glocester bastard, the earle of Lincolne latlie deceased bursten bellie, the earle of Warwike the blacke hound of Arderne, and the earle of Lancaster churle. (p. 551)

Though the "reprochfull" speech acts seem more petty than subversive, Holinshed places them at the start of a political chain reaction, prompting the lords to take revenge against him, and the king to take revenge against them, the "rancour" already "kindled" between the factions now beginning "to blase abroad, and spred so farre" (p. 552). The account makes these affronts more contemptible by aligning them with—and declaring them "woorse" than—Gaveston's previous (sodomitical) "evill manners." In the process, those "evill maners" themselves are also made worse by being represented as part of a continuum of behavior that is finally, directly political and that lays the ground for civil war. Both behaviors thus become doubly incriminated and incriminating, their impact at once spoken and unspeakable.

This process continues as Holinshed merges Gaveston's history into that of the Spensers, who "quicklie crept" into the king's favor, but not (as far as we know) into his bed, after Gaveston's death (p. 552). The chronicle makes no mention of the key distinguishing factor, that this favoritism was not sodomitical. Instead we hear the same old story. Once again the lords turn against the favored as "unprofitable members in the comonwealth" (p. 567), demand and negotiate around their banishment, and finally turn against the king in the civil war already predicted by the "rancour" incited by Gaveston. Whereas before it was the nobility whose "pru-

dent advertisements" were cast aside for the favorite (p. 547), now it is
Isabella, the queen, who "gave good and faithfull counsell," that "was
nothing regarded but by the Spensers meanes cléerelie worne out of the
kings favour" (p. 570).

Beyond invoking the king's earlier neglect of the peers, the mention
of Isabella draws the two narratives together by subtly assigning the second a private, sexual impact. Significantly, Holinshed does not set Edward's relation to Gaveston in conflict with his relation to the queen, even
though that part of the account explicitly raises the issue of desire. (I will
return to this unique moment below.) To the contrary, he nonchalantly
announces the king's marriage almost immediately after describing Gaveston's arrival and influence at court and then later announces Gaveston's
marriage just as nonchalantly. This assumption of compatibility is not in
and of itself so surprising since early modern marriages were not necessarily, exclusively or primarily, a matter of desire, especially in royal house-
holds. What is surprising, however, is that Holinshed does set Edward's
relation to the Spensers, despite its nonsexual nature, in conflict with his
marriage.

With their rise to favor, Isabella becomes not only a discarded coun-
selor but also a discarded wife and sexual partner. In explaining why she
refused, during this time, to return from a diplomatic mission in her native
France, Holinshed offers several equally possible reasons, among them
how "she was used at hir husbands hands, being had in no regard with
him" and that "she was loth to see all things ordered out of frame by the
counsell of the Spensers" (p. 578). Though both excuses are ostensibly
political (like the others in the list), Holinshed then blames her, in more
private terms, for following "evill counsell" rather than upholding the
bond that marriage and sex produce. He declares it:

> a lamentable case, that such division should be betwéene a king and his
> quéene, being lawfullie married, and having issue of their bodies, which
> ought to have made that their copulation more comfortable: but (alas) what
> will not a woman be drawne and allured unto, if by evill counsell she be once
> assaulted? And what will she leave undoone, though never so inconvenient
> to those that should be most déere unto hir, so hir owne fansie and will be
> satisfied? (p. 578)

Though it is Isabella rather than Edward who is accused of showing bad
faith within the marriage, the question Holinshed asks of her—"what will
not a woman be drawne and allured unto, if by evill counsell she be once
assaulted?"—points glaringly though indirectly to Edward, to the one re-

nowned for succumbing to such counsel and his "owne fansie and will." That this excoriation erupts within the account of the Spensers points the finger also at them, setting their position against the queen's, as if their relation to the one "that should be most déere unto hir" is somehow responsible for the division within the marriage.

The point is not that Holinshed "discovers" sodomy here too, but that he presents a situation of political favoritism as disruptive of a bond that, though political as well, is also defined by the "issue of [the king and queen's] bodies." In so doing, he fits the Spensers' story into the space that Gaveston's might otherwise fill and obscures the difference between them. Indeed, when Holinshed sums up the reign and faults Edward for misguided favoritism, again he makes no distinction, treating Gaveston and Spenser, sodomy and statecraft, as inevitably and indistinguishably allied. Favoritism is favoritism—sodomitical or political. The sexual becomes as politically disruptive as the political, the political as sexually disruptive as the sexual. It seems appropriate that the representation of Isabella effects this end indirectly, for it has been by indirection that Holinshed has found directions out, abstraction that has enabled a double-edged incrimination, full of speakable and unspeakable implications.

As Holinshed records Gaveston's beheading and explains why it was a "just reward," he condemns the "scornefull and contemptuous" favorite for treating the nobility with disrespect as for "a rable of other outrages," unspecified and unspeakable, and ends with a condemnation of both:

> But lo the vice of ambition, accompanied with a rable of other outrages, even a reprochfull end, with an everlasting marke of infamie, which he pulled by violent meanes on himselfe with the cords of his owne lewdnesse. (p. 552)

"The everlasting marke of infamie" is so deeply embedded within the sentence, its referent lost (if it exists) within a series of phrases, that what it is remains, ironically and strategically, unclear. In calling attention to that mark while confusing the issue, Holinshed calls attention to its absence, producing here as throughout a sign that by obscuring difference makes that difference everlastingly clear.

Yet the implications of the story and the strategy of occlusion go further still. For the collapse of distinctions allows avoidance of what seems the most direct conclusion that could be drawn from Edward's history—that there is, in fact, an emergent "homosexuality," an innate predilection toward homoerotic desire that threatens to act itself out if not constrained by counsel. Gaveston is clearly, for us, the most flagrant "homosexual" here, dictating and being defined by his "filthie and dishonorable exercises." Yet because his "disordred doings" are merged into politics and into abstraction (p. 547), the nature of his "corrupt humor" cannot and need not be interrogated (p. 549). He is, after all, the foreign other without interiority and soul.

In the case of Edward, however, who sits (and because he sits) in the center of power, interiority and inclination are at stake and at risk, and their centrality may indeed account for the attention Holinshed deflects from Edward and gives instead to his favorites. In the opening pages of the account, Holinshed addresses "the demeanour of this new king, whose disordered maners brought himselfe and manie others unto destruction" (p. 547). Despite a partial retreat to exteriors, to Edward's "maners," Holinshed returns to what lies behind them and assigns him a "nature" that was "given to lightnesse" (p. 547). Though that nature could be and was intially "restreined with the prudent advertisements of certeine of his counsellors," the "gravitie, vertue and modestie" that he displayed in response were merely, we are told, "counterfeited." Because that nature "could not throughlie be so bridled," the king almost inevitably "began to plaie divers wanton and light parts, at the first indeed not outragiouslie, but by little and little, and that covertlie" (p. 547). Edward's actions emerge here as "parts," but slowly and "naturally" evolving parts that are not counterfeit and not for purposes of display. If the self is the sum of its parts, as it seems to be here, those parts tell an unsettling (for the early moderns) story.

In one remarkable passage, Holinshed gives more of that story and confronts the issue of homoerotic desire head on. Breaking the code of silence, as he discusses the influence of Gaveston, he declares it "a wonderfull matter that the king should be so inchanted with the said earle, and so addict himselfe, or rather fix his hart upon a man of such a corrupt humor" (p. 549). Though Gaveston, the sodomitical mover and shaker, is accorded an abstract, desexualized "corrupt humor," the king is assigned a more specific and indelible "fervant affection" which refuses to go away and for which he is largely responsible. The passage underscores his agency, noting that he "addict[ed] himselfe" and "fix[ed] his hart," and was "inchanted with" rather than by his favorite. Attempting to find a precedent for this unorthodox affection, Holinshed calls upon classical authority and quotes (in Latin):

> similar habits are the sparks of love and desire for the similar. Thus a vain person loves the vain, the studious one the studious, and animals are drawn to a kindred group.[26] (p. 549)

The dictum normalizes the attraction by turning it into a general principle of like attracts like and by centering on like "habits" (vanity, studiousness) rather than bodies (except in the case of animals). Yet at the center of the passage are "sparks of love and desire" that require and resist explanation between two men whose bodies are more similar than their "habits." What emerges here, despite Holinshed's efforts to conceal it, is an early recognition of a transgressive desire that goes beyond discrete acts of sodomy, extending beyond corrupt habits to addictive affection—a desire that not only is defined by its object but also defines its subject in a "wonderfull" (i.e., strange) way.

It is in the face of this unsettling addiction that Holinshed turns to Gaveston, displacing the problem outwardly and locating it in a figure whose interiority could (and "should") be erased. The chronicle insistently blames Gaveston for making the king "suddenlie so corrupted, that he burst out into most heinous vices," ultimately giving himself "to wantonnes, [and] passing his time in voluptuous pleasure, and riotous excesse" (p. 547). Yet the repressed returns. The lords' attempts to ostracize Gaveston were based, we are told, on the hope "that the kings mind might happilie be altered into a better purpose, being not altogither converted into a venemous disposition, but so that it might be cured, if the corrupter thereof were once banished from him" (p. 549). That assumption, which Holinshed, it seems, would like to share, proves false after Gaveston's death, when Edward "nothing reformed his maners," undermining the lords' continued but by now less assertive belief that "his nature" was not "altogither evill" (p. 558).

The only way to get away from that evil "nature" seems here to be to decenter it, to merge the issue of "fleshly homoeroticism," which has allowed a safe, depoliticized incrimination of the king's politics, back into a political register (into Gaveston's politicized story), where it disallows incrimination of his sexuality. We are wisely skeptical of discovering "homosexuality" too early on, particularly because the discourse on sodomy was so varied, vague, and inconsistent. Yet the acknowledgment, such as that found in Holinshed, that something "strange" was going on and the attempts to change or displace the subject open up the possibility that the confusion within the discourse marks a resistance to, rather than a lack of awareness of, "the thing that was not."

To "sodomize" the political and to politicize the sodomitical was at once to criminalize questionable but not clearly punishable political moves and also to criminalize and, paradoxically, to deny homosexuality, which was being erased at the moment of its inscription. It was also, to some degree, to criminalize the private, also at the moment of its inscription. If the focus on the king's temporal body makes Edward stand, as Bredbeck suggests, as a subject rather than a king, as "a pattern of fleshly vice," then his history becomes a mirror not only for magistrates but also for their subjects, for their bodies as the Faust tale is for their minds.[27] And because the particular vice at issue is kept in the closet, behind the closed doors of discourse, as it is being displayed, it becomes potentially available and applicable to all. Just as representations of magic turned white all too readily into black by obscuring their subject, so too did the discourse on sodomy, placing the private at risk of being or becoming improprietous, the unspoken at risk of being or becoming unspeakable. To step out of the public sphere is to fall to "heinous vice," to become not self but other. It seems no wonder and no coincidence that it is impossible for us to recuperate a stable and distinct idea of the private as of homosexuality from early modern discourse—not because these ideas did not exist, but because as they were beginning to exist, they were forced into a space of otherness and denied the clear articulation that would give them meaningful, and threatening, presence.

"Fear not to kill the king"

When Marlowe brings Edward's history to center stage he reveals the ways in which the terms and meanings of sodomy were being occluded within a political discourse. Like Holinshed, he also displays a shocking spectacle of sodomy that gets its point across all too forcefully. Yet in Marlowe that spectacle is presented as a rupture rather than as a fitting conclusion to the drama that precedes. Following an unpointed message that must be given point, it becomes a spectacle not of strangeness but of the manipulation of the strange, a manipulation that depends not merely on "unlawful" but on unspeakable things. Though Marlowe does not and cannot give homosexuality a full "modern" presence, in countering its occlusion he begins to open a space that it finally will come to fill.

Perhaps the most appropriate place to begin is at the end, with the shocking murder that Marlowe puts audaciously on display. When the play was recently transformed, under the creative direction of Derek Jarman, into film and into a drama that speaks first and foremost "against the oppression of homosexuals," it was this scene that became the framing moment of the history—but a moment radically rewritten to avoid the tragedy it seems to inscribe.[28] The organizing event of the film is a slowly moving, greatly embellished enactment of Edward's captivity and treatment at the hands of Lightborn, his executioner in Marlowe's text, whom we watch in intermittent segments warming up the coals and preparing the hot spit for (we think) the upcoming murder. The sequence is continually interrupted by "a series of self-contained tableaux" that recreate what comes before in the play in roughly the same chronological order and with something of the same incessant episodic pace.[29] Yet Lightborn chooses to kiss rather than to kill, and the murder we seem to be constantly prompted to anticipate is written out of reality into dream, becoming only Edward's fearful fantasy of how his story will be ended.[30]

It seems more than appropriate that Jarman, in bringing the play's sodomy out of the closet, would begin at the end, with the one scene in which the act of sodomy is so clearly recreated and given center stage. It is at this moment that what is at stake in the play is made finally, unmistakably obvious. Yet if the film was to succeed in reversing the oppression it attacks and in creating a triumphant and affirming place for gay rights, identities, and pleasures, it also had to rewrite the scene. For disturbingly, in Marlowe (as in Holinshed), this flagrant realization of the unspeakable act is also a moment of punishment, ordered by the king's most relentless rival, the Younger Mortimer, and executed by a Lightborn who brings only a kiss of death. Though Jarman's film is filled with homoerotic images and acts, there seems to be only one place for the display of sodomy on Marlowe's stage—and that is in the darkened stench of prison at the moment of death.

Yet it is not Marlowe but Mortimer who is responsible for relegating sodomy to punishment and delimiting its meaning and the meaning of Edward's history. In putting the imprisonment and murder sequence into an extended frame that encompasses the rest and the time of the drama, Jarman amplifies what sets Edward's death significantly apart from that of any of Marlowe's other heroes: its protracted nature. Dido's run into the burning pyre is as erratic and unexpected as Aeneas's departure and the imitative suicides that follow with comic speed and underscore its suddenness. Tamburlaine refuses to stop for death, and even when it stops for him, he keeps playing his game of empire, orchestrating ceremonies of power that, in mapping out the future, seem to forfend his end (as they have in Part 1). Barabas's death depends upon its suddenness and surprise, and although Faustus talks continually of ends, his own among them, death only hits in the very last moments of the play, as the clock ticks off his life with increasing speed.

In *Edward II*, however, we watch for almost a full act as Edward first meets the glowering Mower portending his doom, is placed in confinement, deposed, washed in "puddle-water" and shaved, tortured and taunted in other ways, and then, finally, killed. In prolonging the sequence, Marlowe calls attention to its orchestration, to the fact that what we are watching is a scene not of Edward's doing but of his undoing, torturously executed and embellished (relative to the chronicles) by his captors. While the protracted delay does what it is supposed to on one level, making the king "know the painful cares / That wait upon [his] poor distressed soul" (5.3.37–38), on another, in relation to us, it does not. For instead of turning our sympathies from the king (and so validating the regicide), the abuse turns us toward him and brings out the questionable nature of his treatment at the hands of the opposition.

The method of the murder, which in Holinshed is produced as a fitting end, his authorial retreats notwithstanding, here is disjoined from Edward's history and made to seem all the more arbitrary.[31] The murderer appears, like the Mower, as if out of a morality text, and though he has a name, Lightborn, it smacks of allegory.[32] Commissioned by Mortimer, he is brought in from the outside as a sort of deus (demon?) ex machina—so outside that productions like Jarman's and the recent enactment at the Pit have eroticized the role to bring him in.[33] Otherwise he sounds like Ithamore at his caricatured worst or Barabas parodying him, or like Shakespeare's Aaron, the progenitor of both, boasting of a rich criminal history that seems to belong in another play.

Importantly, too, the means he chooses is correlated to him and not to Edward. Going beyond the chronicle, Marlowe invents a past for Lightborn that defines him as one schooled and accomplished in invasive and invisible techniques. He learned, he tells us,

> in Naples how to poison flowers,
> To strangle with a lawn thrust down the throat,
> To pierce the wind pipe with a needle's point,
> Or, whilst one is asleep, to take a quill,
> And blow a little powder in his ears,
> Or open his mouth, and power quick-silver down,

and insists that he has an even "braver way than"—and implicitly related to—"these" (5.4.30–36). As he chooses his weapon, the implicit becomes explicit, and Edward's death falls congruently into the catalog of crimes, seamlessly into Lightborn's history and not his own.

Rather than fitting the crime, the punishment fits Mortimer's need for a murder and murderer that finally cannot be detected, like the "unpointed" message, "*Edwardum occidere nolite timere bonum est*," that covers its treasonous tracks ("Fear not to kill the king, 'tis good he die") with the exonerating opposite ("Kill not the king, 'tis good to fear the worst") (5.4.8–13). When Mortimer calls Lightborn onstage to carry out the deed, it is clear that they have already spoken and that Mortimer has chosen his accomplice with an eye to creating an invisible event.[34] Mortimer not only cautions him to "be secret" (5.4.27); he also arms him with "a secret token" (5.4.19) that neither we nor Lightborn can see—a token that will mark the murderer for murder and erase all traces of Mortimer's connection to the crime. Though Mortimer leaves the method up to him, insisting that he "care[s] not how it is, so it be not spied" (5.4.39), it is no coincidence on Marlowe's part that the chosen means is a recreation of sodomy—the act that is the ultimate unseeable crime and that is used and obscured throughout the play to condemn an otherwise ostensibly uncondemnable king. What Marlowe puts on display here as throughout is not, as Mortimer would have it, Edward's crime or even Lightborn's, but Mortimer and the peers' relentless efforts to use the unseeable and unspeakable offense to undo the king and make room for their own domination.

The play, as Bredbeck argues in an important recent discussion of it, exposes the ways in which sodomy is "constructed as an affront to order" and then "used to affront order."[35] Homoeroticism provides a crucial site where "politic order and the power it seeks to contain meet and may be negotiated," particularly, Bredbeck argues, in the hands of Mortimer, who takes charge of the negotiations.[36] By "writing" sodomy all over the king, his minions, and his favor, Mortimer is able to "obfuscate motives of politic ambition" and write himself, at least momentarily, into a position at the top of Fortune's wheel, as the Protector of the realm.[37] Otherwise, the baronial revolt would appear as simply and treasonously that—a revolt against the rightful monarch. Because Edward's claims to absolute authority, against the dictates of his father and the advice of his peers, are as legitimate and as problematic as the nobility's assumption of "right," the peers need some unmistakable way of criminalizing the king's action. Sodomy, especially as figured in the boldly extravagant Gaveston, provides that way.

Yet the writing of the sexual/sodomitical onto the political involves more than the conflation of the two and the obfuscation of their difference.[38] It requires the insistent obfuscation of sodomy itself, which might otherwise take on and give meaning in a private register and not provide the necessary ocular proof of the king's violation of power. Crucial to the opposition's strategies (like Holinshed's) is that sodomy be neither seen nor spoken, paradoxically, as it is put on display. For, as Mortimer's uncle (who advocates against overthrowing the monarchy) points out, sodomy in and of itself does not pose an immediate problem for either the king or the kingdom. Insisting that "the mightiest kings have had their minions" (1.4.393) and invoking an impressive list of examples, he advises his nephew to stop the opposition, to

> let his grace, whose youth is flexible,
> And promiseth as much as we can wish,
> Freely enjoy that vain light-headed earl,
> For riper years will wean him from such toys.
>
> (1.4.400–03)

Edward's "wanton humour" (1.4.404) seems almost to be encouraged here, as enabling the kind of flexibility that will make the king, as he ripens, all the more pliable to the nobles' demands. Because the bonds between Edward and his favorites do not necessarily represent a conflict of interests between the ruler and the ruled, the Younger Mortimer, who clearly wants to control rather than to balance the power, must not only politicize sodomy but also obscure it. Its mark of infamy is not of itself enough.

As Kent, finally disenchanted with his brother's rule, prepares to join the queen and the opposition in France, he announces that part of his mission there will be to "certify what Edward's looseness is" (4.1.7). At this point, Edward has begun "to slaughter noble men" (4.1.8), actions which historians have suggested as a legitimate foundation for revolt because he acted without advice and without precedent. (The nobility had never before been executed by a monarch.)[39] What is clearly missing even this late in the play, as all along, and emphasized as absent by Kent's remark is, in fact, certification of what "Edward's looseness" really is. At the outset of the play, the lords attempt to assert their own authority and validate their opposition to the king and to the scapegoated Gaveston in the precise terms of monarchical precedent. The Younger Mortimer declares that they have duly "sworn" to Edward I that Gaveston "should ne'er return unto the realm" in an "oath" overriding the loyalty they "should" also show Edward II (1.1.83–86).[40] Yet Kent quickly undermines the legitimacy of the move, reminding them (and us) of another royal precedent dictating obedience to the king, bringing forth the example of his "father's days" when Percy "brav'd Mowberay in presence of the king" and for the affront "*should* have lost his head" (1.1.109–13; emphasis added) and would have, had not the king decided otherwise. For those who "dare" to "brave the king unto his face," Kent advocates revenge, urging the king to "let these their heads / Preach upon poles, for trespass of their tongues!" (1.1.116–18).[41]

After (if not because) the lords' attempt to claim monarchical precedent meets opposition, they strategically redefine the problem in the less precise and more inclusive terms of Edward's favoritism, making his "minions" a major threat to the realm. Significantly, however, this move is not their only option, a last resort when all other more exclusively political and clearly arguable premises fail. Instead it emerges as a choice, away from definable and contestable national causes toward less definable and so less contestable moral/personalized ones. For although Edward I's voice provides the most solid authorization for their affront, it is not the only legitimate cause. When the Bishop of Coventry is imprisoned and his "goods and body given to Gaveston" (1.2.2), the lords have specific grounds and, via the Church's authority, specific means of protest. Edward himself acknowledges that "the legate of the Pope will be obey'd" (1.4.64) and orders a second banishment when pressured by the Archbishop of Canterbury to do so.

Yet while the nobles allow the treatment of the bishop to enter into their complaints, they do not center on the cause. Instead they defame the king as "wicked" and Gaveston as "accursed" and as a "villain," and declare the "ground . . . corrupted with their steps" (1.2.4–5, 11). As they elaborate, they move in and out of suggestions of sodomy, attacking Gaveston for marching "arm in arm" with and "leaning on the shoulder of" the king, for being received as "'My Lord of Cornwall' now at every word," flattered by "all the court," and waited upon by the guard, and reciprocally for making "happy" those whom he chooses, nodding, scorning, or smiling at his own discretion (1.2.17–24). Flattery, double-edged and double-sided here, takes the stage away from the bishop's plight and explodes the problem of power into a more pervasive and incriminating violation of sexual and social codes.

The nobles never organize around what historians and Kent recognize as possible testimony of tyranny, Edward's execution of the barons (mentioned above), which prompts Kent to declare him a "butcher"

(4.1.4) and Jarman to literalize the label, having Warwick butchered like and on a piece of meat. Though initially the nobles implicate Edward for being too "weak" (2.2.159) and later for being a "tyrant" (3.3.57), they make no issue of the difference, which, in raising the complicated question of tyranny, could work to their advantage.[42] Rather they reiterate the charge of flattery, with Mortimer condemning Edward for choosing to fight "to the last" and "bathe [his] sword in subjects' blood" rather than "banish that pernicious company" (3.3.27–29).

Marlowe provides a glaring instance of the verbal strategies at work here and throughout in Mortimer's appeal to the king for ransom for the Elder Mortimer, who has been captured in foreign war—an appeal that moves consciously into inclusive and sexualized abstraction in order to support an unrelated political demand. Mortimer himself alerts us to the strategic nature (and Marlowe to the rebelliousness) of his speech, promising to "thunder such a peal into his ears / As never subject did unto his king" (2.2.128–29). Because Edward, legitimately, directs the lords themselves to gather the ransom, Mortimer, aided by Lancaster, unleashes a plethora of complaints, creating a "condition of England" speech as extensive and, in its inclusiveness and extremes, as self-defeating as Gaunt's manipulative oration in *Richard II*.[43] Not only is England, we are told, endangered on all sides, by "the wild O'Neill" who "with swarms of Irish kerns, / Lives uncontroll'd within the English pale"; by the Scots who "make road" "unto the walls of York . . . / And, unresisted, drive away rich spoils"; by the "haughty Dane" who "commands the narrow seas," and so on (2.2.164–68). In addition, the kingdom's name is threatened on all fronts, with the Scots making jigs of and "to England's high disgrace" (2.2.189), while the English cast "libels" against the king and make "ballads and rhymes . . . of [his] overthrow" (2.2.177–78).

Significantly, these complaints are framed by incriminations which press Edward's offenses also into a sexual register: the first against the "idle triumphs, masques, lascivious shows, / And prodigal gifts bestow'd on Gaveston" (2.2.157–58), and the last against the display on the battlefield as the king's soldiers "march'd like players, / With garish robes, not armour," while the king himself

> Bedaub'd with gold, rode laughing at the rest
> Nodding and shaking of [his] spangled crest,
> Where women's favours hung like labels down.
>   (2.2.183–87)

Interspersed amid this catalog are other sexualized attacks, complaints that the queen wanders "all forlorn" (2.2.173), while the "northern borderers" "run up and down, / Cursing the name of thee and Gaveston" (2.2.179–81). What gets lost in the confusion, and its ill effects amplified by this movement among the political, the textual, and the sexual, is the real source of contention: Edward's refusal to provide the requested ransom, a refusal of itself not adequate justification for revolt but made contemptible as part of a larger picture. Interestingly, the complaints turn and return to the idea of display—from Gaveston's lascivious shows to Edward's, from Scottish jigs to English ballads—suggesting exhibition as an impediment to power. From our view, however, this focus points not just (if at all) to Edward, whom we never see engaged in such maneuvers, but back to the nobles themselves and to their aversion to display, at least of the sort that hangs "like labels down" to make its meaning contestably clear.

Here and throughout, the sexual/sodomitical transgression is the crucial framing source and subject of obfuscation. In articulating what is wrong with Gaveston's rise to favor, the nobility center on his "baseness," gesturing significantly toward the issue of sodomy. They set the "base and obscure" favorite in direct opposition to themselves, who "naturally would love and honour" the king, presenting Gaveston's base obscurity as the antithesis to their (natural) "love" (1.1.100–101). Yet notably the terms are not dichotomous but shift chiastically between two registers, the political and the sexual, pulling them together while pulling them apart, loading each incriminatingly with the other. Baseness takes on sexual import as it is set against natural "love" and political import as it is set against "honour." And what is "obscure" here, more than Gaveston, is the very nature of their charges. We get nothing of the directness of *Lear*'s Edmund, who attempts to exonerate himself by interrogating the arbitrary relation between baseness and bastardy, the moral abstraction and the sexual signifier. Instead, the nobles perpetuate the confusion, producing Gaveston not only as a "base minion" (1.1.133), but also a "base groom" (1.4.293) and "base flatterer" (2.5.11).

Critics, attempting to clarify the confusion and bring the issue back to power, have tried to locate a cause and have singled out the subversion of class difference as the primary target of the nobles' rejection and "sodomization" of the king's favorites.[44] Yet their condemnations of Gaveston's baseness are neither clearly motivated nor consistently articulated as an issue of class. Lancaster, who leads the charge at first, professes himself ready and willing to sacrifice the four earldoms that substantiate and instantiate his status in order to exile Gaveston—to give up, that is, the very thing he is supposed to be fighting for.

To make matters worse, it is unclear exactly what Gaveston's social status is. Historically (and in the chronicle), although not of a prominent family, he was a "goodlie gentleman."[45] We are wrong to assume, as critics have, that the play has necessarily rewritten history to lower his status and to exacerbate the problem of his rise, for it is only the discourse of the opposition that proffers that conclusion. Mortimer, despite himself, grants Gaveston some noble stature, declaring him "hardly . . . a gentleman by birth" (1.4.81), but a gentleman nonetheless. And though Kent protests when the king invests Gaveston with a plethora of titles (Lord High Chamberlain, Chief Secretary, Earl of Cornwall, and King and Lord of Man), insisting that "the least of these [might] well suffice / For one of greater birth than Gaveston" (1.1.158–59), his indirection leaves open the possibility that "the least" (and no more, rather than none at all) might be appropriate for Gaveston too.

In refusing to resolve the matter and provide a clear foundation for the nobles' charges, Marlowe highlights the indeterminacy not only between those charges and their target but also within them. The nobles *could* presumably tell us what we need to know in order to believe them, but they do not. By moving into abstraction, loading "baseness" with both social and sexual implications, they, like Holinshed, amplify the transgressiveness of both. This is nowhere clearer than when they merge their attack on Gaveston with their attack on the Younger Spenser, a non-sodomitical favorite. Interestingly, although the chronicle focuses on the influence of *both* Spensers after Gaveston's death, Marlowe's nobles narrow the focus to the son, the Younger Spenser, creating a closer parallel between these otherwise unequal instances of favor and justifying equal resistance. Just as the nobles emblematize Gaveston as a "canker" which "gets unto the highest bough" of "a lofty cedar tree" (2.2.16–19), so too do they represent the new favorite as "a putrifying branch / That deads the royal vine" (3.2.165–66).[46] It is because Gaveston's baseness remains so loosely sexualized and so politically loaded that they can do so: that they can unify and reinforce their cause, treating both as "smooth dissembling flatterers" (3.2.172) whose rise threatens the "virtue and nobility" (3.2.170) of the court in extensive and unspeakable ways.[47]

Jarman turns the Younger Spenser's role into that of lover, as if to make sense and to make an anti-gay issue of aggression that seems to have missed its target. Yet the point in Marlowe's play is that it has—that the aggression remains as "anti-gay" as it was before, even though its target is not "gay." The difference between Spenser and Gaveston is as critically important, in its erasure, to the nobles' attempts to "sodomize" the king as it is, in its display, to Marlowe's attempts to disarm them. That Spenser is made to replace Gaveston does not merely underline the political edge of the revolt; it also underlines the simultaneous extension and erasure of sodomy itself, as it becomes at once much more than it is politically and much less than it is sexually. To find sodomy here too is to assign and deny it a separate and meaningful space outside the political, a transgressive space both vital to and obscured by the politic.

In the end, Mortimer's fall is predicated on a move that does make a difference, ultimately restoring, despite himself, the difference between public and private, political and sodomitical, that he and the nobles have so effectively obscured, and giving the private its own self-affirming power. For in efforts to create a punishment that cannot be discovered, Mortimer forces Edward from a problematic position as king to a more sympathetic position as subject.[48] In the process, he brings the unspeakable out of silence, the unseeable out of invisibility, taking off the incriminating edge requiring both silence and absence and exposing the distance between private and public affairs.

The prison, which becomes the locus of the private, seems as if it were more than a world away from the court, a place not to be seen or (in the case of Kent, who goes to Killingworth to free the king and is subsequently executed) entered and survived. While Edward lives in confinement, his voice and vision are filtered out of the political arena. For those at court, "seeing" him is only possible metaphorically, through the mediation of those who would not have him seen, at least not as king. When the prince hesitates to accept the monarchy thrust upon him, the queen, Isabella, urges him to "be content, *seeing* it his highness' pleasure" (5.2.96; emphasis added). But "his highness" is no longer to be seen, and the prince highlights that fact by asking to "let me but see him first" before taking on the kingship, producing that sight (as others do not) as what alone can authorize his voice and give power to his "will" (5.2.97). Yet as Isabella affirms, with Mortimer and herself in charge, "it is impossible" (5.2.99). With the prince and protectorship up for grabs, Edward is denied a political relevance—until, that is, his son takes command and puts his name back on the throne.

Within the confines of prison too, Edward's history is pressed out of a political register into a private one. Like Richard II, who amid captivity is more poet than king, Edward (both before and after his deposition) eschews his role as king even as he attempts to sustain it. When he "call[s] to mind" (5.1.23) that he is a king, he fixates on the "transitory pomp" (5.1.108) and power of the post, asking the inevitable question (like Richard II and Lear after him), "What are kings, when regiment is gone?" (5.1.26). Though he repeatedly excoriates Mortimer and Isabella for usurping his "right" and his "kingdom without cause" (5.1.52–53), he simultaneously personalizes his displacement, defaming Mortimer and the "unconstant queen" for "spot[ting]" his "nuptial bed" (5.1.30–31). With no way and no one to intercede politically, he calls for Isabella's tears and sympathy, remembering when he "for her sake . . . ran at tilt in France" (5.5.71).

Disempowered and displaced, Edward is able to write himself into the position of political and sexual victim. Although his complicity in the crisis of power is not erased, it is softened and our sympathies toward him are encouraged. Detached from the problematic negotiations that have marked his rule, he becomes a private subject, tormented and abused, with Mortimer and Isabella taking on, with his power, his role as sexual and political transgressor. Though he calls to Gaveston, lamenting, "Oh Gaveston, it is for thee that I am wrong'd!" (5.3.41), sodomy, once detached from the political and confined within this private space, loses its incriminating edge. Edward himself revises his terms, insisting instead that it was "for me both thou and both the Spensers died!" (5.3.42), reminding us of what we already know—that it was "for him" and for his power that sodomy was enlisted. Taken out of context and out of the contest for power, sodomy no longer incriminates.

Regicide, however, does. Mortimer's attempts to give Edward's history an unseeable and unspeakable end fail precisely because they are thus separated from the public sphere, unspoken and unseen. Though as Isabella attests, "the murder"—the fact of the murder—"can not be hid" (5.6.46), the means, ironically, are. No one seems to know or care how the murder was effected or "what the matter ment," at least not as Mortimer construed it. The private has become too private, too much its own. When Edward III brings the crime out of the closet, he records only its political implications, dissociating the issue of sodomy from Edward's name.[49] It is Mortimer, in fact, who gets a pole up his head in a loaded public spectacle, establishing once and for all who the offender really is. The spectacle of sodomy, given point and poignancy as illegitimate punishment in a separate, unseeable space, becomes finally a spectacle for us—a spectacle that, instead of telling us what the matter meant, tells us what it did not mean.

"Kill not the king"

But what, outside of these political negotiations, does sodomy mean on Marlowe's stage? Marlowe initiates the drama with the figure of Gaveston, assigning him the theatrical space usually reserved for the alien hero. Just as Barabas and Faustus, after the prologues give way, stand up and identify themselves and their ambitions, bringing all their props of otherness out for show, so also does Gaveston, constructing a homoerotic spectacle that he will use to "draw the pliant king which way [he] please[s]" (1.1.53). Like Barabas and Faustus, instead of being easily readable, Gaveston is constituted by more than the sum of his parts, for his homoeroticism is deeply and inextricably enmeshed in politics. While this intermingling would seem to deny homoerotic desire a place of its own, it is in fact through the political that homoeroticism gains a separate space in this play. Strikingly, in the representations of both Gaveston and Edward, Marlowe begins to open up the stage, state, and status quo to the possibility of homosexuality.[50]

When Gaveston first steps onstage, his position is mediated by and mediator to the political. The letter of the king, calling him back ("My father is deceas'd. Come Gaveston, / And share the kingdom with thy dearest friend" [1.1.1–2]) defines and defends his place on the stage. And it is only when he "stand[s] aside" (1.1.73) to look and listen as Edward and the nobles begin their battle of wills that we are allowed to see the negotiations at court.[51] As it first takes definition, Gaveston's homoeroticism is thus sandwiched within the political as it is within the nobles' discourse, yet with a significant difference. Whereas the precise nature of his desire is lost within the nobility's obfuscating protests, here it is given a distinctive sexual shape.[52] Gaveston rejects, as "not men for me" (1.1.50), the three poor men, who identify themselves in terms of orthodox service and occupations, and then makes clear the kind of men who are for him: wanton poets, pages clad as sylvan nymphs, lovely boys, and so on. The Elder Mortimer is naive to think that Edward's favorites will not impede baronial power, but he is right to notice that Gaveston is indeed a "minion."[53]

That Gaveston is also a shrewd political player is somewhat problematic, rendering the sincerity of his desire suspect. Even as he declares his "great[est] bliss" (1.1.4) being called into the arms and bosom of "him I hold so dear" (1.1.13), he focuses on his own rise in social status and his transcendence of social codes, anticipating being safely "at enmity" "with the world" (1.1.15) and abjuring all "base stooping to the lordly peers"

(1.1.18). After Edward invests him with titles, Gaveston avows that it shall "suffice me to enjoy your love" (1.1.171); yet he embraces power in Tamburlainian fashion, seeing himself

> as great
> As Caesar riding in the Roman street
> With captive kings at his triumphant car.
> (1.1.172–74)

He later speculates, "Were I a king—" (1.4.27) and stops only because the outraged Mortimer cuts him off. Perhaps the most problematic moment comes when Gaveston, banished again, takes leave of the king in a private exchange. While he insists that his deepest sorrow is in leaving not England but Edward, "in whose gracious looks / The blessedness of Gaveston remains" (1.4.121–22), his concern is neither clearly personal nor clearly political. When given the opportunity, he refuses to stay under cover in England, as if the king's "gracious looks" are finally not enough. And he treats Edward's pity as a political accomplishment, noting that "'tis something to be pitied of *a king*" (1.4.131; emphasis added), privileging Edward's status over his desire.

Yet while Gaveston's engagement with power complicates the meaning of his desire, it does not erase it. In fact, it is because he is a political player that his homoeroticism gains a place in the story, and not just within the nobles' discourse. In *Dido*, Ganymede, having no part to play beyond his homoerotic "dandling," is practically dumped from Jupiter's lap as the colonialist contest begins, and he is soon replaced, heteroerotically, by Cupid (probably played by the same actor), who is necessary to Venus's imperialist ploys. In enmeshing Gaveston in the conflict of rule, Marlowe brings him in from the margins, refusing to relegate the homoerotic to the outside, as what "they" do. Indeed, Gaveston's political ambition aligns him with the power-hungry Mortimer, who also uses sexuality to his advantage, forging a vital political alliance through his sexual alliance with the queen. In Mortimer's case, too, it is impossible to know how far love extends beyond politics, but the issue is finally moot. For what is significant here is that sexuality, whether homoerotic or heteroerotic, implements power. In neither case is it obfuscated or erased; it sits in the center and on both sides of the contest, not distractingly other but crucially same.

So, too, does Edward's desire at once surface within his power plays and also stand outside them, more markedly, in fact, than does Gaveston's.[54] In the face of a second exile, Gaveston chooses to leave the king rather than see him only in secret; but Edward searches for other options, proposing first to come to him in exile and then to hide him in England. When his besieged favorite chooses instead to go, Edward becomes visibly "frantic" (1.4.317)—causing Lancaster to exclaim "*Diablo*, what passions call you these?" (4.1.321) and to underscore (with Marlowe's help) their unusual and unorthodox nature.

Though Lancaster will not give those "passions" a name, Marlowe gives them a place, especially as he sets them between Edward and Isabella, as disruptive to their (hetero)sexual bond. Lest we view this as a purely political marriage, like Gaveston's to Edward's niece, Marlowe gives Isabella a voice of desire that supersedes politics, having her look "in vain" for over half the play "for love at Edward's hand" (2.4.62). Gaveston and the desire he incites emerge as a direct challenge to that love. As soon as he first returns, Isabella is displaced from court and defines that displacement in terms of love. She complains to the nobles that "the king regards me not, / But dotes upon the love of Gaveston" (1.2.49–50) and elaborates with a scene of passion: "He claps his cheeks, and hangs about his neck, / Smiles in his face, and whispers in his ears" (1.2.51–52). Once again Marlowe highlights the unconventionality of the desire, having the nobles note (like Holinshed), despite themselves, how "strange" it is that the king "is thus bewitch'd" (1.2.55).[55]

Although Isabella speaks of and through desire throughout the play, the only place Edward allows her is political. In Gaveston's presence, he shuns her; in Gaveston's absence, he enlists her to fight for the favorite's return and, in effect, for her own sexual banishment. Isabella takes on the cause, affirming that if she does not, the king will "ne'er love me" (1.4.199). Clearly, however, even when she succesfully negotiates the return, he never does. In joining with her in a "second marriage" (1.4.337) after her success, he promises her a "golden tongue" (1.4.330), a symbol assigning her a use-value measured by her negotiating power and reducing her body to her tongue, her self to her political voice—with the proviso that she love Gaveston too.[56] In representing Edward's desire for Gaveston thus, as an impediment to his marriage, Marlowe gives the homoerotic bond meaning in a private/sexual space, allowing it to become the thing that defines Edward outside the kingship.

Importantly, however, although Marlowe sets Edward's desire outside the political, he does not condemn it (as the chronicle and nobles do) as an obstacle to rule, but instead brings the sexual back into the contest of rule. Like Mortimer and Gaveston, Edward emerges as a shrewd politician, able to use the sexual for political ends. Just as the nobles set Gaveston before him as a means of opposing his power, so too does he set Gaveston before them as a means of opposing theirs. In words and actions, he answers the Elder Mortimer's ultimatum, "If you love us, my lord, hate Gaveston" (1.1.80), with his own, "They love me not that hate my Gaveston" (2.2.37), embracing the other to exhibit the authorizing power of the self. Tellingly, when he first asks the nobles to "grant me this" (1.1.77), the repeal of Gaveston's exile, the request is already moot; Gaveston has been recalled and stands on the sidelines watching. Instead of a call for permission, Edward's request emerges as a test of obedience, a means of determining how far the peers will press their power and how far he can take his own. His polite meaningless words give way almost immediately to sterner stuff, and he, insisting that he "will have Gaveston," sets his embrace of the favorite up as a means of showing the nobles "what danger 'tis to stand against [their] king" (1.1.96–97). Though he clearly wants to "have" Gaveston, at stake are the parameters of his power. Again and again he raises the issue, asking, "Am I a king, and must be over-rul'd?" (1.1.135) and "Why should a king be subject to a priest?" (1.4.97).[57]

It is through Gaveston that Edward takes action. By displaying his transgressive desire, the king stakes his claim to an absolute authority that transcends all other social and political codes, and not just sexual mores. When the nobles raise the issue of class amid their wide-ranging charges and protest that no "man of noble birth can brook [the] sight" (1.4.12) of Gaveston—"hardly" "a gentleman by birth" (1.4.29)—sitting beside the king, Edward places his will above social hierarchies and threatens: "Were he a peasant, being my minion, / I'll make the proudest of you stoop to him" (1.4.30–31). Keenly aware of their antipathy, he orders the lords to welcome Gaveston home from the second exile with an official "stately triumph" (2.2.12). Though they attempt to subvert the occasion, displaying emblems of Gaveston as a canker to the royal tree, Edward turns the show against them, reminding them that he is that tree and warning them to

> shake me not too much;
> And you the eagles, soar ye ne'er so high,
> I have the jesses that will pull you down.
>
> (2.2.38–40)

With his turn to the Younger Spenser, the political motives behind Edward's displays of favor become particularly clear. The king embraces Spenser, literally and figuratively, in response to the news that the barons have murdered Gaveston, and vows that he will "stain [his] royal standard" (3.2.141) with their blood and "chastise them" "with fire and sword" (3.2.181–83), "march[ing] to make them stoop" (3.2.186). Though Spenser is no sodomite, Marlowe lowers his historically noble stature and makes him a former servant of the newly deceased Earl of Gloucester to make his rise comparably, though not sexually, transgressive. That the new favorite becomes a mouthpiece for absolute monarchical right at once complements and underlines Edward's strategies, revealing his favoritism as a means of power (as well as a product of desire) and not a sign of impotence.

Edward's single most incriminating move comes as he, in trying to avoid reinstating the banishment demanded by the lords, offers up the realm in exchange for "some nook or corner" in which "to frolic with [his] dearest Gaveston" (1.4.72–73), ostensibly sacrificing his kingdom for his minion and fulfilling everyone's worst fears (or in Mortimer's case, fondest hopes). Yet to see this gesture as self-effacing and sincere is to take it out of context. For significantly, Edward renounces his kingdom here only in order to retain it. Faced with the Archbishop of Canterbury's threat (backed by the Church) to "discharge [the] lords / Of duty and allegiance due to thee" (1.4.61–62) if he doesn't suscribe to the exile and knowing that, in the face of this power, "it boots [him] not to threat," he admits in an aside that he "must speak fair" (1.4.63). It is in and only in that "fair" speech that he pretends to value his friend and his frolicking above his realm. Tellingly, he agrees to the banishment after all, rather than lose his kingdom. And when left alone onstage, he casts off and so exposes the guise of submission, vowing to "fire [the] crazed buildings" of "Proud Rome," to force "the papal towers to kiss the lowly ground," and to fill "Tiber's channel" "with slaughter'd priests" (1.4.98–103). Though Gaveston is displaced and the pope obeyed, Edward remains in place and in power, deflecting deposition and disguising his own readiness to fight by assuming the guise of a king "love-sick for his minion" (1.4.87).

It is, ironically, by pressing Edward and Gaveston into the mainstream of the political while assigning them a private (homoerotic) bond that Marlowe legitimates the private and the homoerotic, reclaiming them from an obfuscating discourse in which they can only figure as corruption. Although Edward is "guilty" of exploiting homoeroticism for political gains as the nobles have done, it is not at the expense or through the erasure of his desire, as it is in their case. Rather, his maneuvers expose his own will to power and free the sexual of the public consequences the lords attempt to load upon it, proving him a ruler who, though homoerotically inclined, is not "lewdlie led" away from rule by his favor or his favorites. Instead he has it (and Gaveston) both ways, as a private subject of desire and a public object of negotiation, appropriating the thing that is not while displaying it as what it is—at least as much as seems possible in an era before homosexuality had a local habitation and a name. Whatever sodomitical leanings are in Marlowe, they are not politically corrupt. Though largely unspoken, they are not unspeakable.

Marlowe puts Edward (along with, though more than, Gaveston) in charge of his own otherness, allowing it to authorize the self in the way perhaps that Marlowe himself adopted as he wrote himself into the spectacular role of the atheistic sodomite. Authorized thus, the self becomes a matter of and for public record; but it is a record that allows for the private, giving homoerotic desire a non-problematic if not positive place outside, though through, the politic, defined and determined by the self. Though identity politics will always be politics, it is this idea of self-determination that Marlowe's plays finally support as they expose the constructs and oppose the authorities that would have it otherwise.

Conclusion

It seems appropriate to begin a study of Marlowe and imperialist self-fashioning with *Dido, Queen of Carthage* and to end with *Edward II*—to begin, that is, with an imperialist competition in Africa and to end with a political struggle in England, to begin with the coercive silencing of an other and to end with the exploitation of an other's otherwise silent sin, to begin with myth and to end with history. For what Marlowe's plays show, separately and together, is that the discourse of both external and internal domination, whether in the "dark continent" or on the English throne, was part of a continuum, inexorably dependent upon the circumscription of an other, whose silence was filled with meaning and whose difference was determined as much by myth as by history. As the wheel comes full circle, the bounds between cultural and cross-cultural negotiations blur. Like Tamburlaine's battlefields, Marlowe's plays seem "curiously alike"—not just because they, when viewed as ideology, expose an abstract, existential process, but more because they, when examined for their particular historical relevance, unveil a pervasive representational strategy that itself knew no cultural bounds—except, of course, those that it constructed.

The greatest difference between Elizabethan visions of European and non-European aliens is that at home the subject under question was caught up in a web of accusations that confused and conflated the essential aspects of his or her distinguishing otherness. While representations of sodomitical acts between the Indians of the "New World" generally isolated sodomy (like cannibalism) as a peculiar and peculiarly transgressive ritual, on the home front it was merged almost irretrievably with other offenses, making it difficult for us to determine whether the primary target of accusations of sodomy was sexual, social, political, religious, moral, or even economic. In witch-detecting discourse too, as Marlowe and Scot remind us, black magic was presented as a transgression not only against religion but also against other "orthodox" practices and doctrines such as medicine, law, and humanism. When prosecuted, its practitioners were charged, like sodomites, for other crimes as well, with sodomy, the most inconsistently defined of all, neither surprisingly nor coincidentally among them. Indeed, it seems no coincidence that Faustus's subversive desires and agendas are more difficult to identify than those of Dido, Tamburlaine, or Barabas, at least until Mephastophilis shows up to give them an anti-Christian and ultimately anti-demonic edge.

In contrast, the charges levied at non-European others are more unified and distinctive. While figures such as Tamburlaine or Bajazeth were met with mixed reactions, such types were defined primarily by how—and how barbarously—their politics were played out on the battlefield. And because the Africans were described largely in light of trade negotiations, the essential measure of their identity and of their necessary inferiority was the (always incriminating) degree of their innate civility. Though in these cases too unorthodox religion and villainy were sometimes called in to reinforce social, political, or, in the case of the Jew, economic offenses, designations of the otherness of non-Europeans centered on definable features to a degree that representations of European aliens did not.

This difference reminds us that while the "real" opponents in England's drive toward empire were, of course, the aliens abroad, it was the alien at home whose necessary presence complicated England's attempt to authorize and display its supremacy. Rather than being arbitrary or accidental, the vagueness and inclusiveness of attacks against such figures as the sodomite or conjurer suggest that these kinds of representations were shaped by two contradictory impulses. On the one hand, to spread the consequences of these figures' illicit deeds across several categories was to amplify the severity of those deeds and with it, the power of the authorities who were visibly able to contain them. On the other hand, however, to identify such transgressions in indeterminate terms was, to some degree, to mask them. On the foreign front, there was no need to obscure transgression; Africans could be intrinsically uncivilized and Turks intrinsically barbaric. At home, however, the visible circumscription of internal others conflicted with attempts to project otherness elsewhere, to bound off other worlds as undeniably unlike "ours." And what had to be denied even as it was displayed was the difference within—the horror that in the heart of darkness sat the English themselves, the horror that another Marlowe would uncover centuries later as British imperialism reached its height.

It is fitting then that Christopher Marlowe turns both to Africa and the East, to the two great others defining Europe, as well as to Europe

and England. For the discourses defining all are importantly intercon-
nected, all pointing back to England and to the idea that its difference
depended paradoxically upon an other's. In a few short years Marlowe
made a name for himself in the Renaissance theater, creating expectations
that whatever else happened, his plays would bring spectacles of strangeness to center stage. And it must have been telling to see a dramatist with
such a reputation choose a subject from English history and dramatize that
subject in ways similar to what he had done with more exotic types. However it was perceived, the shift was certainly subversive, evidencing what
makes each of his plays so important, both as a resisting voice to a dominant trend and as an indication of how that trend was manifest. For on
Marlowe's stage there is no denial of the difference within—no denial that
unspeakable acts are rendered unspeakable because of us not them, that
we are "to wonder at unlawful things" in order to see the supremacy of
England and of the status quo, that the darkness of the dark continent as
of the worlds beyond is "ours" rather than "theirs."

Notes

Chapter 1: Strange and Estranging Spectacles

1. I am referring to an often cited mass exodus at a performance of *Doctor Faustus*; see Chapter 4. Steven Mullaney suggests "*the* vernacular," which the learned regarded as "barbarous" in comparison to Latin, as estranged within popular culture because of its accommodation of a plurality of dialects and its continual assimilation of foreign terms; see Mullaney, *The Place of the Stage: License, Play, and Power in Renaissance England* (Chicago: University of Chicago Press, 1988), 76–85.

2. I borrow the phrase from Mullaney, who borrows it from Ben Jonson's description of the antimasque in the *Masque of Queens* (*Place of the Stage*, 64).

3. For an informative discussion of England's economic profile in the mid-sixteenth century, see J. A. Sharpe, *Early Modern England: A Social History 1550–1760* (London: Edward Arnold, 1987), esp. 127–51. Kenneth R. Andrews, *Trade, Plunder, and Settlement: Maritime Enterprise and the Genesis of the British Empire, 1480–1630* (Cambridge: Cambridge University Press, 1984), provides an excellent study of England's early imperialism. See also A. L. Rowse, *The Expansion of Elizabethan England* (London: Macmillan, 1955); James A. Williamson, *The Age of Drake* 2d ed. (London: Adam & Charles Black, 1946); and J. H. Parry, *The Age of Reconnaissance* (Berkeley: University of California Press, 1963).

4. The publication history of this text is offered in Margaret T. Hodgen, *Early Anthropology in the Sixteenth and Seventeenth Centuries* (Philadelphia: University of Pennsylvania Press, 1964), 132–33, which also provides a useful survey of other cross-cultural texts.

5. John Leo Africanus, *The History and Description of Africa and the Notable Things Therein Contained*, trans. John Pory, ed. Robert Brown (London, 1896), 935. The most prominent earlier translations of the Arabic original were Africanus's (1526) Italian version, introduced by Gian Battista Ramusio, the "Italian Hakluyt," in 1550, and Joannes Florianus's (1556) Latin version, which Pory used as the basis of his text. The circulation history is recorded in Brown's introduction (lii–lix); he labels this a "famous worke" on his title page.

6. Rowse, *Elizabethan England*, 159. Richard Helgerson, *Forms of Nationhood: The Elizabethan Writings of England* (Chicago: University of Chicago Press, 1992), 151–91, offers an excellent discussion of Hakluyt and his construction of English nationhood.

7. See Hodgen, *Early Anthropology*, 144–61, on Renaissance collecting.

8. See Mary B. Campbell, *The Witness and the Other World: Exotic European*

Travel Writing, 400–1600 (Ithaca, N.Y.: Cornell University Press, 1988), for a discussion of the ways these myths play into literary traditions.

9. Compare Tzvetan Todorov, *The Conquest of America: The Question of the Other* (New York: Harper & Row, 1984), 49–50, on the ways in which European colonialist texts both "revealed and rejected" cultural difference.

10. See Mullaney, *Place of the Stage*, 26–47.

11. Edward Said, *Orientalism* (New York: Vintage Books, 1978), 54. See also Paul Brown, "'This thing of darkness I acknowledge mine': *The Tempest* and the Discourse of Colonialism," in *Political Shakespeare: New Essays in Cultural Materialism*, ed. Jonathan Dollimore and Alan Sinfield (Ithaca, N.Y.: Cornell University Press, 1985), 48–71; and Stephen Greenblatt, "Invisible bullets: Renaissance Authority and Its Subversion, *Henry IV* and *Henry V*," also in *Political Shakespeare*, 18–47.

12. Robert Young, *White Mythologies: Writing History and the West* (London: Routledge, 1990), provides a useful critique of Said (along with Homi Bhabha, Gayatri Spivak, and others), suggesting that there are really two Orientalisms, one in which the Orient is the imaginary object of colonialist discourse and the other in which it is a real subject of colonialism; see 119–40.

13. Christopher Miller, *Blank Darkness: Africanist Discourse in French* (Chicago: University of Chicago Press, 1985), 14–23. Miller argues that Africa emerges in European discourse as the Other's other, a third term which has no meaning of its own and is inscribed like a blank slate from without.

14. Homi K. Bhabha, "The Other Question: The Stereotype and Colonial Discourse," *Screen* 24 (1983): 18–36. M. M. Bakhtin also offers a useful critique of monologic discourse; his essay on "Discourse in the Novel" in particular has informed my own theoretical position (*The Dialogic Imagination*, trans. Caryl Emerson and Michael Holquist, ed. Michael Holquist [Austin: University of Texas Press, 1981], 259–422).

15. Bhabha, "The Other Question," 23 (quoting Said), 18.

16. See, for example, Raphael Holinshed, *Chronicles of England, Scotland and Ireland* (London, 1807), 2:92, 419. Simon Shepherd, *Marlowe and the Politics of Elizabethan Theatre* (Sussex: Harvester Press, 1986), 142–45, gives a useful overview of the conflicted image of the Turk.

17. Miller, *Blank Darkness*, 64.

18. Compare Janet Adelman, *Suffocating Mothers: Fantasies of Maternal Origin in Shakespeare's Plays*, Hamlet *to* The Tempest (New York: Routledge, 1992), 176–92, who suggests that Antony is inscribed as absence and Cleopatra as presence.

19. For example, see Michael Neill, "Unproper Beds: Race, Adultery, and the Hideous in *Othello*," in *Shakespeare Quarterly* 40 (1989): 383–412, who prefers the term "racialism." See also Winthrop D. Jordan, *The White Man's Burden: Historical Origins of Racism in the United States* (New York: Oxford University Press, 1974) and *White Over Black: American Attitudes Toward the Negro, 1550–1812* (New York: W. W. Norton & Company, 1968).

20. See the Wakefield *Noah* in *The Wakefield Mystery Plays*, ed. Martial Rose (New York: W. W. Norton, 1961), 88–106; or the York *Flood, Herod and the Magi,*

The Slaughter of the Innocents, and *Christ Before Herod* in *York Mystery Plays: A Selection in Modern Spelling*, ed. Richard Beadle and Pamela M. King (Oxford: Clarendon Press, 1984).

21. From the epilogue, 2. David M. Bevington, *Tudor Drama and Politics: A Critical Approach to Topical Meaning* (Cambridge, Mass.: Harvard University Press, 1968), 156–57.

22. For an excellent study of the theater's social place and the ways other cultures were "rehearsed" within it, see Mullaney, *Place of the Stage*. Jean-Chritophe Agnew, *Worlds Apart: The Market and the Theater in Anglo-American Thought, 1550–1750* (Cambridge: Cambridge University Press, 1987), also gives an excellent discussion of the early theater's place in society. See also Michael Bristol, *Carnival and Theater: Plebian Culture and the Structure of Authority in Renaissance England* (New York: Methuen, 1985).

23. Muly Hamet appears in *The Famous History of the Life and Death of Captain Thomas Stuckeley*. See the discussion in Anthony Gerard Barthelemy, *Black Face, Maligned Race: The Representation of Blacks in English Drama from Shakespeare to Southerne* (Baton Rouge: Louisiana State University Press, 1987), 86–91.

24. I refer to the by now well-known allegation that in one performance an extra devil was conjured up; see John M. Bakeless, *The Tragicall History of Christopher Marlowe* (Cambridge, Mass.: Harvard University Press, 1942), 1:299–300.

25. For an intriguing discussion of the set speech, see Thomas Cartelli, "Ideology and Subversion in the Shakespearean Set Piece," *English Literary History* 53 (1986): 1–25.

26. Johannes Birringer, *Marlowe's Dr. Faustus and Tamburlaine: Theological and Theatrical Perspectives* (New York: Verlag Peter Lang, 1984), 105. Harry Levin's claim for hyperbole as Marlowe's dominating mode has influenced other critics—such as Frank Fieler, C. L. Barber, and William Blackburn—to see the plays as expressing either attainable or unattainable hyperbolic possibilities. See Levin, *The Overreacher: A Study of Christopher Marlowe* (Cambridge, Mass.: Harvard University Press, 1952). Even critics who adopt a darker view of the Elizabethan and Marlovian "world picture" emphasize the hyperbolic dimensions of Marlovian drama, finding within it communities of "supervillain[s] among knaves" (William Godshalk, *The Marlovian World Picture* [The Hague: Mouton, 1974], 28), patterns of obsessive histrionic "ravishment" (Michael Goldman, "Marlowe and the Histrionics of Ravishment" in *Two Renaissance Mythmakers: Christopher Marlowe and Ben Jonson*, ed. Alvin Kernan [Baltimore: Johns Hopkins University Press, 1977], 23), provocations of "over-inflated" audience expectations (Judith Weil, *Christopher Marlowe: Merlin's Prophet* [Cambridge: Cambridge University Press, 1977], 1), representations of extraordinary disasters, and stage properties which suggest metonymically, allegorically, and hyperbolically more than they show (Felix Bosonnet, *The Function of Stage Properties in Christopher Marlowe's Plays* [Switzerland: Franche Verlag Bern, 1978], 84–89).

27. For discussion of Marlowe's association with the School of Night (or, as it was also called, of atheism), see William Urry, *Christopher Marlowe and Canterbury*, ed. Andrew Butcher (London: Faber & Faber, 1988), 69–71.

28. From *Acts of the Privy Council*, quoted in C. F. Tucker Brooke, *The Life of Marlowe and the Tragedy of Dido, Queen of Carthage* (New York: Gordian Press, 1930), 58. Other useful biographies include: Bakeless, *Tragicall History*; A. L. Rowse, *Christopher Marlowe: His Life and Work* (New York: Harper & Row, 1964); Urry, *Marlowe and Canterbury*; and Frederick Boas, *Christopher Marlowe: A Biographical and Critical Study* (Oxford: Clarendon Press, 1940).

29. Kyd's letters to Sir John Puckering and the Baines note are cited in Brooke, *Life of Marlowe*, 98–108. See also Urry, *Marlowe and Canterbury*, 71–79.

30. Brooke, *Life of Marlowe*, 101; David Riggs, "Authorship, Atheism and Tamburlaine," a paper presented at the annual Shakespeare Association of America Convention, Vancouver, British Columbia, 23 March 1991.

31. Brooke, *Life of Marlowe*, 113.

32. Jonathan Goldberg, "Sodomy and Society: The Case of Christopher Marlowe," *Southwest Review* 69 (1984): 377.

33. See Leah S. Marcus, "Textual Indeterminacy and Ideological Difference: The Case of *Doctor Faustus*," *Renaissance Drama* 20 (1989): 16, who quotes the libel.

34. From the "glosse" on the "Sonet" appended to the *New Letter of Notable Contents* (1593), reproduced in Brooke, *Life of Marlowe*, 111–12. The point of these poems is not very clear; Brooke declares them "cloudy drivel" (112).

35. Urry surveys these "facts," the documents which record them, and the theories built around them (*Marlowe and Canterbury*, 80–98).

36. Ibid., 98.

37. Sometime before 1633, Thomas Heywood added a prologue to *The Jew of Malta*, "crav[ing] pardon" for "so boldly dar[ing]" to reanimate a figure and a play which "hath pass'd so many censures"; from the "Prologue Spoken at Court," in E. D. Pendry's edition of Marlowe's *Complete Plays and Poems* (London: J. M. Dent & Sons, 1976), 5. In an introduction to *The Jew of Malta*, N. W. Bawcutt, ed. (Baltimore: Johns Hopkins University Press, 1978), 2, reads this as an apology for the play's old-fashionedness. The accompanying epilogue, however, with its disclaimer that "if aught here offend . . . / We only act and speak what others write," suggests more subversive reasons for rebuke.

38. Stephen Greenblatt, *Renaissance Self-Fashioning: From More to Shakespeare* (Chicago, University of Chicago Press, 1980), 194. See also Shepherd, who tries "to lose Marlowe's works within a wider context" of "the politics of Elizabethan theatre," situates the plays amidst a variety of cultural documents and dramatic traditions, and begins to explore the relation between the audience, dominant Elizabethan ideologies, and "the questioning/affirming strategies of the individual text" (*Marlowe and the Politics of Elizabethan Theatre*, xvii–xviii). In covering such a vast ideologic and dramatic terrain, his study, though useful, does indeed "lose" Marlowe's works and at times the full impact of the contexts in which they are situated. Jonathan Dollimore's chapter on *Faustus* in *Radical Tragedy: Religion, Ideology and Power in the Drama of Shakespeare and His Contemporaries* (Chicago: University of Chicago Press, 1984), has also contributed to the rehistoricizing of Marlowe, and I will return to his argument in Chapter 5.

39. Greenblatt, *Renaissance Self-Fashioning*, 212, 197, 203.

40. These terms come from Keir Elam, *The Semiotics of Theatre and Drama*

(London: Methuen, 1980), 17–18, who argues that "when theatrical semiosis is alienated, made 'strange' rather than automatic, the spectator is encouraged to take note of the semiotic *means*, to become aware of the sign-vehicle and its operations."

41. Other critics have also suggested that the plays "encourag[e] the spectators to compare what they see with what the characters see," but without respect to external codes and to different ends than I propose here (Weil, *Merlin's Prophet*, 19).

42. A. M. Nagler, *Shakespeare's Stage*, enlarged ed. (New Haven: Yale University Press, 1981), 32–37; Alan Dessen, *Elizabethan Stage Conventions and Modern Interpreters* (Cambridge: Cambridge University Press, 1984), 84–104; Michael Hattaway, *Elizabethan Popular Theatre: Plays in Performance* (London: Routledge & Kegan Paul, 1982), 34–40.

43. Elam, citing the Russian formalist and folklorist Petr Bogatyrev, argues that "even in the most determinedly realistic of dramatic representations," theatrical signs "point beyond the denotation to some ulterior cultural signification" (*Semiotics of Theatre*, 10).

44. Greenblatt, *Renaissance Self-Fashioning*, 195–96.

45. Bevington discusses this group of plays and their use of setting in *Tudor Drama and Politics*, 156–57, cited above. Marlowe's *Tamburlaine* plays follow in the tyrant play tradition.

46. All references to *Damon and Pythias* are from Robert Dodsley, *A Select Collection of Old English Plays*, 4th ed., ed. W. Carew Hazlitt (London: Reeves & Turner, 1874), 11–104.

47. Simon Shepherd, *Amazons and Warrior Women: Varieties of Feminism in Seventeenth Century Drama* (New York: St. Martin's Press, 1981), 13.

48. Marlowe's texts have invited comparisons to Spenser before; see, for example, Roy Battenhouse, *Marlowe's Tamburlaine: A Study in Renaissance Moral Philosophy* (Nashville, Tenn.: Vanderbilt University Press, 1941), 178–92.

49. Hattaway presents convincing—though, as he admits, not conclusive—evidence that the dragon may have been brought onstage with Mephostophilis, as an ominous sign of "the powers which [Faustus] has unleashed" but, ironically, does not see or does not fear (*Elizabethan Popular Theatre*, 171).

50. Muriel C. Bradbrook, "*The Jew of Malta* and *Edward II*," in *Marlowe: A Collection of Critical Essays*, ed. Clifford Leech (Englewood Cliffs, N.J.: Prentice Hall, 1964), 127. For example, Levin, who sees the historicity of the material as a constraint upon the playwright's "artistic conception," argues that Edward is "more deeply grounded within the psychological range of his creator" and that his "sensations are relayed to us more fully and faithfully" (*The Overreacher*, 86–87). J. B. Steane sets the play apart for its "unelaborated prosaic manner" (*Marlowe: A Critical Study* [Cambridge: Cambridge University Press, 1964], 213), and Claude J. Summers for "examin[ing] the very center of Tudor political concerns . . . with an immediacy which his plays set in the Orient and Malta necessarily lack" (*Christopher Marlowe and the Politics of Power* [Salzburg: Institut für Englische Sprache und Literatur, 1974], 155).

51. See, for example, Constance Kuriyama, *Hammer or Anvil: Psychological*

Patterns in Christopher Marlowe's Plays (New Brunswick, N.J.: Rutgers University Press, 1980), 195.

52. This is the costume recorded on the Henslowe property list; see Hattaway, *Elizabethan Popular Drama*, 86.

53. Miller, *Blank Darkness*, 131.

54. Dollimore, too, suggests Marlovian drama as an important antecedent to Jacobean tragedy (*Radical Tragedy*, 119).

55. Jacques Derrida, *Dissemination*, trans. Barbara Johnson (Chicago: University of Chicago Press, 1981), 25.

56. I am evoking Lancaster's assertion that "in no respect can contraries be true" (*Edward II* 1.4.251).

57. Marjorie Garber discusses the implications of audience complicity in "'Vassal Actors': The Role of Audience in Shakespearean Tragedy" in *Renaissance Drama* 9 (1978): 71–89.

58. Marlowe's plays stand, in this regard (among others), in contrast to Shakespeare's later tragedies in which, as Richard Hapgood has suggested, the "dramatic life is so generally distributed" that the plays encourage a variety of identifications or experiences ("Shakespeare and the Included Spectator," in *Reinterpretations of Elizabethan Drama*, ed. Norman Rabkin [New York: Columbia University Press, 1969], 126).

59. Goldman, "Histrionics of Ravishment," 24.

60. My approach clearly departs from that of Spivak and the "subaltern studies" group, who are interested in recuperating that voice. See Gayatri Chakravorty Spivak, *In Other Worlds: Essays in Cultural Politics* (New York: Routledge, 1988) and *The Post-Colonial Critic: Interviews, Strategies, Dialogues*, ed. Sarah Harasym (New York: Routledge, 1990).

61. Because the dating of the plays is so uncertain, I have made no attempt to organize them chronologically, except in the case of *Dido* and *Tamburlaine*, which are generally accepted as the first and second of Marlowe's plays. I have chosen also not to treat *The Massacre at Paris* at great length because of the problems of the text. Though the play can be safely attributed to Marlowe, there is much uncertainty about whether the existing text has been somehow "mangled" by him or others; see Bakeless, *Tragicall History*, 1:69–71.

62. Shepherd, *Marlowe and the Politics of Elizabethan Theatre*, 182; see also 178–197.

63. See, for example, the recent Indigo Girls' song, "Ghost," *Rites of Passage* (Sony Music Entertainment, 1992).

Chapter 2: Reproducing Africa

1. Critics generally assign *Dido* to this early period. See, for example, H. J. Oliver's introduction to his edition of *Dido, Queen of Carthage and The Massacre at Paris* (Cambridge, Mass.: Harvard University Press, 1968), xx–xxvi.

2. Because "colonialism" emerges from "imperialism," I treat the two as parts of a continuum. Strictly speaking, the travel narratives I focus on below are

part of an imperialist, and the play, colonialist (or anti-colonialist) discourse, but the strategies and agendas they employ or address are essentially the same.

3. I borrow the terminology from M. M. Bakhtin, *The Dialogic Imagination*, trans. Caryl Emerson and Michael Holquist, ed. Michael Holquist (Austin: University of Texas Press, 1981), following the model of Peter Hulme in *Colonial Encounters: Europe and the Native Caribbean, 1492–1797* (London: Methuen, 1986), whose work on colonialist discourse has vitally informed my own.

4. Hulme, *Colonial Encounters*; Tzvetan Todorov, *The Conquest of America: The Question of the Other* (New York: Harper & Row, 1984); Stephen Greenblatt, "Learning to Curse: Aspects of Linguistic Colonialism in the Sixteenth Century," in *Learning to Curse: Essays in Early Modern Culture* (New York: Routledge, 1990). As Hulme writes: "Such a monologic encounter can only masquerade as a dialogue: it leaves no room for alternative voices" (p. 9). See also: James A. Boon, *Other Tribes, Other Scribes: Symbolic Anthropology in the Comparative Study of Cultures, Histories, Religions, and Texts* (Cambridge: Cambridge University Press, 1982) and Mary Louise Pratt, "Scratches on the Face of the Country; or What Mr. Barrow Saw in the Land of the Bushmen," *Critical Inquiry* 12 (1985): 119–43.

5. Hulme, *Colonial Encounters*, 166.

6. All quotations from Richard Hakluyt, *The Principal Navigations, Voyages, Traffiques & Discoveries of the English Nation* (Glasgow: James Maclehose & Sons, 1903–5), in this chapter are from volume 6.

7. Hulme, *Colonial Encounters*, 21; Christopher Miller, *Blank Darkness: Africanist Discourse in French* (Chicago: University of Chicago Press, 1985), introduced in Chapter 1 above. Hulme sets the "discourse of savagery" beside the "discourse of Oriental civilization" as "archives of topics and motifs that can be traced back to the classical period"; see also pp. 13–43.

8. See, for example, Edmund Hogan's account of his encounter with the Moorish emperor, Mully Abdelmelech (Hakluyt, *Principal Navigations*, 285–93).

9. From Joannes Boemus, *The Fardle of Facions*, trans. William Waterman (New York: Da Capo Press, 1970). This text has no page numbers; all quotations come from the section on "Affricke" unless otherwise noted. The mythic Christian emperor, Prester John, appears again and again in representations of Africa as sort of a cult hero, alive and well from the twelfth to the seventeenth[!] centuries, civilizing the heart of Ethiopia (often described as Africa's darkest region). For an excellent discussion of this myth and its significances, see Miller, *Blank Darkness*, 34–39, 58–62.

10. From the preface, Boemus, *The Fardle of Facions*.

11. Margaret T. Hodgen, *Early Anthropology in the Sixteenth and Seventeenth Centuries* (Philadelphia: University of Pennsylvania Press, 1964), 131–43, suggests that Boemus's description of laws and customs, which emerged at the same time as Machiavelli, is designed also to promote "improved political morality."

12. I discuss these differences and similarities at greater length in "Imperialist Beginnings: Richard Hakluyt and the Construction of Africa," *Criticism* 34 (1992): 517–38.

13. A subsequent account mentions "certaine wild Negros not accustomed to trade," suggesting an equivalence between being "wild" and being "not accustomed to trade" (Hakluyt, *Principal Navigations*, 215). Hulme and others have

documented how this divide functions in New World discourse. Todorov argues that "adjectives of the *good/wicked* type teach us nothing; not only because these qualities depend on the point of view adopted but also because they correspond to specific states and not to stable characteristics, because they derive from the pragmatic estimate of a situation and not from the desire to know" (*The Conquest of America*, 38).

14. See my essay, "Making More of the Moor: Aaron, Othello, and Renaissance Refashionings of Race," *Shakespeare Quarterly* 41 (1990): 438–42.

15. For a discussion of the play's sources, see John M. Bakeless, *The Tragicall History of Christopher Marlowe* (Cambridge, Mass.: Harvard University Press, 1942), 2:58–64.

16. Chaucer follows Ovid and his emphasis on love stands in contrast also to what we find in Virgil and Marlowe. He uses the tale in *The House of Fame* to "speke of love" (*The Works of Geoffrey Chaucer* 2d ed., ed. F. N. Robinson [Boston: Houghton Mifflin Company, 1957], 247) and similarly in *The Legend of Good Women* to address the question of what makes "sely wemen, ful of innocence, / Ful of pite, or trouthe, and conscience," trust men (*Works of Geoffrey Chaucer*, 1254–55).

17. All translations are from Allen Mandelbaum, trans. *The Aeneid of Virgil* (Berkeley: University of California Press, 1971, translation copyright © 1971 by Allen Mandelbaum), and are reprinted with the permission of Allen Mandelbaum and Bantam Books, a division of Bantam Doubleday Dell Publishing Group, Inc. I have used Publius Vergilius Maro, *The Aeneid*, ed. J. W. Mackail (Oxford: Clarendon Press, 1930) in citing the original Latin text. Because the line numbers of these editions vary, the translations are marked with Mandelbaum's numeration and the Latin text with Mackail's.

18. "bellum ingens geret Italia populosque ferocis / contundet moresque viris et moenia ponet" (1:263–64).

19. "rerum dominos" (1:282); "his ego nec metas rerum nec tempora pono: / imperium sine fine dedi" (1:278–79).

20. Hulme, *Colonial Encounters*, 249. See also Richard Monti, *The Dido Episode and the Aeneid: Roman Social and Political Values in the Epic* (Leiden, Neth.: E. J. Brill, 1981), which Hulme draws on.

21. Hulme, *Colonial Encounters*, 253.

22. "quam tu urbem, soror, hanc cernes, quae surgere regna / coniugio tali! Teucrum comitantibus armis / Punica se quantis attollet gloria rebus!" (4:47–49).

23. "hoc praeteixt nomine culpam" (4:172). Richard Stanyhurst, *The First Four Books of the Aeneid of Virgil* (Edinburgh, 1877), 97. Mandelbaum's translation (of "*culpam*" as "fault") is clearly more faithful to the Latin.

24. Mackail makes this point about the role of "Elemental Powers" (*Aeneid*, 138, n. 166).

25. "turpique cupidine captos" (4:194); "tam ficti pravique tenax quam nuntia veri" (4:188).

26. "neque enim specie famave movetur" (4:170).

27. "nec coniugis umquam / praetendi taedas aut haec in foedera veni" (4:338–39).

28. "hoc solum nomen quoniam de coniuge restat" (4:324).

29. Though the play was once received as a "slavish" dramatization of Virgil,

critics now recognize important differences. See, for example: Christopher Leech, *Christopher Marlowe: Poet for the Stage*, ed. Anne Lancashire (New York: AMS Press, 1986), 26–41, and Mary Elizabeth Smith, *"Love Kindling Fire": A Study of Christopher Marlowe's* The Tragedy of Dido Queen of Carthage (Salzburg: Institut für Englische Sprache und Literatur, 1977), 74.

30. Critics have often commented on the diminution of the gods' omnipotence and grandeur. See, for example, Simon Shepherd, *Marlowe and the Politics of Elizabethan Theatre* (Sussex: Harvester Press, 1986), 52, and Smith, *"Love Kindling Fire"*, 59–83.

31. I discuss this further in Chapter 6.

32 Stephen Greenblatt categorizes Aeneas along with Barabas as the "alien," without noting what seem essential differences in their types (*Renaissance Self-Fashioning: From More to Shakespeare* [Chicago: University of Chicago Press, 1980], 194). Barabas, like each of Marlowe's other heroes, represents a type culturally circumscribed as other, but Aeneas does not. As I discuss below, the play makes an issue of his dual position as at once the insider, relative to Europe, and the outsider, relative to Carthage, bringing out the relativity and subjectivity of any such designation.

33. See Hulme, *Colonial Encounters*, 167, and Todorov, *The Conquest of America*, 29.

34. Ironically, his attempts to bound off a symbolic Troy stand in contrast to his countrymen's fatal failure to enforce the physical boundaries of Troy, for they willingly embraced both "false" Sinon and the "Trojan" horse full of Greeks within their city's walls.

35. Elsewhere, he reports that Pyrrhus's harness is "dropping blood" (2.1.214); Hecuba is "hanging" on his eyelids and "howling" as she is swung into the "empty air" (2.1.245, 248); Priam is "beating" his breast and "falling on the ground" with her, and "forgetting both his want of strength and hands" (2.1.228, 252). Aeneas reenforces this immediacy by voicing Greek and Trojan cries, which twice elicit Dido's interjections. Gerald Pinciss has also noted the prevalence of participles, suggesting that they create a sense of "frenzied activity" (*Christopher Marlowe* [New York: Frederick Ungar Publishing Co., 1975], 115).

36. "Aeneas, quamquam lenire dolentem / solando cupit et dictis avertere curas, / multa gemens magnoque animum labefactus amore" (4:393–95).

37. One might compare Marlowe's juxtaposition of Aeneas and Dido to Shakespeare's juxtaposition of Antony and Cleopatra, in *Antony and Cleopatra*, which revolves around a similar polarization of worlds. For various interpretations of how that division is schematized, see: Richard P. Wheeler, "'Since first we were dissevered': Trust and Autonomy in Shakespearean Tragedy and Romance" and Madelon Gohlke, "'I wooed thee with my sword': Shakespeare's Tragic Paradigms," both in *Representing Shakespeare: New Psychoanalytic Essays*, ed. Murray Schwartz and Coppelia Kahn (Baltimore: Johns Hopkins University Press, 1980), 150–87). See also John Danby, "*Antony and Cleopatra*: A Shakespearian Adjustment," in *Modern Shakespearean Criticism: Essays on Style, Dramaturgy, and the Major Plays*, ed. Alvin B. Kernan (New York: Harcourt, Brace, Jovanovich, 1970), 407–27.

38. For further discussion of Carthaginian history and myths, see A. H. L.

Heeren, *Historical Researches into the Politics, Intercourse, and Trade of the Carthaginians, Ethiopians and Egyptians* (New York: Negro Universities Press, 1969), and B. H. Warmington, *Carthage*, rev. ed. (New York: Frederick A. Praeger Publishers, 1969).

39. See also *Dido* 5.1.279–82.

40. Irus, as J. B. Steane notes, was "a beggar who fought Ulysses" (Christopher Marlowe, *The Complete Plays*, ed. J. B. Steane [Baltimore: Penguin Books, 1975], 56).

41. The degree of Cupid's influence is highly questionable. Though he does eroticize the relation and, when he touches Dido with his arrow, cause her to vacillate erratically from embracing to rejecting Iarbas too, his impact is greatest on the nurse. As Shepherd has suggested, Marlowe privileges human agency over the interventions of the gods (*Marlowe and the Politics of Elizabethan Theatre*, 52). The eroticism that Cupid inspires feeds into rather than disrupts Dido's agenda, fueling the sexual discourse she has already initiated as a means to her political ends.

42. She might be anticipating citizen resistance to a "mixed" marriage rather than to an illicit bond.

43. "sperate deos memores fandi atque nefandi" (1:543).

Chapter 3: East of England

1. I have chosen to treat the two parts both separately (in separate sections) and together (in the same chapter) because they were produced both separately and together. While the chances are good that Marlowe intended to construct a two-part play, the first part was often performed as a separate unit. For a useful discussion of how *Tamburlaine* fits into a tradition of two- (and even four-) part plays, see Mary Thomas Crane, "The Shakespearean Tetralogy," *Shakespeare Quarterly* 36 (1985): 282–99.

2. The seminal work on Europe's confrontation with the East is Edward Said, *Orientalism* (New York: Vintage Books, 1978), preceded by Raymond Schwab, *La Renaissance orientale*. The translation (*The Oriental Renaissance: Europe's Rediscovery of India and the East, 1680–1880*, trans. Gene Patterson-Black and Victor Reinking [New York: Columbia University Press, 1984]), which I have used, includes an interesting foreword by Said.

3. For a brief survey of this activity, see editor Richard David's "General Introduction" to *Hakluyt's Voyages* (Boston: Houghton Mifflin Company, 1981), 17–32.

4. Schwab's "Oriental Renaissance" is a second Renaissance (not a description of the first), engendered by the recovery and decoding of Eastern civilization. While Said looks primarily at the ways Europe projected its own negative image onto the East, Schwab sees Orientalism as a positive, culturally enriching embrace of an extraordinary civilization. Their differences may derive in part from the ways they circumscribe the Orientalist field, which for Schwab is primarily

academic and for Said, more broadly and politically based. Yet the divergence also points to the ambivalence of Europe's visions of the East, discussed below.

5. Samuel Chew, *The Crescent and the Rose: Islam and England during the Renaissance* (New York: Oxford University Press, 1937), which informs my discussion, offers an extensive survey of Renaissance England's knowledge and experience of the Orient.

6. Chew discusses this impact of Christianity (*The Crescent and the Rose*, 55–99).

7. See Margaret T. Hodgen, *Early Anthropology in the Sixteenth and Seventeenth Centuries* (Philadelphia: University of Pennsylvania Press, 1964), 17–77, 111–54.

8. See Richard Hakluyt, *The Principal Navigations, Voyages, Traffiques & Discoveries of the English Nation* (Glasgow: James Maclehose & Sons, 1903–5), volume I, in particular.

9. Both the expenditures for the Turkish costumes and the composition of Gascoigne's masque occurred in 1571, probably as a celebratory result of the Turkish setback at Lepanto (Chew, *The Crescent and the Rose*, 125–27).

10. For a useful survey of the Renaissance's "Eastern" plays, see Robert Cawley, *The Voyagers and Elizabethan Drama* (London: Oxford University Press, 1938), 107–231, and Chew, *The Crescent and the Rose*, 469–540.

11. Quoted in Chew, *The Crescent and the Rose*, 484.

12. Peter Hulme, *Colonial Encounters: Europe and the Native Caribbean, 1492–1797* (London: Methuen, 1986), 21.

13. Said gives more credit to both sides than does Schwab, and admits that the darker side of the vision pertains mostly to Islam (*Orientalism*, 70).

14. See Chew, *The Crescent and the Rose*, 205–38.

15. In a vigorously anti-Moslem appendix to his translation of Africanus's *Geographical Historie of Africa*, John Pory, for example, divides Mohammedanism into four sects: the Turkish, which is "libertine" and martial; the Tartarian, which is simple; the Arabian, which is "most superstitious and jealous"; and the Persian, which "stand[s] more upon reason and nature" (John Leo Africanus, *The History and Description of Africa and the Notable Things Therein Contained*, trans. John Pory, ed. Robert Brown [London, 1896], 1010). See also Chew, *The Crescent and the Rose*, 223–38.

16. See Simon Shepherd, *Marlowe and the Politics of Elizabethan Theatre* (Sussex: Harvester Press, 1986), 143–44. For further discussion of the manifestations of anti-Moslem and anti-Ottoman sentiment, particularly as they intersected with the discourse on blackness, see Anthony Gerard Barthelemy, *Black Face, Maligned Race: The Representation of Blacks in English Drama from Shakespeare to Southerne* (Baton Rouge: Louisiana State University Press, 1987), 1–17, and Elliot H. Tokson, *The Popular Image of the Black Man in English Drama, 1550–1688* (Boston: G. K. Hall, 1982), 106–19.

17. George Whetstone also excoriates Mahomet for his "devilish policies" which finally were "nourished with the blood of many thousands" (*The English Mirror* [London, 1586], 55). Whetstone's account is a recounting of the version in Thoman Fortescue's *The Foreste*, which itself is a rather loose translation of Pedro

Mexia's *Silva de varia lecion* (1544). Marlowe may have used any of these, but critics usually accept Whetstone as the most likely source. See: T. C. Izard, "The Principal Source for Marlowe's *Tamburlaine*" in *Modern Language Notes* 58 (1943): 411–17; John D. Jump's introduction to *Tamburlaine the Great, Parts I and II* (Lincoln: University of Nebraska, 1967); and John M. Bakeless, *The Tragicall History of Christopher Marlowe* (Cambridge, Mass.: Harvard University Press, 1942), 1:204–5, who differs with this "commonly received opinion."

18. "The Queen's Letter to the great Turke 1582," reprinted in Hakluyt, *Principal Navigations*, 5:226.

19. The quote is from the letter cited above (n. 18), in Hakluyt, *Principal Navigations*, 5:227. The second letter mentioned here and quoted below is "The answere of her Majestie to the aforesaid Letters of the Great Turke, sent the 25 of October 1579," in Hakluyt, *Principal Navigations*, 5:175–78.

20. Hakluyt, *Principal Navigations*, 5:177.

21. The summation of Perondinus is from Jump's introduction, *Tamburlaine*, xiii.

22. The full subtitle reads, "A Regard wherein all estates may beholde the Conquestes of Envy."

23. Other treatments of the text's ambivalence include: David M. Bevington, *From "Mankind" to Marlowe: Growth of Structure in the Popular Drama of Tudor England* (Cambridge, Mass.: Harvard University Press, 1962); William Godshalk, *The Marlovian World Picture* (The Hague: Mouton, 1974); Charles G. Massington, *Christopher Marlowe's Tragic Vision: A Study in Damnation* (Athens: Ohio University Press, 1972); and Shepherd, *Marlowe and the Politics of Elizabethan Theatre*, 151–52.

24. Compare Lawrence Benaquist, who also argues that the play offers no prefabricated "ethical standards," but who suggests that the spectators are pressed to tolerate and admire Tamburlaine nonetheless (*The Tripartite Structure of Christopher Marlowe's* Tamburlaine *Plays and* Edward II [Salzburg: Institut für Englische Sprache und Literatur, 1975], 22).

25. Their destructiveness does not seem quite as severe here as it is for Tamburlaine's foes in Part 2, where, as I argue below, the violence escalates and becomes the modus operandi of imperialism across the board. In each case, however, the civility or incivility of Tamburlaine's actions seems comparable to that of his competitors.

26. David Thurn, "Sights of Power in *Tamburlaine*," *English Literary Renaissance* 19 (1989): 5, 8. Thurn's work on spectacle in Marlowe is stellar.

27. Tamburlaine also embraces the soldan as the "happy father of Zenocrate" and rewrites Egypt's political defeat as a familial victory, declaring the role of father "higher than thy Soldan's name"—higher, that is, than the name Tamburlaine has divested of power and meaning (5.2.372–73).

28. I am referring to *Tamb.* 5.2.97–127. For other readings of the effect of this turn, see Godshalk, *The Marlovian World Picture*, 122–23, and Benaquist, *Tripartite Structure in* Tamburlaine *and* Edward II, 66–67.

29. Their exchange at this point is also reciprocally eroticized. Bajazeth swears that he will turn Tamburlaine into his "chaste and lustless eunuch" (3.3.77),

and Tamburlaine refuses to say "how I'll handle thee," but assures him that "every common soldier" will smile to see it (3.3.85).

30. See their interchange, *Tamb.* 1.2.138–251.

31. See, for example, Thurn, "Sights of Power in *Tamburlaine*"; Stephen Greenblatt, *Renaissance Self-Fashioning: From More to Shakespeare* (Chicago: University of Chicago Press, 1980), 210–13; Bevington, *From "Mankind" to Marlowe*, 208; and Harry Levin, *The Overreacher: A Study of Christopher Marlowe* (Cambridge, Mass.: Harvard University Press, 1952), 31–53.

32. See *Tamb.* 2.5.50–54.

33. The soldan's use of myth aggrandizes his position while defaming Tamburlaine's. If Tamburlaine is the Calydonian boar, the Egyptians become the "brave Argolian knights" who heroically saved their homeland, and if Tamburlaine is "the wolf that angry Themis sent / To waste and spoil sweet Aonian fields," the Egyptians are Cephalus and the "lusty Theban youths" who saved Thebes (as they cannot save Egypt) from a terrorizing beast.

34. The parallel scenes are: *Tamb.* 1:1.2, 2:1.3, and 2:3.4.

35. See *Tamb.* 1:1.2.87–105 and 2:1.3.28–53.

36. Others have noticed the emphasis on these accruing numbers but accept them as an affirmation rather than a destabilization of power. See, for example, Frank Fieler, *Tamburlaine, Part I and Its Audience* (Gainesville: University of Florida Press, 1961), 30. The account-taking is uniquely precise in Part 2, where the precision of the numbers undermines their limitlessness and their saturation undermines their meaningfulness.

37. See his description of Tamburlaine's "world of people," 2:1.1.67–76.

38. We must take Tamburlaine's word on this, since the retreat happens off-stage, but the fact that Callapine, after exiting to do battle, "re-enter[s] presently" lends credence to Tamburlaine's report (stage direction).

39. Greenblatt, *Renaissance Self-Fashioning*, 202. If this is Mahomet's revenge, he is otherwise falling down on his duty, for Callapine's defeat leaves the Mahometan empire in ruins.

40. See my discussion of Robert Greene's attack on Marlowe in Chapter 1.

41. As King of Persia he plans to direct his empire-building from his "native city Samarcanda" (2:4.3.107), a city northeast of Persia but under Persian rule. While hoping still to become "emperor of the three-fold world" (2:4.3.118) of Africa, Asia, and Europe, he anticipates making it a "princely seat," "famous through the furthest continents" (2:4.3.109–10), with treasures collected from all parts of the conquered Eastern world.

42. This is the mission Whetstone assigns him. Unlike his predecessor in Part 1, the Tamburlaine of Part 2 seems almost to have read, and incorporated into his own self-presentation, Whetstone's vision of his rule—a vision whose unity both parts of the play (as well as Whetstone's text itself) disrupt.

43. Peter Donaldson, "Conflict and Coherence: Narcissism and Tragic Structure in Marlowe" in *Narcissism and the Text: Studies in Literature and the Psychology of Self*, ed. Lynne Layton and Barbara Ann Shapiro (New York: New York University Press, 1989), 39.

44. William Armstrong, who also points to this as "the dominant image in

Part Two," notes the significance of the chariot as a sign of "the pride that must take a fall" in *Marlowe's* Tamburlaine*: The Image and the Stage* (Hull, England: University of Hull Publications, 1966), 17.

45. For an interesting treatment of the psychoanalytic implications of the desexualized relation between Tamburlaine and Zenocrate, see Donaldson, "Conflict and Coherence: Narcissism and Tragic Structure in Marlowe."

46. See *Tamb.* 2:1.6.85–86.

47. Compare Greenblatt, *Renaissance Self-Fashioning*, 210–12.

48. This gesture, a sign and not an authentic measure of his martial prowess, points to the remarkable fact that he has not been wounded during more than five acts full of battles, evidence of his ability to "harmless run among the deadly pikes" (2:1.4.46), or of a detachment from actual fighting. (It is unclear how involved he actually is in his battles; the most clearly indicated involvement emerges, in fact, at moments when he sets himself up to be seen.)

49. These terms are from Whetstone's title to his chapter on Tamburlaine, which announces that his "large kingdom" was "overthrowne by the envy and discord of his two sonnes." Tamburlaine, Whetstone laments, "left behind him two sons, every way far unlike their father: between whose envy sowed such dissention, that through their incapacities to govern the conquests of their father, the children of Bajazet . . . stole into Asia, and so won the people to disobedience" (*The English Mirrour*, 82).

50. To some his death signals a "bare fact of fortune," reflecting "the stillness of the universe" (Judith Weil, *Christopher Marlowe: Merlin's Prophet* [Cambridge: Cambridge University Press, 1977], 116); to others, proof that he is "nothing more or less than a man" (Levin, *The Overreacher*, 36); to yet others, a sign that it is not he but "the playwright who holds the powerful pen" (Marjorie Garber, "'Here's Nothing Writ': Scribe, Script, and Circumscription in Marlowe's Plays," *Theatre Journal* [October 1984], 308). Even those linking it to the gods betray uncertainty. Gerald Pinciss, for example, argues that Tamburlaine is "*possibly* struck down by an angry god for blasphemy and *possibly* subsumed into the godhead itself" (*Christopher Marlowe* [New York: Frederick Ungar Publishing Co., 1975], 38; emphasis added).

51. Paul Kocher also argues that Elizabethan theatrical conventions "would almost certainly have required Marlowe to make this connection expressly"; (*Christopher Marlowe: A Study of His Thought, Learning, and Character* [Chapel Hill: University of North Carolina Press, 1946], 90). Kocher's conclusion that "time had arrived for ending, so he made one," however, misses the significance of this gap.

Chapter 4: Capitalizing on the Jew

1. Ithamore "worships" his master's nose, and William Rowley, in *The Search for Money* (1609), mentions a figure with features "like the artificiall Jewe of Maltae's nose." We cannot be sure whether Barabas, Shylock's prototype, shared

Shylock's red wig and beard (mentioned in reference to Richard Burbage's performance as "the red-hair'd Jew"). I share Michael Hattaway's assumption, however, that the likelihood is great (*Elizabethan Popular Theatre: Plays in Performance* [London: Routledge & Kegan Paul, 1982], 81). The quotes above appear in John M. Bakeless, *The Tragicall History of Christopher Marlowe* (Cambridge, Mass.: Harvard University Press, 1942), 2:368.

2. These issues have been addressed prominently in Jean-Marie Maguin, "*The Jew of Malta*: Marlowe's Ideological Stance and the Play-World's Ethos," *Cahiers Elisabethains: Études sur la Pre-Renaissance et la Renaissance Anglaises* 27 (1985): 17–26; George K. Hunter, "The Theology of Marlowe's *The Jew of Malta*" in *Dramatic Identities and Cultural Traditions: Studies in Shakespeare and His Contemporaries* (New York: Barnes & Noble, 1978), 60–102; and Alfred Harbage, "Innocent Barabas," *Tulane Drama Review* 8 (1964): 47–58.

3. These performances ran concurrently during *The Jew of Malta*'s 1592 season. I have compiled this information from G. B. Harrison's *The Elizabethan Journals: Being a Record of Those Things Most Talked of during the Years 1591–1603* (Ann Arbor: University of Michigan Press, 1955), 97–187.

4. See Richard Helgerson, who argues that imperialist texts, such as Richard Hakluyt's *Principal Navigations*, had to reshape England to make otherwise "unheroic" material gain a valid goal (*Forms of Nationhood: The Elizabethan Writings of England* [Chicago: University of Chicago Press, 1992], 151–91).

5. Though the historical documents were less accessible to the illiterate populace than the mystery plays, for example, which demonized the Jew, they nonetheless helped shape popular conceptions of the Jew.

6. For a full discussion of these other charges, and their manifestations in literary texts in particular, see: Esther L. Panitz, *The Alien in Their Midst: Images of Jews in English Literature* (London: Associated University Press, 1981); Edgar Rosenberg, "The Jew in Western Drama," in *The Jew in English Drama: An Annotated Bibliography*, comp. Edward D. Coleman (New York: New York Public Library and KTAV Publishing House, 1968); Joshua Trachtenberg, *The Devil and the Jews: The Medieval Conception of the Jew and Its Relation to Modern Antisemitism* (Cleveland, Ohio: World Publishing Company, 1961); M. J. Landa, *The Jew in Drama* (Port Washington, N.Y.: Kennikat Press, 1926); Jacob Lopez Cardozo, *The Contemporary Jew in the Elizabethan Drama* (Amsterdam: H. J. Paris, 1925); and R. Po-Chia Hsia, *The Myth of Ritual Murder: Jews and Magic in Reformation Germany* (New Haven, Conn.: Yale University Press, 1988).

7. My discussion of the history of the Jews has been informed primarily by Cecil Roth, *A History of the Jews in England*, 3d ed. (Oxford: Clarendon Press, 1964); Donald S. Katz, *Philo-Semitism and the Readmission of the Jews to England 1603–1655* (Oxford: Clarendon Press, 1982); and Harold Pollins, *Economic History of the Jews in England* (Rutherford, N.J.: Fairleigh Dickinson University Press, 1982).

8. Roth, *History of the Jews in England*, 52.

9. Raphael Holinshed, *Chronicles of England, Scotland, and Ireland* (London, 1807), 2:211.

10. John Stow, *A Summarie of Englyshe Chronicles* (London, 1565), 92.

11. Ibid.

12. Jean-Christophe Agnew, *Worlds Apart: The Market and the Theater in Anglo-American Thought, 1550–1750* (Cambridge: Cambridge University Press, 1986), 71. I return to the issue of usury below.

13. William Harrison, *The Description of England*, ed. Georges Edelen (Ithaca: Cornell University Press, 1968), 203.

14. Philip Stubbes, *The Anatomie of Abuses*, ed. William Turnbull (London, 1836), 142.

15. I disagree with critics who argue that Elizabethans viewed Judaism always as "a lie" or "a delusion bordering at times on the ludicrous and at times on the tragic" (Coburn Freer, "Lies and Lying in *The Jew of Malta*," in *"A Poet and a filthy Play-maker: New Essays on Christopher Marlowe*, ed. Kenneth Friedenreich [New York: AMS Press, 1988], 159). Freer is agreeing with Hunter's assessment in the essay cited above (n.2).

16. The quotations here are taken from Holinshed, *Chronicles*, 2:453–54. The wording is similar in Stow.

17. Stubbes, *The Anatomie of Abuses*, 158.

18. See Katz, *Philo-Semitism and the Readmission of the Jews*, 43–88, 158–89.

19. The banishment was probably motivated primarily by financial factors, by the Crown's belief that it no longer needed the Jews' capital. See Roth, *History of the Jews in England*, 68–90, and Pollins, *Economic History of the Jews in England*, 22.

20. The decree is now lost, but historians generally agree that the reasons were unstated. See D'Blossiers Tovey, who surveys the historical and public records concerning the Jews (*Anglia Judaica: or The History and Antiquities of the Jews in England* [Oxford, 1738], 233).

21. These and other contemporary plays including Jews are surveyed in Landa, *The Jew in Drama*, esp. 47–55, 86–104, and Cardozo, *The Contemporary Jew in the Elizabethan Drama*.

22. Simon Shepherd, *Marlowe and the Politics of Elizabethan Theatre* (Sussex: Harvester Press, 1986), 170. My discussion of the history of Malta and the Knights of St. John has been informed by Alison Hoppen, *The Fortification of Malta: By the Order of St. John, 1530–1798* (Edinburgh: Scottish Academic Press, 1979); Quentin Hughes, *Fortress: Architecture and Military History in Malta* (London: Lund Humphries, 1969); Eric Brockman, *Last Bastion: Sketches of the Maltese Islands* (London: Darton, Longman & Todd, 1961); and Maturin M. Ballou, *The Story of Malta* (Boston, 1893).

23. J. B. Steane, *Marlowe: A Critical Study* (Cambridge: Cambridge University Press, 1964), 169.

24. In the Revels edition of *The Jew of Malta* (Baltimore: Johns Hopkins University Press, 1978), the editor, N. W. Bawcutt, makes this emendation, explaining that "the King of Spain would not wish to expel the Knights of Malta" (103 [n. 38]).

25. Hoppen, *The Fortification of Malta*, 4. See also Hughes, *Fortress: Architecture and Military History in Malta*, 17–50.

26. Ballou, *The Story of Malta*, 6.

27. Stephen Greenblatt, *Renaissance Self-Fashioning: From More to Shakespeare* (Chicago: University of Chicago Press, 1980), 203.

28. Compare Thomas Cartelli, "Endless Play: The False Starts of Marlowe's *Jew of Malta*," in *"A Poet and a filthy Play-maker"*, 17–28. Cartelli sees the false start working to "neutralize audience resistance by failing to providence an unequivocal source of moral gravity that would serve to inhibit audience involvement" (p. 118).

29. As critics have noted, Machevill does not seem to follow Machiavelli but Innocent Gentillet, whose *Discours sur les moyens de bien gouverner et maintenir en bonne paix un royaume . . . Contre Nicholas Machiavel Florentin* (1576) in protesting Machiavellianism also misrepresented it. The effect, however, is the same, for Barabas follows neither. For further discussion of the ways Machiavellianism is represented or misrepresented in the play, see Bob Hodge, "Marlowe, Marx, and Machiavelli: Reading into the Past," in *Literature, Language and Society in England, 1580–1680*, ed. David Aers et al. (Dublin: Gill & Macmillan, 1981), 1–22; and Howard B. Babb, "'Policy' in Marlowe's *The Jew of Malta*," *English Literary History* 24 (1957): 85–94.

30. Ballou, *The Story of Malta*, 276; Brockman, *Last Bastion*, 127.

31. Hoppen, *The Fortification of Malta*, 9.

32. Roth, *History of the Jews in England*, 20.

33. Although Ferneze asserts of the Christians that "to stain our hands with blood / Is far from us and our profession" (1.2.148–49), he silences Barabas's attempts to exonerate the Jews, retorting: "Sham'st thou not to justify thyself, / As if we knew not thy profession?" (1.2.123–24).

34. The earliest use recorded in the Oxford English Dictionary is 1541.

35. Hakluyt, *Principal Navigations*, 5:6.

36. See Agnew, *Worlds Apart*, 101–48.

37. Ibid., 121.

38. Quoted in Agnew, *Worlds Apart*, 121.

39. Harry Levin, *The Overreacher: A Study of Christopher Marlowe* (Cambridge, Mass.: Harvard University Press, 1952), 62; Greenblatt, *Renaissance Self-Fashioning*, 196; Charles Lamb, *Specimens of English Dramatic Poets* (London, 1808), quoted in Bawcutt's introduction to the play (*The Jew of Malta*, 18).

40. Greenblatt grants him an "'indigenous' Judaism" (*Renaissance Self-Fashioning*, 207).

41. Hunter, "The Theology of Marlowe's *The Jew of Malta*," discusses other theological discrepancies and is seconded by Freer, "Lies and Lying in *The Jew of Malta*."

42. Greenblatt, *Renaissance Self-Fashioning*, 208.

43. Levin, *The Overreacher*, 73.

44. Greenblatt, *Renaissance Self-Fashioning*, 220.

45. Pollins, *Economic History of the Jews in England*, 17.

46. See, for example, Bakeless, *Tragicall History*, 1:328.

47. It is this catalog that Shakespeare appropriates (or misappropriates) in *Titus Andronicus*, as he fashions Aaron, the Moor, from Barabas, the Jew; see *Titus Andronicus* 5.1.125–44.

48. Shepherd has noted too that "his stories of murder are extraneous to the play," and, I would add, to his character (*Marlowe and the Politics of Elizabethan Theatre*, 175).

49. Barabas's detection and fall become increasingly likely as his direct participation in his plots increases.

50. I discuss the problems that Ithamore's stereotyped characterization poses to Marlowe's ideological agenda in the introduction.

51. In 1.2 Calymath grants Ferneze a month to collect the payment, and before the Turk returns (in 3.5), to announce that "the time you took for respite is at hand" (3.5.8), Barabas is already loaded, enough to buy a house as fine as the governor's.

52. No one in Malta seems to leave anything up to the justice of heaven, especially not Ferneze, who has imposed policies that (as Barabas notes) seem anything but Christian.

53. Ferneze does indicate to his men that he plans to free them, but he does not make clear whether he hopes to use his embrace of Barabas to do so. His naïveté in his earlier dealings with the Jew leads us to doubt his foresight.

54. Thomas Sanders, for example, writes of the janissaries' domination over the King of Barbary (the region of the Moors), explaining that "these janissaries are soldiers there under the Great Turk, and their power is above the king's" (Richard David, *Hakluyt's Voyages* [Boston: Houghton Mifflin Company, 1981], 142).

Chapter 5: Demonizing Magic

1. All references to the play are to Michael Keefer's edition of the A-text unless otherwise noted. I have adopted Keefer's spelling of Mephastophilis throughout, except when discussing texts with alternative spellings (which I then use).

I agree with Keefer's and Leah S. Marcus's stipulation that the A-text comes closest to an original Marlowe. See Keefer, Introduction to *Christopher Marlowe's Doctor Faustus: A 1604-Version Edition* (Peterborough, Can.: Broadview Press, 1991), xi–xxii, and Marcus, "Textual Indeterminacy and Ideological Difference: The Case of *Doctor Faustus*," *Renaissance Drama* 20 (1989): 13–22 esp. See also Michael J. Warren, "*Doctor Faustus*: The Old Man and the Text," *English Literary Renaissance* 11 (1981): 111–47. For a creative (though somewhat farfetched) account of how censorship may have come into play, see William Empson, *Faustus and the Censor: The English Faustbook and Marlowe's Doctor Faustus*, ed. John Henry Jones (New York: Basil Blackwell, 1987). Roy T. Eriksen offers a useful survey of the changing critical preferences for the versions (*"The Forme of Faustus Fortunes": A Study of the Tragedie of Doctor Faustus (1616)* [Atlantic Highlands, N.J.: Humanities Press International, 1987], 9–13).

2. This is the argument put forth by Marcus, "Textual Indeterminacy," 5, which I return to at the end of the chapter.

3. For an interesting study of the significance of enclosure in Marlowe, see Marjorie Garber, "'Infinite Riches in a Little Room': Closure and Enclosure in Marlowe," in *Two Renaissance Mythmakers: Christopher Marlowe and Ben Jonson*, ed. Alvin Kernan (Baltimore: Johns Hopkins University Press, 1977), 3–21.

4. M. H. Abrams, et al., eds., *The Norton Anthology of English Literature*, 5th ed. (New York: W. W. Norton & Company, 1986), 1:792. The editors dismiss the more controversial parts of his life as "sensational information" of which we cannot be sure (1:792).

5. Ibid., 1:814.

6. Robert Greene, for example, as I mention in Chapter 1, targets "that Atheist *Tamburlan*." And, as David Riggs ("Authorship, Atheism and Tamburlaine," a paper presented at the annual Shakespeare Association of America Convention, Vancouver, B.C., 23 March 1991) and Marcus have pointed out, the authors of the Dutch Church libel threatened to rebel violently "Per Tamburlaine" (quoted in Marcus, "Textual Indeterminacy," 16). I am much indebted to David Riggs for drawing my attention to this document and its implications.

7. See A. L. French, who discusses the critical shift from a "guiltless Faustus to a culpable one" ("The Philosophy of *Dr. Faustus*," *Essays in Criticism* 20 [1970]: 123). Critics have also argued for ambiguity, as they do about Marlowe's plays in general, but the tendency is largely in the case of *Faustus* to opt for one extreme or the other. See Max Bluestone, "*Libido Speculandi*: Doctrine and Dramaturgy in *Doctor Faustus*," in *Reinterpretations of Elizabethan Drama*, ed. Norman Rabkin (New York: Columbia University Press, 1969), 33–88.

8. René Girard is right, I think, to question the assumptions behind the question, to ask instead, "Why should a well-educated young man have second thoughts when it comes to killing a close relative who also happens to be the king . . . and the husband of his own mother?" ("Hamlet's Dull Revenge," in *Literary Theory/Renaissance Texts*, ed. Patricia Parker and David Quint [Baltimore: Johns Hopkins University Press, 1986], 299).

9. See Marcus, "Textual Indeterminacy," and Keefer, Introduction to *Doctor Faustus*.

10. See my discussion in Chapter 3.

11. Compare Johannes Birringer's treatment of Faustus "alone with himself" (*Marlowe's Dr. Faustus and Tamburlaine: Theological and Theatrical Perspectives* [New York: Verlag Peter Lang, 1984], 76). The absence of God problematizes readings that turn *Faustus* into moral drama, or even readings such as Jonathan Dollimore's (discussed below), for it is not he but Lucifer who is present to set the terms of damnation. See also Robert H. West, "The Impatient Magic of *Dr. Faustus*," *English Literary Renaissance* 4 (1974): 218–40.

12. Stephen Greenblatt, *Renaissance Self-Fashioning: From More to Shakespeare* (Chicago: University of Chicago Press, 1980), 197.

13. Jonathan Dollimore argues that Faustus wants to "escape agonized irresolution" (*Radical Tragedy: Religion, Ideology and Power in the Drama of Shakespeare and His Contemporaries* [Chicago: University of Chicago Press, 1984], 113), as I mention below. See also Greenblatt, *Renaissance Self-Fashioning*, 197, also mentioned below.

14. Giovanni Pico della Mirandola, *Oration on the Dignity of Man*, trans. A. Robert Caponigri (Chicago: Henry Regnery Company, 1956), 53.

15. Greenblatt (*Renaissance Self-Fashioning*) has provided the seminal work on this topic.

16. In Franco Zefferelli's recent film version, which otherwise attempts to produce a very knowable action-adventure Hamlet (à la Mel Gibson), the soliloquy stands out as a signficant rupture.

17. Even as early as 1946, W. W. Greg finds the complaint frequently reiterated, especially by critics who see the discrepancy as proof of multiple authorship, and attempts to make sense of it as Marlowe's deliberate strategy ("The Damnation of Faustus," in *Marlowe: A Collection of Critical Essays*, ed. Clifford Leech [Englewood Cliffs, N.J.: Prentice Hall, 1964], 92–107).

18. Dollimore, *Radical Tragedy*, 112–13; Greenblatt, *Renaissance Self-Fashioning*, 197.

19. For a useful survey of representations of magicians before (as well as during) the Renaissance, see Barbara Howard Traister, *Heavenly Necromancers: The Magician in English Renaissance Drama* (Columbia: University of Missouri Press, 1984).

20. John S. Mebane surveys these texts in *Renaissance Magic and the Return of the Golden Age: The Occult Tradition and Marlowe, Jonson and Shakespeare* (Lincoln: University of Nebraska Press, 1989), 96–108. Keith Thomas dates the witch craze 1550–1675 in his important study of *Religion and the Decline of Magic: Studies in Popular Beliefs in Sixteenth and Seventeenth Century England* (London: Weidenfeld & Nicholson, 1971). Other useful studies of this phenomenon include: Alan Macfarlane, *Witchcraft in Tudor and Stuart England* (London: Routledge & Kegan Paul, 1970); Hugh Trevor-Roper, *The European Witch-Craze of the Sixteenth and Seventeenth Centuries* (Harmondsworth, England: Penguin, 1956); and Wallace Notestein, *A History of Witchcraft in England from 1558 to 1718* (New York: Russell & Russell, 1911).

21. We know only secondhand of the first collection (the Erfurt collection, probably by Wolf Wambach). The oldest surviving text is the Nuremberg manuscript of the 1570s. Throughout the 1560s and 1570s, oral Faust tales seem to have been commonly circulated throughout Europe. The Stationers' Register of 1589 lists "A ballad of the life and death of Doctor Faustus the greater cungerer," which may or may not have been the same as the extant "Judgement of God shewed upon one John Faustus," included in a seventeenth-century collection of ballads. For a fuller discussion of this history, see H. G. Haile, Introduction to *The History of Doctor Johann Faustus* (Urbana: University of Illinois Press, 1965), 1–13, and John Henry Jones, Introduction to Empson, *Faustus and the Censor*, 1–36. See also Keefer, *Doctor Faustus*, xxxvii–xlv.

22. Marlowe was almost certainly familiar with the English Faustbook, at the least. See John M. Bakeless, *The Tragicall History of Christopher Marlowe* (Cambridge, Mass.: Harvard University Press, 1942), 1:275–77.

23. William Prynne reports in his *Histriomastix* (1633) of the "visible apparition of the Devill on the stage at the Belsavage Play-house, in Queen Elizabeths

dayes, (to the great amazement both of the Actors and Spectators) whiles they were there prophanely playing the History of *Faustus* (the truth of which I have heard from many now alive, who well remember it,) there being some distracted with that fearefull sight." Others, less intent on circulating antitheatrical propaganda, tell a similar story, and their accounts attest to the exotic appeal (and not the truth) of the subject. Excerpts of these accounts are quoted in Bakeless, *Tragicall History*, 1:299–301.

24. Other magician plays include George Peele's *The Old Wives Tales*, and the anonymous *John of Bordeaux, or the Second Part of Friar Bacon* and *The Merry Devill of Edmonton*.

25. Thomas, *Religion and the Decline of Magic*, as well as Frances A. Yates, *The Occult Philosophy in the Elizabethan Age* (London: Routledge & Kegan Paul, 1979), and Mebane, *Renaissance Magic*, have been particularly useful to my discussion of the place of magic in early modern England. See also Ernst Cassirer, *The Individual and the Cosmos in Renaissance Philosophy*, trans. Mario Domandi (New York: Harper & Row, 1964); Wayne Shumaker, *The Occult Sciences in the Renaissance: A Study in Intellectual Patterns* (Berkeley: University of California Press, 1972); Brian Vickers, ed., *Occult and Scientific Mentalities in the Renaissance* (Cambridge: Cambridge University Press, 1984); and Joan P. Couliano, *Eros and Magic in the Renaissance*, trans. Margaret Cook (Chicago: University of Chicago Press, 1987). For studies pointing more directly to Marlowe and magic, see: James Robinson Howe, *Marlowe, Tamburlaine, and Magic* (Athens: Ohio University Press, 1976); Eriksen, *"The Forme of Faustus Fortunes"*; and William George Blackburn, *Perilous Grace: The Poet as Protean Magician in the Works of Marlowe, Jonson, and Spenser* (Ann Arbor, Mich.: University Microfilms International, 1978).

26. See, for example, Pico della Mirandola, *Oration*, 25–29.

27. Reginald Scot, *The discoverie of witchcraft* (London, 1584), 244.

28. Mebane, *Renaissance Magic*, 53–72.

29. Thomas, *Religion and the Decline of Magic*, offers the seminal treatment of the rivalary between religion and magic, and Mebane, *Renaissance Magic*, discusses the conflict between magic and other disciplines. See also Stephen Ozmont, *Mysticism and Dissent: Religious Ideology and Social Protest in the Sixteenth Century* (New Haven, Conn.: Yale University Press, 1973), and Christina Larner, *Witchcraft and Religion: The Politics of Popular Belief* (New York: Blackwell, 1984).

30. Yates, *Occult Philosophy*, 89–90.

31. Thomas discusses these practices and the attempts to regulate them (*Religion and the Decline of Magic*, 234–47). He records, for example, a law instituted in 1542 that declared it a "felony to use magic for treasure-seeking, for recovery of stolen goods, or 'to provoke any person to unlawful love'" (p. 245). Although it was revoked five years later, a similar though less stringent law was reinstated in 1563, and the penalties were made more severe in 1604 (not surprisingly, shortly after James I took office).

32. Thomas, *Religion and the Decline of Magic*, 476–79. See also Mebane, *Renaissance Magic*, 98.

33. Scot, *The discoverie of witchcraft*, 1.

34. I am much indebted to David Riggs for suggestions about the implications of Calvinism in this context.

35. Haile, Introduction to *The History of Doctor Johann Faustus*, 4–5. See also Keefer, *Doctor Faustus*, xxxiii–xxxvii.

36. From a letter written by Abbot Trithemius of Wurzburg (1507), quoted in William Rose, ed., Introduction to *The Historie of the Damnable Life and Deserved Death of Doctor John Faustus* (South Bend, Ind.: University of Notre Dame, 1963), 3; Philipp Melanchton, quoted in Jones, Introduction to Empson, *Faustus and the Censor*, 7; quoted in Haile, Introduction to *The History of Doctor Johann Faustus*, 4.

37. See Keefer, *Doctor Faustus*, xxxvi.

38. Jones, Introduction to Empson, *Faustus and the Censor*, 7–8.

39. I am using H. Logeman's edition of *The Historie of the Damnable life and Deserved Death of Doctor John Faustus*, by P. F., Gent (Gand: Librarie H. Englecke, 1900), 3.

40. Haile, Introduction to *The History of Doctor Johann Faustus*, 6. I am referring here to the Erfurt collection of tales.

41. Thomas makes this point in *Religion and the Decline of Magic*.

42. Quoted in Jones, Introduction to Empson, *Faustus and the Censor*, 13.

43. Haile, Introduction to *The History of Doctor Johann Faustus*, 8.

44. Because the dates of both Greene's play and Marlowe's are uncertain, we cannot know which preceded.

45. The seminal essay is Paul Brown, "This thing of darkness I acknowledge mine': *The Tempest* and the Discourse of Colonialism," in *Political Shakespeare: New Essays in Cultural Materialism*, ed. Jonathan Dollimore and Alan Sinfield (Ithaca: Cornell University Press, 1985), 48–71. See also Cartelli, "Prospero in Africa: *The Tempest* as Colonialist Text and Pretext," in *Shakespeare Reproduced: The Text in History and Ideology*, ed. Jean E. Howard and Marion F. O'Connor (New York: Methuen, 1987), 99–115, as well as Meredith Skura's critique of colonialist readings ("Discourse and the Individual: The Case of Colonialism in *The Tempest*," *Shakespeare Quarterly* 40 [1989]: 42–74).

46. From Scot's dedicatory epistle to "Maister Doctor Coldwell, Deane of Rochester and M. D. Readman, Archdeacon of Canterburie," in *The discoverie of witchcraft*. The title page includes the following warning: "Beleeve not everie spirit, but trie the spirits, whether they are of God; for manie false prophets are gone out into the world."

47. Dedicatory epistle to Sir Roger Manwood in Scot, *The discoverie of witchcraft*.

48. Ibid.

49. Scot, Epistle to Maister Doctor Coldwell, *The discoverie of witchcraft*.

50. "The Jewes," Scot writes, "held one kind of diabolical sacrifice, never taught them by Moses, namelie, to offer their children to Moloch, making their sonnes and their daughters to runne through the fire; supposing such grace and efficacie to have beene in that action, as other witches affirme to be in charmes and words" (*The discoverie of witchcraft*, 190).

51. Discussions of Scot tend to highlight this as the most important reve-

lation of the text, not the idea of social or political coercion and victimization of the already disadvantaged. See Notestein, *A History of Witchcraft*, 67–72.

52. James I, *Daemonologie*, ed. G. B. Harrison (New York: Barnes and Noble, 1924), xi. Weyer's work, *De praestigiis daemonum* (1563), was less well known in England. See Yates, *Occult Philosophy*, 69.

53. From Thomas Beard, *The Theater of Gods Judgements*, quoted above; see Chapter 1.

54. Dollimore, *Radical Tragedy*, 110.

55. Ibid., 115.

56. Others too (in different ways) have argued that the idea of heaven's conspiracy problematizes morality readings of the play. See, for example, Bluestone, "Doctrine and Dramaturgy in *Doctor Faustus*."

57. Compare David M. Bevington, who offers the seminal treatment of *Faustus*'s relation to the morality tradition, in *From "Mankind" to Marlowe: Growth of Structure in the Popular Drama of Tudor England* (Cambridge, Mass.: Harvard University Press, 1962). See also: James A. Reynolds, *Repentance and Retribution in Early English Drama* (Salzburg: Universitat Salzburg, Institut für Anglisktick und Amerikanistik, 1982); Richard Waswo, "Damnation, Protestant Style: *Faustus, Macbeth*, and the Christian Tragedy," *Journal of Medieval and Renaissance Studies* 4 (1974): 63–99; and Margaret O'Brien, "Christian Belief in *Doctor Faustus*," *English Literary History* 37 (1970): 1–11.

58. Birringer, *Marlowe's Dr. Faustus and Tamburlaine*, 227. H. W. Matalene characterizes Faustus as one who "hates 'learning'—though he loves 'knowing'" and who indulges not in scholarly exploration but in "learning-avoidance" ("Marlowe's *Faustus* and the Comforts of Academicism," *English Literary History* 39 [1972]: 594–95). This "shallowness of study," Matalene argues, is the protagonist's "means of coming to feel his own potential, his power and worth as against other men" (p. 507).

59. For discussion of how Christian cabalism presumably safeguarded magical practice, see Yates, *Occult Philosophy*, 75.

60. See *Faustus* 2.3.69–85.

61. These readings are numerous and varied. Greg first implicated the scene as upsetting "the nice balance between possible salvation and imminent damnation," because here Faustus commits the unforgivable sin of "demoniality" ("bodily intercourse with demons") ("The Damnation of Faustus," 92–107). More recent interpretations have treated the scene as a symbolic rather than literal turning point. Kay Stockholder, for example, has argued that "Faustus associates sensuality both with forbidden knowledge and power, and with ensuing diabolic punishment" ("'Within the massy entrails of the earth': Faustus's Relation to Women," in *"A Poet and a filthy Play-maker": New Essays on Christopher Marlowe*, ed. Kenneth Freidenreich [New York: AMS Press, 1988], 205) and that, in joining with Helen, he pays the "psychic consequences" of this association (p. 216). "The tragedy," she contends, "is not that Faustus is damned, but that he thinks himself damned for his desires" (p. 217). See also C. L. Barber, "'The Forme of Faustus' Fortunes Good or Bad," *Tulane Drama Review* 8 (1964): 94–119.

62. W. W. Greg (among others) makes this identification of Saba as the Queen of Sheba, whose story is told in 1 Kings x; *Marlowe's* Doctor Faustus*: Parallel Texts* (Oxford: Clarendon Press, 1950), 332, n. 546.

63. The sultan actually checks up on Faustus's harem activities to see how powerful the conjurer really is, though at things other than conjuring.

64. Although Stockholder argues that what Faustus is coming to terms with is heterosexual desire rather than, as I contend, the idea of immortality, she too sees Helen as embodying "an alternative to Christian immortality" ("'Within the massy entrails,'" 214).

65. He does use an inappropriate (though not surprising, in light of his situation) rhetoric of bargaining, showing that his idea of salvation is not exactly orthodox.

66. In *Troilus and Cressida*, for example, which looks at the discrepancies within her representation, Troilus and Paris put her on a pedestal while Cressida defames her as a wanton "merry Greek" (1.1.112).

67. Marcus, "Textual Indeterminacy," 5.

68. Keefer gives an excellent discussion of these differences (Introduction to *Doctor Faustus*, lx–lxix). See also Marcus, "Textual Indeterminacy," and Warren, "The Old Man and the Text." For alternative readings of the import of the comic sequences, see Robert Ornstein, "The Comic Synthesis in *Doctor Faustus*," *English Literary Renaissance* 22 (1955): 165–72, and John H. Crabtree, Jr., "The Comedy in Marlowe's *Doctor Faustus*," *Furman Studies* 9 (1961): 1–9.

69. Although there seems to be no historical analogue for Bruno, the name calls up Marlowe's contemporary, Giordano Bruno, and brings the representation home to the contemporary situation of magicians. The fact that Bruno was living in England between 1583 and 1585 makes the reference more timely. See Eriksen, *"The Forme of Faustus Fortunes"*, 59.

Chapter 6: The Show of Sodomy

1. Raphael Holinshed, *Chronicles of England, Scotland, and Ireland* (London, 1807), 587. All references to Holinshed in this chapter refer to volume 2.

2. See Karen Cunningham, "Renaissance Execution and Marlovian Elocution: The Drama of Death," *PMLA* 105 (1990): 209–22.

3. The fact that he had first been deposed softens the blow, though the legitimacy of the deposition was itself questionable.

4. Definitions of sodomy were so inclusive and so vague that one might wonder whether rape with a hot spit would qualify, making the event a "real" rather than symbolic act of sodomy.

5. In Part 2, Tamburlaine's ill-fated son, Calyphas, sets his characterizing antimilitarism, though not in line with homoerotic desire, suggestively against heteroeroticism, boasting that he fears swords and cannons as little as he does "a naked lady in a net of gold" (*Tamb.* 2:4.1.69), while refusing adamantly to fight.

6. See Harry Redner, *In the Beginning Was the Deed: Reflections on the Passage of Faust* (Berkeley: University of California Press, 1982), 192.

7. Jonathan Goldberg has talked about Bartolome de Las Casas and New World sodomy ("Sodomy in the New World," paper presented at Rutgers University, New Brunswick, N.J., 1 April 1991). Sodomy was also boldly described in classical texts, which might be the exception or further proof of the rule, depending on how "other" the classical world was perceived to be. See the discussion below. Alan Bray makes the point, too, that sodomy was habitually ascribed to foreigners, especially Italians and Turks (*Homosexuality in Renaissance England* [London: Gay Men's Press, 1982], 71).

8. The seminal work on the subject has been Bray, *Homosexuality in Renaissance England*. My discussion has also been informed by: Vern L. Bullough, *Homosexuality: A History from Ancient Greece to Gay Liberation* (New York: New American Library, 1979) and *Sexual Variance in Society and History* (New York: John Wiley & Sons, 1976); James M. Saslow, *Ganymede in the Renaissance: Homosexuality in Art and Society* (New Haven, Conn.: Yale University Press, 1986); Gregory W. Bredbeck, *Sodomy and Interpretation: Marlowe to Milton* (Ithaca, N.Y.: Cornell University Press, 1991); Bruce R. Smith, *Homosexual Desire in Shakespeare's England: A Cultural Poetics* (Chicago: University of Chicago Press, 1991); David F. Greenberg, *The Construction of Homosexuality* (Chicago: University of Chicago Press, 1988); and Jonathan Goldberg, "Sodomy and Society: The Case of Christopher Marlowe," *Southwest Review* 69 (1984): 371–78.

9. Seymour Kleinberg, for example, has argued that homosexuality seems to have been tolerated "for men who had already done their service to society and posterity in marriage and paternity" ("*The Merchant of Venice*: The Homosexual as Anti-Semite in Nascent Capitalism," in *Literary Visions of Homosexuality*, ed. Stuart Kellogg [New York: Haworth Press, 1983], 115). As Bray (*Homosexuality in Renaissance England*) and others point out, the term did not appear in England until the late nineteenth century, not coincidentally with the emergence of psychiatry.

10. From St. Antonino, *Confessionale*, quoted in Bullough, *Homosexuality*, 33; a manual for justices of the peace, quoted in Peter Laslett, *The World We Have Lost Further Explored*, 3d. ed. (New York: Charles Scribner's Sons, 1984), 157. Officially the charge of sodomy seems to have been levied for the most part (as far as we know) at those accused of other crimes; see Bray, *Homosexuality in Renaissance England*, 13, and Vern L. Bullough, "Heresy, Witchcraft, and Sexuality," *Journal of Homosexuality* 1 (1974): 192. As Alan Bray has argued, a large part of the perceived problem was not the act itself but the implications of the act, the fact that it overturned established hierarchies, allowing servants to dominate masters and transgress bounds of class, authority, and service. See "Homosexuality and the Signs of Male Friendship in Elizabethan England," *History Workshop* 29 (1990): 1–19. For fuller treatments of homosexuality and the law, see also: Cynthia B. Herrup, "Law and Morality in Seventeenth Century England," *Past and Present* 106 (1985): 102–23; Martin Ingram, *Church Courts, Sex and Marriage in England, 1570–1640* (Cambridge: Cambridge University Press, 1987); and Sir William Holdsworth, *A History of English Law*, Vol. 4 (London: Methuen, 1924).

11. James M. Saslow has argued that a distinction was drawn between feelings, associated only with chaste bonds, and acts, associated with sodomy ("Homosexuality in the Renaissance: Behavior, Identity and Artistic Expression," in

Hidden from History: Reclaiming the Gay and Lesbian Past, ed. Martin Duberman, et al. [New York: New American Library, 1989], 96–97). Yet as the example of Holinshed, discussed at length below, suggests, the distinction did not hold.

12. Saslow argues, for example, that the Neoplatonists "always ranked Ganymede far more highly as a symbol of chaste intellectual intercourse than of its fleshly counterpart" (*Ganymede in the Renaissance*, 33), while Bray sees the latter as the privileged meaning (*Homosexuality in Renaissance England*, 55). See also Byrne R. Fone, who argues that Ganymede had already become a "code word for homosexual" ("This Other Eden: Arcadia and the Homosexual Imagination" in *Literary Visions of Homosexuality*, 14).

13. Bredbeck, *Sodomy and Interpretation*, xii.

14. See, for example: Saslow, *Ganymede in the Renaissance*; Greenberg, *The Construction of Homosexuality*, esp. 124–83; and Bullough, *Sexual Variance*, esp. 93–158.

15. Smith, *Homosexual Desire in Shakespeare's England*, 121–22.

16. Others have noticed that sodomy was manifest as "the secret sin" "not to be named" (Bullough, *Sexual Variance*, 423, 427), but have not realized the full impact of this silence and obfuscation on the use of sodomy as a means of incrimination. Some have argued for more neutral explanations, suggesting that sodomy was kept "secret" to avoid encouraging it (by giving hints, etc.), or that sins were automatically and indiscriminately conceived of as part of a continuum, with one leading inevitably to another (Herrup, "Law and Morality in Seventeenth Century England," 109).

17. Though the dominant tendency is still to believe that "homosexuality" as a unique sexual identity did not exist in the early modern period, and that sodomy was seen only as a discrete act not a predilection, critics and historians are beginning to acknowledge traces within texts that argue otherwise. See, for example, Smith, *Homosexual Desire in Shakespeare's England* (mentioned below) and Fone, "This Other Eden."

18. Holinshed is Marlowe's primary source. The play also draws upon Stow's *Annals of England*, particularly for the scene in which Edward's captors wash him in puddle water and beard him. For discussion of the play's relation to its sources, see the introduction in the H. B. Charlton and R. D. Waller edition of *Edward II* (London: Methuen, 1933), 31–52.

19. Natalie Fryde gives a useful account of the political issues and conflicts involved in the reign and of their place in England's political history (*The Tyranny and Fall of Edward II, 1321–26* [Cambridge: Cambridge University Press, 1979]). Her study does not give much attention to the charges of sodomy, perhaps in part because it centers on the last half of the reign, when the Despensers were in power.

20. Ibid., 13.

21. Ibid. Interestingly, as Fryde makes clear, this excuse was not unique to the opposition under Edward; throughout the medieval period, as the powers of the kingship were being defined and contested, the same strategy was deployed.

22. Bredbeck, *Sodomy and Interpretation*, 53–54.

23. Bredbeck also sees the private as inscribed as part of the politic. Yet for him this happens subversively in Marlowe, not coercively in earlier accounts such

as Holinshed's. Bredbeck focuses primarily on the political incorporation of sodomy, and overlooks the reciprocity here and what happens outside the politic (ibid., 33–86). Compare also Smith, who argues that in Holinshed the politics of Edward's reign are by and large "sexual politics" (*Homosexual Desire in Shakespeare's England*, 217).

24. Poidras declares "that by means of a false nursse he was stolne out of his cradle, and this Edward the second being a carters son was brought in and laid in his place" (Holinshed, *Chronicles*, 2:557).

25. Cunningham, "Renaissance Execution and Marlovian Elocution," 211.

26. "——vetus autorum sententia, mores / Quòd similes, simile & studium sunt fomes amoris, / Sic vanus vanum, studiosus sic studiosum / Diligit, & socios adeunt animalia coetus." The translation is by Mary Crane.

27. Bredbeck, *Sodomy and Interpretation*, 54–55.

28. Stephen Holden, "Historical Edward II and Gay Issues Today," *The New York Times*, 2 March 1992.

29. Ibid.

30. That Edward fantasizes thus, of course, raises other questions about his sense of his place in his own story.

31. Though David H. Thurn differs on the significance of this event, his argument that the play insists on the arbitrary nature of sights of sovereignty is relevant here; see "Sovereignty, Disorder and Fetishism in Marlowe's *Edward II*," *Renaissance Drama* 21 (1990): 115–41. Compare also Smith who argues that "the punishment suits the crime" (*Homosexual Desire in Shakespeare's England*, 220).

32. Bray notes too that the "one clear statement of Edward's sodomitical sin is put in the hands of a man called Lightborne, whose name is but an anglicized echo of Lucifer, the father of all lies" ("Homosexuality and the Signs of Male Friendship," 10). Bray does not see this move, as I do, as a strategy for undermining the charges of sodomy, but presents it rather as part of an unresolved tension between the representation of friendship and of a sodomitical bond.

33. In the production at the Barbican Pit (London, 1991), Lightborn does kill Edward, but after erotic embraces.

34. Lightborn later assures Edward that his hands "were never stain'd with innocent blood" (5.5.83) and though his statement is misleading, it is probably true; his methods keep the blood and destruction undetectably inside.

35. Bredbeck, *Sodomy and Interpretation*, 75.

36. Ibid., 71.

37. Ibid., 61.

38. This is Bredbeck's primary focus.

39. Fryde, *The Tyranny and Fall of Edward II*, 59.

40. See Bredbeck on the legitimacy and implications of this precedent (*Sodomy and Interpretation*, 61–62).

41. J. B. Steane has called Kent "the mouthpiece of some fundamental Tudordoxy" (*Marlowe: A Critical Study* [Cambridge: Cambridge University Press, 1964], 214) and he is to some degree, though this position is complicated by the fact that the opposition also has a legitimate counterclaim.

42. In the first case they are protesting against Gaveston and the king's dis-

regard of his kingdom, in the second, against Spenser and Edward's threat to "make England's civil towns huge heaps of stones" (3.3.31) if he has to.

43. I am referring to Gaunt's famous speech in *Richard II* 2.1.31–68 in which he idealizes England as an "other Eden" for a "happy breed of men." While Gaunt idealizes and Mortimer declaims, the exaggeration in each case works similarly.

44. See, for example, Smith, *Homosexual Desire in Shakespeare's England*, 215.

45. Holinshed, *Chronicles*, 2:548.

46. The first instance comes as they "welcome" Gaveston back from a second exile, armed (secretly) with plans to kill him and (publicly) with shields whose emblems reflect and condemn his position.

47. These terms, too, are marked by abstraction, "nobility" resonating with moral and economic implications.

48. Compare Thomas Cartelli, *Marlowe, Shakespeare, and the Economy of Theatrical Experience* (Philadelphia: University of Pennsylvania Press, 1991), 132–35.

49. In an intriguing move, director Derek Jarman keeps the issue in play by putting Edward III in a stunning ensemble of earrings and heels in his 1991 film version of *Edward II* (Fine Line Features).

50. Compare Bredbeck, *Sodomy and Interpretation*, 56–60.

51. That Gaveston is mediating our gaze is made all the clearer as Marlowe brings us into the court situation *in medias res*.

52. As Thurn points out, Gaveston's homoerotic vision does contain sexual ambiguities ("Sovereignty, Disorder and Fetishism in Marlowe's *Edward II*," 191–21); yet the homoeroticism is still clear.

53. I use the term loosely here to indicate a sexual favorite. I agree with Smith that Gaveston does not quite fit the "minion" role in other ways; see *Homosexual Desire in Shakespeare's England*, 213–15.

54. Compare Stephen Orgel, who suggests that Marlowe's representation of Edward's sexuality may have been "a way of protecting the play, a way of keeping what it says about power in tact" ("Nobody's Perfect: Or Why Did the English Stage Take Boys for Women?" *South Atlantic Quarterly* 88 [1989]: 25).

55. As in the cultural discourse, here too sodomy is demonized into witchcraft.

56. It is no wonder that she turns finally to Mortimer, repeating the sins of the past, engaging herself to another whose "desire" for her is written out in political terms, though this time without competing sexual interests.

57. Though Edward is often condemned as a weak king like Mycetes, the differences between them are instructive, leading us to expect the Persian king to be overthrown before the first act and Edward to survive until the end.

Works Cited

Abrams, M. H. et al., eds. *The Norton Anthology of English Literature*. 5th ed. 2 vols. New York: W. W. Norton & Company, 1986.

Adelman, Janet. *Suffocating Mothers: Fantasies of Maternal Origin in Shakespeare's Plays*, Hamlet *to* The Tempest. New York: Routledge, 1992.

Africanus, John Leo. *The History and Description of Africa and the Notable Things Therein Contained*. Translated by John Pory. Edited by Robert Brown. London: Printed for the Hakluyt Society, 1896.

Agnew, Jean-Christophe. *Worlds Apart: The Market and the Theater in Anglo-American Thought, 1550–1750*. Cambridge: Cambridge University Press, 1986.

Andrews, Kenneth R. *Trade, Plunder, and Settlement: Maritime Enterprise and the Genesis of the British Empire, 1480–1630*. Cambridge: Cambridge University Press, 1984.

Armstrong, William. *Marlowe's* Tamburlaine*: The Image and the Stage*. Hull, England: University of Hull Publications, 1966.

Babb, Howard B. "'Policy' in Marlowe's *The Jew of Malta*." *English Literary History* 24 (1957): 85–94.

Bakeless, John M. *The Tragicall History of Christopher Marlowe*. 2 vols. Cambridge, Mass.: Harvard University Press, 1942.

Bakhtin, M. M. *The Dialogic Imagination*. Translated by Caryl Emerson and Michael Holquist. Edited by Michael Holquist. Austin: University of Texas Press, 1981.

Ballou, Maturin M. *The Story of Malta*. Boston: Houghton, Mifflin and Company, 1893.

Barber, C. L. "'The Form of Faustus' Fortunes Good or Bad.'" *Tulane Drama Review* 8 (1964): 94–119.

Bartels, Emily C. "Imperialist Beginnings: Richard Hakluyt and the Construction of Africa." *Criticism* 34 (1992): 517–38.

———. "Making More of the Moor: Aaron, Othello, and Renaissance Refashionings of Race." *Shakespeare Quarterly* 41 (1990): 1–15.

Barthelemy, Anthony Gerard. *Black Face, Maligned Race: The Representations of Blacks in English Drama from Shakespeare to Southerne*. Baton Rouge: Louisiana State University Press, 1987.

Battenhouse, Roy W. *Marlowe's Tamburlaine: A Study in Renaissance Moral Philosophy*. Nashville, Tenn.: Vanderbilt University Press, 1941.

Bawcutt, N. W., ed. *The Jew of Malta*, by Christopher Marlowe. Baltimore: Johns Hopkins University Press, 1978.

Benaquist, Lawrence. *The Tripartite Structure of Christopher Marlowe's* Tamburlaine

Plays and Edward II. Salzburg: Institut für Englische Sprache und Literatur, 1975.

Bevington, David M. *From "Mankind" to Marlowe: Growth of Structure in the Popular Drama of Tudor England*. Cambridge, Mass.: Harvard University Press, 1962.

―――. *Tudor Drama and Politics: A Critical Approach to Topical Meaning*. Cambridge, Mass.: Harvard University Press, 1968.

Bhabha, Homi K. "The Other Question: The Stereotype and Colonial Discourse." *Screen* 24 (1983): 18–36.

Birringer, Johannes. *Marlowe's* Dr. Faustus *and* Tamburlaine*: Theological and Theatrical Perspectives*. New York: Verlag Peter Lang, 1984.

Blackburn, William George. *Perilous Grace: The Poet as Protean Magician in the Works of Marlowe, Jonson, and Spenser*. Ann Arbor, Mich.: University Microfilms International, 1978.

Bluestone, Max. "*Libido Speculandi*: Doctrine and Dramaturgy in Contemporary Representations of Marlowe's *Doctor Faustus*." In *Reinterpretations of Elizabethan Drama*, edited by Norman Rabkin, 33–88. New York: Columbia University Press, 1969.

Boas, Frederick. *Christopher Marlowe: A Biographical and Critical Study*. Oxford: Clarendon Press, 1940.

Boemus, Joannes. *The Fardle of Facions*. Translated by William Waterman. New York: Da Capo Press, 1970.

Boon, James A. *Other Tribes, Other Scribes: Symbolic Anthropology in the Comparative Study of Cultures, Histories, Religions, and Texts*. Cambridge: Cambridge University Press, 1982.

Bosonnet, Felix. *The Function of Stage Properties in Christopher Marlowe's Plays*. Switzerland: Franche Verlag Bern, 1978.

Bradbrook, Muriel C. "*The Jew of Malta* and *Edward II*." In *Marlowe: A Collection of Critical Essays*, edited by Clifford Leech, 120–27. Englewood Cliffs, N.J.: Prentice Hall, 1964.

Bray, Alan. "Homosexuality and the Signs of Male Friendship in Elizabethan England." *History Workshop* 29 (1990): 1–19.

―――. *Homosexuality in Renaissance England*. London: Gay Men's Press, 1982.

Bredbeck, Gregory W. *Sodomy and Interpretation: Marlowe to Milton*. Ithaca, N.Y.: Cornell University Press, 1991.

Bristol, Michael. *Carnival and Theater: Plebian Culture and the Structure of Authority in Renaissance England*. New York: Methuen, 1985.

Brockman, Eric. *Last Bastion: Sketches of the Maltese Islands*. London: Darton, Longman & Todd, 1961.

Brooke, C. F. Tucker. *The Life of Marlowe and the Tragedy of Dido, Queen of Carthage*. New York: Gordian Press, 1930.

Brown, Paul. "'This thing of darkness I acknowledge mine': *The Tempest* and the Discourse of Colonialism." In *Political Shakespeare: New Essays in Cultural Materialism*, edited by Jonathan Dollimore and Alan Sinfield, 48–71. Ithaca, N.Y.: Cornell University Press, 1985.

Bullough, Vern L. "Heresy, Witchcraft, and Sexuality." *Journal of Homosexuality* 1 (1974): 183–201.

————. *Homosexuality: A History from Ancient Greece to Gay Liberation*. New York: New American Library, 1979.

————. *Sexual Variance in Society and History*. New York: John Wiley & Sons, 1976.

Campbell, Mary B. *The Witness and the Other World: Exotic European Travel Writing, 400–1600*. Ithaca, N.Y.: Cornell University Press, 1988.

Cardozo, Jacob Lopez. *The Contemporary Jew in the Elizabethan Drama*. Amsterdam: H. J. Paris, 1925.

Cartelli, Thomas. "Endless Play: The False Starts of Marlowe's *The Jew of Malta*." In *"A Poet and a filthy Play-maker": New Essays on Christopher Marlowe*, edited by Kenneth Friedenreich, 117–28. New York: AMS Press, 1988.

————. "Ideology and Subversion in the Shakespearean Set Piece." *English Literary History* 53 (1986), 1–25.

————. *Marlowe, Shakespeare, and the Economy of Theatrical Experience*. Philadelphia: University of Pennsylvania Press, 1991.

————. "Prospero in Africa: *The Tempest* as Colonialist Text and Pretext." In *Shakespeare Reproduced: The Text in History and Ideology*, edited by Jean E. Howard and Marion F. O'Connor, 99–115. New York: Methuen, 1987.

Cassirer, Ernst. *The Individual and the Cosmos in Renaissance Philosophy*. Translated by Mario Domandi. New York: Harper & Row, 1964.

Cawley, Robert Ralston. *The Voyagers and Elizabethan Drama*. London: Oxford University Press, 1938.

Charlton, H. B., and Waller, R. D., eds. *Edward II*, by Christopher Marlowe. London: Methuen, 1933.

Chaucer, Geoffrey. *The Works of Geoffrey Chaucer*. 2d ed. Edited by F. N. Robinson. Boston: Houghton Mifflin Company, 1957.

Chew, Samuel. *The Crescent and the Rose: Islam and England during the Renaissance*. New York: Oxford University Press, 1937.

Couliano, Ioan P. *Eros and Magic in the Renaissance*. Translated by Margaret Cook. Chicago: University of Chicago Press, 1987.

Crabtree, John H., Jr. "The Comedy in Marlowe's *Doctor Faustus*." *Furman Studies* 9 (1961): 1–9.

Crane, Mary Thomas. "The Shakespearean Tetralogy." *Shakespeare Quarterly* 36 (1985): 282–99.

Cunningham, Karen. "Renaissance Execution and Marlovian Elocution: The Drama of Death." *PMLA* 105 (1990): 209–22.

Danby, John. "*Antony and Cleopatra*: A Shakespearean Adjustment." In *Modern Shakespearean Criticism: Essays on Style, Dramaturgy, and the Major Plays*, edited by Alvin B. Kernan, 407–27. New York: Harcourt, Brace, Jovanovich, 1970.

David, Richard, ed. *Hakluyt's Voyages*. Boston: Houghton Mifflin Company, 1981.

Derrida, Jacques. *Dissemination*. Translated by Barbara Johnson. Chicago: University of Chicago Press, 1981.

Dessen, Alan. *Elizabethan Stage Conventions and Modern Interpreters*. Cambridge: Cambridge University Press, 1984.

Dodsley, Robert. *A Select Collection of Old English Plays*. 4th ed. Edited by W. Carew Hazlitt. London: Reeves & Turner, 1874.

Dollimore, Jonathan. *Radical Tragedy: Religion, Ideology and Power in the Drama of*

Shakespeare and His Contemporaries. Chicago: University of Chicago Press, 1984.

Donaldson, Peter S. "Conflict and Coherence: Narcissism and Tragic Structure in Marlowe." In *Narcissism and the Text: Studies in Literature and the Psychology of Self*, edited by Lynne Layton and Barbara Ann Shapiro, 36–63. New York: New York University Press, 1989.

Elam, Keir. *The Semiotics of Theatre and Drama.* London: Methuen, 1980.

Empson, William. *Faustus and the Censor: The English Faust-book and Marlowe's Doctor Faustus.* Edited by John Henry Jones. New York: Basil Blackwell, 1987.

Eriksen, Roy T. *"The Forme of Faustus Fortunes": A Study of the Tragedie of Doctor Faustus (1616).* Atlantic Highlands, N.J.: Humanities Press International, 1987.

Fieler, Frank. Tamburlaine, Part I *and Its Audience.* Gainesville: University of Florida Press, 1961.

Fone, Byrne R. "This Other Eden: Arcadia and the Homosexual Imagination." In *Literary Visions of Homosexuality*, edited by Stuart Kellogg, 13–34. New York: Haworth Press, 1983.

Fraser, Russell, and Norman Rabkin, eds. *Drama of the English Renaissance.* 2 vols. New York: Macmillan, 1976.

Freer, Coburn. "Lies and Lying in *The Jew of Malta.*" In *"A Poet and a filthy Playmaker": New Essays on Christopher Marlowe*, edited by Kenneth Friedenreich, 143–166. New York: AMS Press, 1988.

French, A. L. "The Philosophy of *Dr. Faustus.*" *Essays in Criticism* 20 (1970): 123–42.

Fryde, Natalie. *The Tyranny and Fall of Edward II, 1321–26.* Cambridge: Cambridge University Press, 1979.

Garber, Marjorie. "'Here's Nothing Writ': Scribe, Script, and Circumscription in Marlowe's Plays." *Theatre Journal* (October 1984): 301–20.

———. "'Infinite Riches in a Little Room': Closure and Enclosure in Marlowe." In *Two Renaissance Mythmakers: Christopher Marlowe and Ben Jonson*, edited by Alvin Kernan, 3–21. Baltimore: Johns Hopkins University Press, 1977.

———. "'Vassal Actors': The Role of the Audience in Shakespearean Tragedy." *Renaissance Drama* 9 (1978): 71–89.

Girard, René. "Hamlet's Dull Revenge." In *Literary Theory/Renaissance Texts*, edited by Patricia Parker and David Quint, 280–302. Baltimore: Johns Hopkins University Press, 1986.

Godshalk, William. *The Marlovian World Picture.* The Hague: Mouton, 1974.

Gohlke, Madelon. "'I wooed thee with my sword': Shakespeare's Tragic Paradigms." In *Representing Shakespeare: New Psychoanalytic Essays*, edited by Murray Schwartz and Coppelia Kahn, 170–87. Baltimore: Johns Hopkins University Press, 1980.

Goldberg, Jonathan. "Sodomy and Society: The Case of Christopher Marlowe." *Southwest Review* 69 (1984): 371–78.

———. "Sodomy in the New World." Paper presented at Rutgers University, New Brunswick, N.J., 1 April 1991.

Goldman, Michael. "Marlowe and the Histrionics of Ravishment." In *Two Renais-*

sance Mythmakers: Christopher Marlowe and Ben Jonson, edited by Alvin Kernan. Baltimore: Johns Hopkins University Press, 1977.

Greenberg, David F. *The Construction of Homosexuality*. Chicago: University of Chicago Press, 1988.

Greenblatt, Stephen. "Invisible Bullets: Renaissance Authority and Its Subversion, *Henry IV* and *Henry V*." In *Political Shakespeare: New Essays in Cultural Materialism*, edited by Jonathan Dollimore and Alan Sinfield, 18–47. Ithaca, N.Y.: Cornell University Press, 1985.

———. "Learning to Curse: Aspects of Linguistic Colonialism in the Sixteenth Century." In *Learning to Curse: Essays in Early Modern Culture*. New York: Routledge, 1990.

———. *Renaissance Self-Fashioning: From More to Shakespeare*. Chicago: University of Chicago Press, 1980.

Greg, W. W. "The Damnation of Faustus." In *Marlowe: A Collection of Critical Essays*, edited by Clifford Leech, 92–107. Englewood Cliffs, N.J.: Prentice Hall, 1964.

———. *Marlowe's* Doctor Faustus: *Parallel Texts*. Oxford: Clarendon Press, 1950.

Haile, H. G., Introduction to *The History of Doctor Johann Faustus*. Urbana: University of Illinois Press, 1965.

Hakluyt, Richard. *The Principal Navigations, Voyages, Traffiques & Discoveries of the English Nation*. 12 vols. Glasgow: James Maclehose & Sons, 1903–5.

Hapgood, Richard. "Shakespeare and the Included Spectator." In *Reinterpretations of Elizabethan Drama*, edited by Norman Rabkin, 117–36. New York: Columbia University Press, 1969.

Harbage, Alfred. "Innocent Barabas." *Tulane Drama Review* 8 (1964): 47–58.

Harrison, G. B. *The Elizabethan Journals: Being a Record of Those Things Most Talked of during the Years 1591–1603*. Ann Arbor: University of Michigan Press, 1955.

Harrison, William. *The Description of England*. Edited by Georges Edelen. Ithaca, N.Y.: Cornell University Press, 1968.

Hattaway, Michael. *Elizabethan Popular Theatre: Plays in Performance*. London: Routledge & Kegan Paul, 1982.

Helgerson, Richard. *Forms of Nationhood: The Elizabethan Writings of England*. Chicago: University of Chicago Press, 1992.

Heeren, A. H. L. *Historical Researches into the Politics, Intercourse, and Trade of the Carthaginians, Ethiopians, and Egyptians*. Vol 1. Translated from the German. 1832. Reprint. New York: Negro Universities Press, 1969.

Herrup, Cynthia B. "Law and Morality in Seventeenth Century England." *Past and Present* 106 (1985): 102–23.

The Historie of the Damnable Life, and Deserved Death of Doctor John Faustus, by P. F., Gent. Edited by H. Logeman. Gand: Librarie H. Engelcke, 1900.

Hodge, Bob. "Marlowe, Marx and Machiavelli: Reading into the Past." In *Literature, Language and Society in England 1580–1680*, edited by David Aers et al., 1–22. Dublin: Gill & Macmillan, 1981.

Hodgen, Margaret T. *Early Anthropology in the Sixteenth and Seventeenth Centuries*. Philadelphia: University of Pennsylvania Press, 1964.

Holden, Stephen. "Historical Edward II and Gay Issues Today." *The New York Times* 20 March 1992.

Holdsworth, Sir William. *A History of English Law*. Vol. 4. London: Methuen, 1924.

Holinshed, Raphael. *Chronicles of England, Scotland, and Ireland*. 6 vols. London: Printed for J. Johnson et al., 1807.

Hoppen, Alison. *The Fortification of Malta: By the Order of St. John, 1530–1798*. Edinburgh: Scottish Academic Press, 1979.

Howe, James Robinson. *Marlowe, Tamburlaine, and Magic*. Athens: Ohio University Press, 1976.

Hsia, R. Po-Chia. *The Myth of Ritual Murder: Jews and Magic in Reformation Germany*. New Haven, Conn.: Yale University Press, 1988.

Hughes, Quentin. *Fortress: Architecture and Military History in Malta*. London: Lund Humphries, 1969.

Hulme, Peter. *Colonial Encounters: Europe and the Native Caribbean, 1492–1797*. London: Methuen, 1986.

Hunter, George K. "The Theology of Marlowe's *The Jew of Malta*." In *Dramatic Identities and Cultural Traditions: Studies in Shakespeare and His Contemporaries*, 60–102. New York: Barnes & Noble, 1978.

Indigo Girls, "Ghost." *Rites of Passage*. Sony Music Entertainment, 1992.

Ingram, Martin. *Church Courts, Sex and Marriage in England, 1570–1640*. Cambridge: Cambridge University Press, 1987.

Izard, T. C. "The Principal Source for Marlowe's *Tamburlaine*." *Modern Language Notes* 58 (1943): 411–17.

James I. *Daemonologie*. Edited by G. B. Harrison. New York: Barnes and Noble, 1924.

Jarman, Derek, dir. *Edward II*. Fine Line Features, 1991.

Jordan, Winthrop D. *The White Man's Burden: Historical Origins of Racism in the United States*. New York: Oxford University Press, 1974.

———. *White over Black: American Attitudes Toward the Negro, 1550–1812*. New York: W. W. Norton & Company, 1968.

Jump, John D., ed. *Tamburlaine the Great, Parts I and II*, by Christopher Marlowe. Lincoln: University of Nebraska Press, 1967.

Katz, David S. *Philo-Semitism and the Readmission of the Jews to England 1603–1655*. Oxford: Clarendon Press, 1982.

Keefer, Michael. Introduction to *Christopher Marlowe's Doctor Faustus: A 1604-Version Edition*. Peterborough, Can.: Broadview Press, 1991.

Kleinberg, Seymour. "*The Merchant of Venice*: The Homosexual as Anti-Semite in Nascent Capitalism." In *Literary Visions of Homosexuality*, edited by Stuart Kellogg, 113–26. New York: Haworth Press, 1983.

Knappen, M. M. *Tudor Puritanism*. Chicago: University of Chicago Press, 1939.

Kocher, Paul. *Christopher Marlowe: A Study of His Thought, Learning, and Character*. Chapel Hill: University of North Carolina Press, 1946.

Kuriyama, Constance. *Hammer or Anvil: Psychological Patterns in Christopher Marlowe's Plays*. New Brunswick, N.J: Rutgers University Press, 1980.

Landa, M. J. *The Jew in Drama*. Port Washington, N.Y.: Kennikat Press, 1926.

Larner, Christina. *Witchcraft and Religion: The Politics of Popular Belief.* New York: Blackwell, 1984.

Laslett, Peter. *The World We Have Lost Further Explored.* 3d. ed. New York: Charles Scribner's Sons, 1984.

Leech, Clifford. *Christopher Marlowe: Poet for the Stage,* edited by Anne Lancashire. New York: AMS Press, 1986.

Levin, Harry. *The Overreacher: A Study of Christopher Marlowe.* Cambridge, Mass.: Harvard University Press, 1952.

Macfarlane, Alan. *Witchcraft in Tudor and Stuart England.* London: Routledge & Kegan Paul, 1970.

Maguin, Jean-Marie. "*The Jew of Malta*: Marlowe's Ideological Stance and the Play-World's Ethos." *Cahiers Elisabethains: Études sur la Pre-Renaissance et la Renaissance Anglaises* 27 (1985): 17–26.

Mandelbaum, Allen, trans. *The Aeneid of Virgil.* Berkeley: University of California Press, 1971.

Marcus, Leah S. "Textual Indeterminacy and Ideological Difference: The Case of *Doctor Faustus.*" *Renaissance Drama* 20 (1989): 1–29.

Marlowe, Christopher. *The Complete Plays.* Edited by J. B. Steane. Baltimore: Penguin Books, 1975.

———. *Complete Plays and Poems.* Edited by E. D. Pendry. London: J. M. Dent & Sons, 1976.

Massington, Charles G. *Christopher Marlowe's Tragic Vision: A Study in Damnation.* Athens: Ohio University Press, 1972.

Matalene, H. W. III. "Marlowe's *Faustus* and the Comforts of Academicism." *English Literary History* 39 (1972): 495–519.

McElroy, John F. "Repetition, Contrariety, and Individualization in *Edward II.*" *Studies in English Literature, 1500–1900* 24 (1984): 205–224.

Mebane, John S. *Renaissance Magic and the Return of the Golden Age: The Occult Tradition and Marlowe, Jonson, and Shakespeare.* Lincoln: University of Nebraska Press, 1989.

Miller, Christopher. *Blank Darkness: Africanist Discourse in French.* Chicago: University of Chicago Press, 1985.

Milton, John. *Complete Poems and Major Prose.* Edited by Merritt Y. Hughes. Indianapolis: Odyssey Press, 1957.

Monti, Richard C. *The Dido Episode and the Aeneid: Roman Social and Political Values in the Epic.* Leiden, Neth.: E. J. Brill, 1981.

Mullaney, Steven. *The Place of the Stage: License, Play, and Power in Renaissance England.* Chicago: University of Chicago Press, 1988.

Nagler, A. M. *Shakespeare's Stage.* Enlarged ed. New Haven, Conn.: Yale University Press, 1981.

Neill, Michael. "Unproper Beds: Race, Adultery, and the Hideous in *Othello.*" *Shakespeare Quarterly* 40 (1989): 383–412.

Notestein, Wallace. *A History of Witchcraft in England from 1558 to 1718.* New York: Russell & Russell, 1911.

O'Brien, Margaret. "Christian Belief in *Doctor Faustus.*" *English Literary History* 37 (1970): 1–11.

Oliver, H. J., ed. *Dido, Queen of Carthage and The Massacre at Paris,* by Christopher Marlowe. Cambridge, Mass.: Harvard University Press, 1968.

Orgel, Stephen. "Nobody's Perfect: Or Why Did the English Stage Take Boys for Women?" *South Atlantic Quarterly* 88 (1989): 7–29.

Ornstein, Robert. "The Comic Synthesis in *Doctor Faustus.*" *English Literary Renaissance* 22 (1955): 165–72.

Ozmont, Stephen. *Mysticism and Dissent: Religious Ideology and Social Protest in the Sixteenth Century.* New Haven, Conn.: Yale University Press, 1973.

Panitz, Esther L. *The Alien in Their Midst: Images of Jews in English Literature.* London: Associated University Press, 1981.

Parry, J. H. *The Age of Reconnaissance.* Berkeley: University of California Press, 1963.

Pico della Mirandola, Giovanni. *Oration on the Dignity of Man.* Translated by A. Robert Caponigri. Chicago: Henry Regnery Company, 1956.

Pinciss, Gerald. *Christopher Marlowe.* New York: Frederick Ungar Publishing Co., 1975.

Pollins, Harold. *Economic History of the Jews in England.* Rutherford, N.J.: Fairleigh Dickinson University Press, 1982.

Pratt, Mary Louise. "Scratches on the Face of the Country; or What Mr. Barrow Saw in the Land of the Bushmen." *Critical Inquiry* 12 (1985): 119–43.

Redner, Harry. *In the Beginning Was the Deed: Reflections on the Passage of Faust.* Berkeley: University of California Press, 1982.

Reynolds, James A. *Repentance and Retribution in Early English Drama.* Salzburg: Universität Salzburg, Institut für Anglisktick und Amerikanistik, 1982.

Riggs, David. "Authorship, Atheism and Tamburlaine." Paper presented at the annual Shakespeare Association of America Convention, Vancouver, British Columbia, 23 March 1991.

Rose, William, ed. Introduction to *The Historie of the Damnable Life, and Deserved Death of Doctor John Faustus.* South Bend, Ind.: University of Notre Dame, 1963.

Rosenberg, Edgar. "The Jew in Western Drama." In *The Jew in English Drama: An Annotated Bibliography,* compiled by Edward D. Coleman. New York: New York Public Library and KTAV Publishing House, 1968.

Roth, Cecil. *A History of the Jews in England.* 3d ed. Oxford: Clarendon Press, 1964.

Rowse, A. L. *Christopher Marlowe: His Life and Work.* New York: Harper & Row, 1964.

———. *The Expansion of Elizabethan England.* London: Macmillan, 1955.

Said, Edward. *Orientalism.* New York: Vintage Books, 1978.

Saslow, James M. *Ganymede in the Renaissance: Homosexuality in Art and Society.* New Haven, Conn.: Yale University Press, 1986.

———. "Homosexuality in the Renaissance: Behavior, Identity, and Artistic Expression." In *Hidden from History: Reclaiming the Gay and Lesbian Past,* edited by Martin Duberman et al. New York: New American Library, 1989.

Schwab, Raymond. *The Oriental Renaissance: Europe's Rediscovery of India and the East, 1680–1880.* Translated by Gene Patterson-Black and Victor Reinking. New York: Columbia University Press, 1984.

Scot, Reginald. *The discoverie of witchcraft.* London, 1584.

Shakespeare, William. *The Riverside Shakespeare.* Edited by G. Blakemore Evans et al. Boston: Houghton Mifflin Company, 1974.

Sharpe, J. A. *Early Modern England: A Social History 1550–1760.* London: Edward Arnold, 1987.

Shepherd, Simon. *Amazons and Warrior Women: Varieties of Feminism in Seventeenth Century Drama.* New York: St. Martin's Press, 1981.

———. *Marlowe and the Politics of Elizabethan Theatre.* Sussex: Harvester Press, 1986.

Shumaker, Wayne. *The Occult Sciences in the Renaissance: A Study in Intellectual Patterns.* Berkeley: University of California Press, 1972.

Skura, Meredith Anne. "Discourse and the Individual: The Case of Colonialism in *The Tempest.*" *Shakespeare Quarterly* 40 (1989): 42–74.

Smith, Bruce R. *Homosexual Desire in Shakespeare's England: A Cultural Poetics.* Chicago: University of Chicago Press, 1991.

Smith, Mary Elizabeth. *"Love Kindling Fire": A Study of Christopher Marlowe's The Tragedy of Dido Queen of Carthage.* Salzburg: Institut für Englische Sprache und Literatur, 1977.

Spivak, Gayatri Chakravorty. *In Other Worlds: Essays in Cultural Politics.* New York: Routledge, 1988.

———. *The Post-Colonial Critic: Interviews, Strategies, Dialogues.* Edited by Sarah Harasym. New York: Routledge, 1990.

Stanyhurst, Richard, trans. *The First Four Books of the Aeneid of Virgil.* Edinburgh: Edinburgh Printing Company, 1877.

Steane, J. B. *Marlowe: A Critical Study.* Cambridge: Cambridge Univ. Press, 1964.

Stockholder, Kay. "'Within the massy entrails of the earth': Faustus's Relation to Women." In *"A Poet and a filthy Play-maker": New Essays on Christopher Marlowe,* edited by Kenneth Friedenreich, 203–19. New York: AMS Press, 1988.

Stow, John. *A Summarie of Englyshe Chronicles.* London, 1565.

Stubbes, Philip. *The Anatomie of Abuses.* Edited by William Turnbull. London: W. Pickering, 1836.

Summers, Claude J. *Christopher Marlowe and the Politics of Power.* Salzburg: Institut für Englische Sprache und Literatur, 1974.

Thomas, Brook. *The New Historicism and Other Old-Fashioned Topics.* Princeton, N.J.: Princeton University Press, 1991.

Thomas, Keith. *Religion and the Decline of Magic: Studies in Popular Beliefs in Sixteenth and Seventeenth Century England.* London: Weidenfeld & Nicolson, 1971.

Thurn, David H. "Sights of Power in *Tamburlaine.*" *English Literary Renaissance* 19 (1989): 3–21.

———. "Sovereignty, Disorder, and Fetishism in Marlowe's *Edward II.*" *Renaissance Drama* 21 (1990): 115–41.

Todorov, Tzvetan. *The Conquest of America: The Question of the Other.* New York: Harper & Row, 1984.

Tokson, Elliot H. *The Popular Image of the Black Man in English Drama, 1550–1688.* Boston: G. K. Hall, 1982.

Tovey, D'Blossiers. *Anglia Judaica or The History and Antiquities of the Jews in England*. Oxford, 1738.

Trachtenberg, Joshua. *The Devil and the Jews: The Medieval Conception of the Jew and Its Relation to Modern Antisemitism*. Cleveland, Ohio: World Publishing Company, 1961.

Traister, Barbara Howard. *Heavenly Necromancers: The Magician in English Renaissance Drama*. Columbia: University of Missouri Press, 1984.

Trevor-Roper, Hugh. *The European Witch-Craze of the Sixteenth and Seventeenth Centuries*. Harmondsworth, England: Penguin, 1956.

Urry, William. *Christopher Marlowe and Canterbury*. Edited by Andrew Butcher. London: Faber & Faber, 1988.

Vergilius Maro, Publius. *The Aeneid*. Edited by J. W. Mackail. Oxford: Clarendon Press, 1930.

Vickers, Brian, ed. *Occult and Scientific Mentalities in the Renaissance*. Cambridge: Cambridge University Press, 1984.

The Wakefield Mystery Plays. Edited by Martial Rose. New York: W. W. Norton, 1961.

Warmington, B. H. *Carthage*. Rev. ed. New York: Frederick A. Praeger Publishers, 1969.

Warren, Michael J. "*Doctor Faustus*: The Old Man and the Text." *English Literary Renaissance* 11 (1981): 111–47.

Waswo, Richard. "Damnation, Protestant Style: *Faustus, Macbeth*, and Christian Tragedy." *Journal of Medieval and Renaissance Studies* 4 (1974): 63–99.

Weil, Judith. *Christopher Marlowe: Merlin's Prophet*. Cambridge: Cambridge University Press, 1977.

West, Robert H. "The Impatient Magic of Dr. Faustus." *English Literary Renaissance* 4 (1974): 218–40.

Wheeler, Richard P. "'Since first we were dissevered': Trust and Autonomy in Shakespearean Tragedy and Romance." In *Representing Shakespeare: New Psychoanalytic Essays*, edited by Murray Schwartz and Coppelia Kahn, 150–69. Baltimore: Johns Hopkins University Press, 1980.

Whetstone, George. *The English Mirrour*. London, 1586.

Williamson, James A. *The Age of Drake*. 2d ed. London: Adam & Charles Black, 1946.

Yates, Frances A. *The Occult Philosophy in the Elizabethan Age*. London: Routledge & Kegan Paul, 1979.

York Mystery Plays: A Selection in Modern Spelling. Edited by Richard Beadle and Pamela M. King. Oxford: Clarendon Press, 1984.

Young, Robert. *White Mythologies: Writing History and the West*. London: Routledge, 1990.

Index

Abigail, 21, 26, 98, 99

Adelman, Janet, 178 n.18

Africa: and colonialist discourse, 4, 5–6, 29–33, 81; double vision of, 7, 31–33; and the East, 54, 55–56, 59, 81; in Marlowe, 15–16, 19, 29–30, 44–46, 52 (see also *Dido, Queen of Carthage*); as "other," xiii, 114, 124, 173–75, 178 n.13. *See also* Moors; Negroes

Africanus, John Leo, *The Geographical Historie of Africa*, xiv, 4, 177 n.5, 187 n.15

Agnew, Jean-Christophe, 97, 179 n.22, 192 n.12

Agrippa, Cornelius: historical figure, 118, 123; in Marlowe, 114, 116, 130

alien, the: cultural place of (in England), xiii–xv, 3–9; and geographic difference, 38–39, 173–75; in Marlowe, xv, 10–26 (see also *Dido, Queen of Carthage*; *Doctor Faustus*; *Edward II*; *Jew of Malta, The*; *Tamburlaine*); on the stage, 9–10. *See also* Colonialist discourse; Stereotypes

Amazons, 16, 79

Andrews, Kenneth R., 177 n.3

Antony and Cleopatra, 7, 8, 185 n.37

Armstrong, William, 189–90 n.44

Babb, Howard B., 193 n.29

Bacon, Francis, 125

Baines, Richard, 11, 12

Bajazeth: in *Tamburlaine*, 6, 19, 56, 60, 62–65, 69–70, 78; in sources, 57, 58

Bakeless, John M., 179 n.24, 180 n.28, 182 n.61, 184 n.15, 188 n.17, 193 n.46, 196 n.22

Bakhtin, M. M., 178 n.14, 183 n.3

Ballou, Maturin M., 192 nn. 22, 26, 193 n.30

Barabas: contextualization of, 17, 18, 19, 20–21, 22; and Judaism, 97–98; as Machiavel, 92 (*see also* Machevill); and Malta, 87–88, 91, 92–96, 99, 100, 107; as "other," 24, 82, 87, 93, 95–96, 100–108,

158; self-constructions, 96–107; as subject of domination, 22, 92–96, 107; and usury, 6, 94–95. See also *Jew of Malta, The*; Jews

Barber, C. L., 179 n.26, 199 n.61

Bartels, Emily C., 183 n.12, 184 n.14

Barthelemy, Anthony Gerard, 179 n.23, 187 n.16

Bartholomew Fair, 96

Battenhouse, Roy, 181 n.48

Bawcutt, N. W., 180 n.37, 192 n.24

Beard, Thomas, *Theatre of Gods Judgements*, 11, 199 n.53

Benaquist, Lawrence, 188 nn. 24, 28

Bevington, David, 9–10, 181 n.45, 188 n.23, 189 n.31, 199 n.57

Bhabha, Homi K., 6, 7, 178 n.12

Birringer, Johannes, 179 n.26, 195 n.11, 199 n.58

Blackburn, William, 179 n.26, 197 n.25

Bluestone, Max, 195 n.7, 199 n.56

Boas, Frederick, 180 n.28

Bodin, Jean, *De la demonomanie des sociers*, 117, 118, 123

Boemus, Joannes, *The Fardle of Facions*, xiv, 4, 31–32, 55, 183 n.9

Boon, James A., 183 n.4

Bossonet, Felix, 179 n.26

Bourgogne, Jean de, *Travels of Sir John Mandeville*, 55

Bradbrook, Muriel C., 181 n.50

Bray, Alan, 145, 201 nn. 7–10, 202 n.12, 203 n.32

Bredbeck, Gregory, 146, 148, 156, 159, 201 n.8, 202–3 n.23, 204 n.50

Bristol, Michael, 179 n.22

Brockman, Eric, 192 n.22, 193 n.30

Brooke, C. F. Tucker, 180 nn.28–30, 34

Brown, Paul, 178 n.11, 198 n.45

Bruno, Giordano, 200 n.69

Bullough, Vern L., 201 nn. 8, 10, 202 nn. 14, 16

Calvinism, 119, 125, 126

Calymath: and the Jew, 94, 98–99, 105, 106; and Malta, 88–91, 107; as Turk, 6, 24–25. See also *Jew of Malta, The*

Campbell, Mary B., 177–78 n.8

capitalism, 96–97

Cardozo, Jacob Lopez, 191 n.6, 192 n.21

Cartelli, Thomas, 179 n.25, 193 n.28, 198 n.45, 204 n.48

Cassirer, Ernst, 197 n.25

Catholicism: conceptions of, 85, 121, 124 (*see also* Knights of St. John); in Marlowe, 25, 26, 121, 139–40, 142

Cawley, Robert, 187 n.10

Chew, Samuel, 187 nn. 5–6, 9–10, 14–15

Colonialism. *See* Imperialism

colonialist discourse: dialogism and, 34–36, 37–52, 53–54, 66–67; and domestic discourse, xiv–xv, 5, 107–8, 141–42, 145, 173–75; in the Elizabethan era, xiv, xv, 4–5, 55; and Marlowe, xv, xvii, 3–4, 9–10, 12–14, 23 (see also *Dido, Queen of Carthage*; *Jew of Malta, The*; *Tamburlaine*); monologism in, 29–33, 38, 81, 183 n.4; self/other dichotomies in, xiv, 3–4, 5–9, 38, 55–59, 81, 113–14, 183–84 n.13; stereotypes and, 6–9, 94, 96; and *The Tempest*, xiv, 122. *See also* Stereotypes

Comedy of Errors, The, 96

Cosroe, 19, 60, 65, 67, 68–69, 70, 71

Couliana, Joan P., 197 n.25

Coxe, Francis, *A short treatise declaring the detestable wickedness of magical sciences*, 117

Crabtree, John H., Jr., 200 n.68

Crane, Mary Thomas, 186 n.1, 203 n.26

Cunningham, Karen, 150, 200 n.2

Daborne, Robert, *A Christian Turn'd Turk*, 88

Danby, John, 185 n.37

David, Richard, 186 n.3

Dee, John, 118

Derrida, Jacques, 182 n.55

Dessen, Alan, 14

Dido: in classical legend, 15, 45, 46, 51; as colonialist, in Marlowe, 44–52. See also *Dido, Queen of Carthage*

Dido, Queen of Carthage, 29–52; Aeneas as colonizer in, 37–44; and the *Aeneid*, 34–36, 37, 44, 45, 46, 51–52; and colonialist discourse, xiv, 29–33, 38, 39–40, 46; and *Edward II*, 46, 157, 173; eroticism in, 25, 41–42, 43–44, 47–51; gods in, 15, 37, 40, 47, 48–49, 168, 186 n.41; guest/host relations in, 40–44 (*see also* Virgil, *Aeneid*); homoeroticism in, 37, 48–49, 144, 168; and *The Jew of Malta*, 45, 83; setting, 15–16 (*see also* Africa, in Marlowe); the "stranger" in, 18, 19, 37–40, 50, 185 n.32; and *Tamburlaine*, 81

Doctor Faustus, 111–42; Chorus, 127–28, 137; damnation in, 113, 116, 125, 131–33, 136–37, 139, 140; eroticism in, 133–37, 144–45; exoticism of, 3, 10, 16; and the European subject, 111–17; and *Edward II*, 111, 112, 115, 117, 156, 157, 167; imperialism, 138–42; and the magician, 114–15, 117, 123, 125, 126–29, 137, 141; and Marlowe's "imperialist" plays, 61, 107–8, 111, 114–16, 127, 139, 174; morality tradition in, 22, 114, 127–28, 132–33, 137; Protestantism in, 126, 127, 137–38 (*see also* Protestantism); texts of, 111–12, 113, 116, 138–39, 141–42, 194 n.1. *See also* Faust, the legend; Faustus

Dollimore, Jonathan, 116, 126, 127, 137, 180 n.38, 182 n.54, 195 n.11

Donaldson, Peter, 77, 190 n.45

Drake, Sir Francis, 4

Dutch Church libel, 12, 24, 195 n.6

East, the, 53–59: and Africa, 54, 55–56, 59, 81; and English imperialism, 4, 53–54, 56–58, 59, 174–75; and Orientalism, 5–6, 54–56, 60, 79, 81; in *Tamburlaine*, 59–60, 79, 81. *See also* Persians; *Tamburlaine*; Turks

Eden, Richard, *Historye of Travayle*, 55

Edward II (Marlowe's): contextualization of, 18–20, 22; and Gaveston, 22, 159, 160–65, 166, 167–72, in historical sources, 143–44, 147–56, 158, 160, 161; and homoerotic desire, 17, 46, 167–72; the nobility versus, 156–66; as political player, 46, 157, 165–66, 168–69, 170–72; and Spenser, the Younger, 22, 164–65, 166, 171. See also *Edward II*

Edward II, 143–72; and the chronicles, 143–44, 147–56, 158, 160, 202 n.18; and *Dido, Queen of Carthage*, 46, 157, 173; as a "domestic" play, 3, 16–17, 108, 111–12, 115, 117, 145, 156, 167; and Jarman's *Edward II*, 156–57, 158, 162, 164, 204 n.49; and *The*

Jew of Malta, 107–8, 157, 158, 167; the nobility in, 157–58, 159–65, 166, 167–68, 170–71; the private in, 149, 155–56, 165–66, 171–72; the regicide in, 156–59, 166; sodomy in, 144–45, 156–72 (*see also* Sodomy); and *Tamburlaine*, 17, 144, 157. See also Edward II

Edwards, Richard, *Damon and Pythias*, xiii, 15

Elam, Keir, 180–81 n.40, 181 n.43

Empson, William, 194 n.1

Eriksen, Roy T., 194 n.1, 197 n.25, 200 n.69

European subject, the: and interiority, 111, 113–14, 142; in Marlowe, 16–17, 29, 108, 173–75; versus non-European subjects, xiv–xv, 5, 111–17, 138, 141–42. See also *Doctor Faustus*; *Edward II*

Faust, the legend, 112, 117, 119–21, 122, 129, 130, 134, 135

Faustbooks, 117, 120–21, 122, 129, 130, 134

Faustus, 126–38; contextualization of, 18, 19, 20–21, 22; and divinity, 127, 128–38; and Helen, 132–38; and interiority, 111–12, 113–17; and magic, 114–16, 123, 125, 126, 128–29, 140–41 (*see also* Magician, Renaissance); as transgressor, 111, 116, 126–38. See also *Doctor Faustus*

Ficino, Marsilio, 118

Fieler, Frank, 179 n.26, 189 n.36

Fone, Byrne R., 202 nn. 12, 17

Ford, John, 18

Freer, Coburn, 192 n.15, 193 n.41

French, A. L., 195 n.7

Fryde, Natalie, 202 n.19, 203 n.39

Ganymede, 37, 48–49, 144, 145–46, 168

Garber, Marjorie, 182 n.57, 190 n.50, 195 n.3

Gascoigne, George, "A devise of a Masque," 55

Gast, Johannes, 120

Gaveston, Piers de: in *Edward II*, 18, 22, 159, 160–65, 166, 167–72; in Holinshed, 149–55, 164

Gentillet, Innocent, 193 n.29

Girard, René, 195 n.8

Godshalk, William, 179 n.26, 188 nn. 23, 28

Gohlke, Madelon, 185 n.37

Goldberg, Jonathan, 11, 201 nn. 7, 8

Goldman, Michael, 22, 179 n.26

Greenberg, David F., 201 n.8, 202 n.14

Greenblatt, Stephen: on colonialist discourse, 30, 178 n.11; on *Doctor Faustus*, 116, 195 nn.12–13; on *The Jew of Malta*, 98, 193 nn. 27, 39, 40, 44, 185 n.32; on Marlovian strategies, 13, 15, 21, 185 n.32; on *Tamburlaine*, 15, 71, 74–75, 189 n.31

Greene, Robert: *Friar Bacon and Friar Bungay*, 117, 121–22; on Marlowe, 11, 75, 195 n.6

Greg, W. W., 196 n.17, 199 n.61, 200 n.62

Haile, H. G., 196 n.21, 198 nn. 35, 40, 43

Hakluyt, Richard, *Principal Navigations*: on Africa, 30–31, 32–33, 38, 40; on the East, 55, 188 nn.18–19, 193 n.35; and English imperialism, xiv, 4–5

Hamlet, 113, 116

Hapgood, Richard, 182 n.58

Harbage, Alfred, 191 n.2

Harrison, G. K., 191 n.3

Harrison, William, *Description of England*, 85

Harvey, Gabriel, 12

Hattaway, Michael, 14, 181 n.49, 182 n.52, 191 n.1

Haughton, William, *Englishmen for My Money*, 88

Heeren, A. H. L., 185–86 n.38

Helen (of Troy), 25, 120, 132–38

Helgerson, Richard, 177 n.6, 191 n.4

Herrup, Cynthia B., 201 n.10, 202 n.16

Heywood, Thomas, 180 n.37

Hodge, Bob, 193 n.29

Hodgen, Margaret T., 177 nn. 4, 7, 183 n.11, 187 n.7

Holden, Stephen, 203 n.28

Holdsworth, Sir William, 201 n.10

Holinshed, Raphael, *Chronicles*: and the alien, xiv–xv, xvi; Jews in, 84–87, 178 n.16, 191 n.9; Knights of St. John in, 89; sodomy in, 143–44, 145, 147–56, 157, 158, 160, 204 n.45

homoeroticism: cultural place of (in England), 146, 153–56; in *Dido, Queen of Carthage*, 37, 48–49, 144, 168; in *Doctor Faustus*, 144–45; in *Edward II*, 144–45, 159–60, 167–69, 171–72; in *Tamburlaine*, 188–89 n.29, 200 n.5. See also Homosexuality, Renaissance; Sodomy

homosexuality, Renaissance: emergence of, 147, 148, 153–56; in Marlowe, 156, 164–65, 167–69, 171–72. See also Homoeroticism; Sodomy

Hoppen, Alison, 192 nn. 22, 25, 193 n.31
Howe, James Robinson, 197 n.25
Hsia, R. Po-Chia, 191 n.6
Hughes, Quentin, 192 nn. 22, 25
Hulme, Peter, 30, 31, 35, 55, 183–84 nn. 3, 5, 13, 185 n.33
Hunter, George K., 191 n.2, 192 n.15, 193 n.41

imperialism, English: and capitalism, 96; versus colonialism, 182–83 n.2; in the Elizabethan era, xiii–xv, 3–9, 10; in the East, 54, 88, 89; and Marlowe, xv, 3–4, 9, 10–13, 15, 23–24, 173–75 (*see also names of individual plays*). *See also* Colonialist discourse
Indigo Girls, 182 n.63
Ingram, Martin, 201 n.10
Isabella, Queen: in Holinshed, 152–53; in Marlowe, 160, 165, 166, 169
Islam, 56, 57–58, 74–75. *See also* Mohammed
Ithamore: and the Jew, 20, 21, 24, 95–96, 99, 101–3, 105, 106; as Turk, 6, 25, 94, 158
Izard, T. C., 188 n.17

James I, *Daemonologie*, 117, 118, 125
Jarman, Derek, *Edward II*, 156–57, 158, 162, 164, 204 n.49
Jew of Malta, The, 82–108: and capitalism, 96–97; and *Dido, Queen of Carthage*, 45, 83, 88; and *Doctor Faustus*, 107–8, 111, 114–16, 127, 174; and *Edward II*, 107–8, 157, 158, 164; Establishment/Outsider dichotomy in, 89–91, 108; and imperialism, xiv, 82–83; the Jew in, 6, 22, 82, 87, 92–108 (*see also* Barabas); Malta in, 87–91, 92, 93–94 (*see also* Malta); and *Tamburlaine*, 66, 81, 83, 88, 97, 100, 106; the Turk in, 6, 100–103 (*see also* Ithamore; Turks)
Jews: conceptions of, 6–7, 21, 83–84, 102, 124, 192 n.15; in history, 83–87, 99; on the stage, 9, 17, 24, 96. *See also Jew of Malta, The*
John of Bordeaux, or the Second Part of Friar Bacon, 197 n.24
Jones, John Henry, 196 n.21, 198 n.38
Jonson, Ben, xiii, 10, 96, 117, 123, 177 n.2
Jordan, Winthrop, 178 n.19
Jump, John D., 188 n.17

Katz, Donald S., 191 n.7, 192 n.18
Keefer, Michael, 194 n.1, 195 n.9, 198 nn. 35, 37, 200 n.68
King Lear, 115, 163
Kleinberg, Seymour, 201 n.9
Knights of St. John, 89, 90–91, 93. *See also Jew of Malta, The*
Kocher, Paul, 190 n.51
Kuriyama, Constance, 181–82 n.51
Kyd, Thomas, 11

Lamb, Charles, 193 n.39
Landa, M. J., 191 n.6, 192 n.21
Larner, Christina, 197 n.29
Las Casas, Bartolome de, 145
Leech, Christopher, 184–85 n.29
Levant Company, 54
Levin, Harry, 179 n.26, 181 n.50, 189 n.31, 190 n.50, 193 n.39, 193 n.43
Lightborn, 156–57, 158–59
Lodge, Thomas, *Alarm Against Usurers*, 97

Macfarlane, Alan, 196 n.20
Machevill, 17, 82, 92, 96, 127, 193 n.29
Machiavellianism: cultural place of (in England), xiii, 57, 97, 183 n.11, 193 n.29; in *The Jew of Malta*, 92, 127. *See also* Machevill
Mackail, J. W., 184 nn. 17, 24
magician, Renaissance: cultural place of (in England), xiv, 8–9, 114–15, 117–25, 173–74; and sodomy, 145, 146, 150–51, 156; on the stage, 117, 121–23. *See also Doctor Faustus*
Maguin, Jean-Marie, 191 n.2
Malta: history of, 88–89, 90–91, 93; in *The Jew of Malta*, 87–91, 92–96, 100, 105, 107. *See also Jew of Malta, The*
Mandelbaum, Allen, 184 n.17
Marcus, Leah, 138, 180 n.33, 194 nn.1–2, 195 nn. 6, 9, 200 n.68
Marlowe, Christopher: and the alien, xv, 10–13, 13–26; constructions of, xvi–xvii, 10–13, 54, 112–13, 125, 138, 145, 175; dating of the plays, 182 nn. 61, 1; imperialist versus domestic plays, 23–24, 112, 138–39, 141–42, 173; reinforcement of stereotypes in, 24–26; settings in, 3, 13–17, 53, 83, 88–91, 93, 111–12, 173–75; women in, 25–26 (*see also* Abigail; Dido; Isabella, Queen; Zenocrate). *See also names of individual plays*

Mary, Queen of Scots, 64
Masque of Moors, 55
Masque of Queens, 177 n.2
Massacre at Paris, The: the alien in, 3, 16, 25, 115, 145; text, xvi, 24, 112, 182 n.61
Massington, Charles G., 188 n.23
Matalene, H. W., 199 n.58
Mebane, John S., 196 n.20, 197 nn. 25, 28, 29, 32
Merchant of Venice, The, 6, 10, 96
Merry Devil of Edmonton, The, 197 n.24
Miller, Christopher, 6, 7, 18, 31, 178 n.13, 183 n.9
Milton, John, *Paradise Lost*, 137
Mohammed, 55, 57, 70, 75, 77, 80
Mohammedanism. *See* Islam.
Monti, Richard, 184 n.20
Moors: in colonialist discourse, xiv, 31, 32–33, 40, 55; cultural place of (in England), 5, 55; on the stage, xiii, 8, 10, 78, 193 n.47. *See also* Africa
Muenster, Sebastian, *Cosmography*, 55
Mullaney, Steven, 3, 177 n.2, 178 n.10, 179 n.22
Mully Mullocco, 83
Munday, Anthony, *John a Kent and John a Cumber*, 117
Muscovy Company, 54, 55

Nagler, A. M., 14
Negroes, 32–33, 55, 79. *See also* Africa
Neill, Michael, 178 n.19
new historicism, xv–xvi
Newton, Thomas, *Notable History of the Saracens*, 55
A New Way to Pay Old Debts, 96
New World, the: cultural place of (in England), 4, 5; and the East, 54, 55; as "other," 144, 145
Norton Anthology of English Literature, 112, 113, 128
Notestein, Wallace, 196 n.20, 199 n.51

O'Brien, Margaret, 199 n.57
Orgel, Stephen, 204 n.54
Orientalism: and Africa, 5–6, 55–56, 183 n.7; and the East, 5–6, 54–56, 60, 178 n.12. *See also* Said, Edward
Orlando Furioso, 83
Ornstein, Robert, 200 n.68
Othello, 5, 8, 19, 54, 93

Ovid, *Heroides*, 34
Ozmont, Stephen, 197 n.29

Panitz, Esther L., 191 n.6
Parry, J. H., 177 n.3
Peele, George, *The Old Wives Tales*, 197 n.24
Perondinus, Petrus, *Vita magni Tamerlanis*, 58
Persians: conceptions of, 15, 56–57, 58, 81; cultural place of (in England), xiii, 9–10, 55; in *Tamburlaine*, 19, 60, 65, 68–69, 72, 73, 76 (*see also* Cosroe). *See also* East, the
Pico della Mirandola, Giovanni, 118, 196 n.14
Pinciss, Gerald, 185 n.35, 190 n.50
Poidras, John, 150–51
Pollins, Harold, 191 n.7, 192 n.19, 193 n.45
Pory, John, *The History and Description of Africa*, xiv, 4, 177 n.5, 187 n.15
Pratt, Mary Louise, 183 n.4
Prester John, 31, 79
Preston, Thomas, *Cambyses*, xiii, 9–10, 15, 55, 56, 57
private, the, 147, 155–56, 165–66, 171–72
Protestantism: and *Doctor Faustus*, 126, 127, 137–38 (see also *Doctor Faustus*); and the magician, 112, 119–21, 123, 125
Prynne, William, 196–97 n.23

Ralegh, Sir Walter, 4
Redner, Harry, 200 n.6
Reynolds, James A., 199 n.57
Richard II, 162, 165–66
Riggs, David, 11, 12, 195 n.6, 198 n.34
Rosenberg, Edgar, 191 n.6
Roth, Cecil, 191 nn.7–8, 192 n.19, 193 n.32
Rowley, William, 190 n.1
Rowse, A. L., 177 nn. 3, 6, 180 n.28

Said, Edward, 5–6, 7, 54, 56, 178 n.12, 186 n.2. *See also* Orientalism
Saslow, James M., 201 n.8, 201–2 n.11, 202 nn. 12, 14
School of Night, 11, 12
Schwab, Raymond, *La Renaissance orientale*, 54, 56, 186 n.2
Scot, Reginald, *The discoverie of witchcraft*, xv, 123–25, 173, 197 n.27
self: in Marlowe, 38–39, 111–17, 142; versus the "other," xiv, 3–4, 5–6, 56, 141–42, 173–75; regulation of, 112, 119, 123, 138–39,

self (*continued*)
145, 172. *See also* Colonialist discourse;
European subject, the
*Selimus, The First Part of the Tragicall
Raigne of*, 55
settings: in Marlowe, 3, 13–17, 53, 83, 88–91,
93, 111–12, 173–75; non-European, xiii,
15–16; staging of, 14
Shakespeare, William: and the alien, xiii,
xiv, 7–8, 10, 52, 96, 163, 185 n.37, 200 n.66;
Jews in, 6, 10; the magician in, 117, 122–
23; Moors in, 5, 8, 10, 158, 193 n.47; Turks
in, 54, 93, 96; and the self, 113, 115, 162,
165–66. *See also names of individual plays*
Sharpe, J. A., 177 n.3
Shepard, Simon: on Marlowe, 25, 180 n. 38,
185 n.30, 186 n.41, 188 n.23, 194 n.48; on
"others," 178 n.16, 181 n.47, 187 n.16, 192
n.22
Shumaker, Wayne, 197 n.25
Sir John Mandeville, 83
Skura, Meredith, 198 n.45
Smith, Bruce, 146, 201 n.8, 202 n.17, 203 nn.
23, 31, 204 nn. 44, 53
Smith, Mary Elizabeth, 184–85 nn. 29, 30
sodomy: cultural place of (in England),
xiv–xv, 8–9, 118, 143–47; as incrimination, 143–44, 146–47, 148–53, 155–56,
157–66; incrimination of, 146–47, 148,
150–56, 164–65; and Marlowe, xvi, 11–12,
145 (see also *Edward II*); obfuscation of,
143–44, 146–47, 148, 150–51, 153, 155–56,
159–66, 173–74. *See also* Homosexuality,
Renaissance
Soliman and Persida, 55
Spanish Comedy, The, 83
Spanish Tragedy, The, 83
Spenser, Edmund, 15, 16
Spensers: in Holinshed, 151–53, 164; in Marlowe, 22, 164–65, 166, 171
Spivak, Gayatri Chakravorty, 178 n.12, 182
n.60
Stanyhurst, Richard, 36
Steane, J. B., 89, 181 n.50, 186 n.40, 203 n.41
stereotypes: cultural place of (in England),
xiv–xv, 9–10, 94; in Marlowe, xv, 12–14,
17–26 (*see also names of individual plays*);
theoretical conceptions of, 6–9, 96, 100.
See also Colonialist discourse
Stockholder, Kay, 199 n.61, 200 n.64

Stow, John, *Chronicles*, 20, 84, 86–87, 202
n.18
Stubbes, Philip, *Anatomie of Abuses*, 85, 86
subaltern, the, 23
Summers, Claude J., 181 n.50

Tamburlaine, 59–81: centrality of, 20, 22, 67,
72–73; contextualization of, 17–19; and
divinity, 65–66, 68–69, 70, 74–76, 77,
80; homogenization of, 71–81; imperialist
self-constructions, 59–66, 67, 76–81; as
object of imperialism, 10, 66–71; and Persia, 60, 65, 68–69, 70, 72, 73, 76–77 (*see
also* Cosroe); relation to Bajazeth, 6, 62,
63, 64–65, 69–70, 78 (*see also* Bajazeth);
seduction of Zenocrate, 62–64, 70, 71,
72–73, 76–77, 79 (*see also* Zenocrate);
in sources, 58–59, 76, 80. See also
Tamburlaine
Tamburlaine, 53–81; ambivalence in, 19,
22–23, 60–61; cultural place of (in England), xiv, 24, 112–13; and the discourse
on the East, 53–59, 59–60, 81; and *Dido,
Queen of Carthage*, 81; and *Doctor Faustus*,
111, 114–16, 127, 139, 174; and *Edward II*,
17, 144, 157; and *The Jew of Malta*, 66, 81,
83, 88, 97, 100, 106; relation between the
two parts, 65, 71–72, 76, 78, 186 n.1; religion in, 65, 66, 68–69, 70, 71, 74–76, 77,
80, 113; rhetoric of power in, 67, 72–74,
76, 78–79, 104, 106. *See also* Tamburlaine
Tempest, The, xiv, 117, 122–23
Thomas, Keith, 119, 196 n.20, 197 nn. 25, 29,
31, 198 n.41
Thurn, David, 60, 189 n.31, 203 n.31, 204
n.52
Timon of Athens, 96
Titus Andronicus, xiii, 10, 158, 193 n.47
Todorov, Tzvetan, 30, 178 n.9, 183–84 n.13,
185 n.33
Tokson, Elliot H., 187 n.16
Tourneur, Cyril, 18
Tovey, D'Blossiers, 192 n.20
Trachtenberg, Joshua, 191 n.6
Traister, Barbara Howard, 196 n.19
Travels of Three English Brothers, The, 88
Trevor-Roper, Hugh, 196 n.20
Troilus and Cressida, 200 n.66
Turks: conceptions of, 6–7, 8, 56, 57–58, 96,
174, 194 n.54, 201 n.7; cultural place of (in

Turks (*continued*)

England), xiv, 54, 55, 81; and English imperialism, 5, 54, 57–58, 88, 89, 90–91; and
Islam, 57–58 (*see also* Islam); in *The Jew of
Malta*, 6, 19, 24–25, 54, 88–96, 99, 101–3,
105–6, 107 (see also *Jew of Malta, The*); in
Tamburlaine, Part 1, 6, 19, 56, 60, 62, 63,
64–65, 69–70; in *Tamburlaine, Part 2*, 72,
73–74, 75, 76–77, 78, 79. *See also* East,
the; *Tamburlaine*

Urry, William, 179 n.27, 180 nn.28–29,
35–36
usury, 83, 84, 85, 87, 97, 145. *See also* Jews

Vickers, Brian, 197 n.25
Virgil, *Aeneid*: and *Dido, Queen of Car-
thage*, 44, 46 (see also *Dido, Queen of
Carthage*); and imperialism, 34–36, 37,
45, 51–52
Volpone, 96

Warmington, B. H., 185–86 n. 38
Warren, Michael J., 194 n.1, 200 n.68

Waswo, Richard, 199 n.57
Webster, John, 18
Weil, Judith, 179 n.26, 181 n.41, 190 n.50
West, Robert H., 195 n.11
Weyer, Johann, 125, 199 n.52
Wheeler, Richard P., 185 n.37
Whetstone, George, *The English Mirrour*,
57, 58–59, 76, 187–88 n.17, 189 n.42, 190
n.49
Williamson, James A., 177 n.3
Wilson, Robert, *The Three Ladies of London*,
88
witch. *See* Magician, Renaissance

Yates, Frances A., 197 nn. 25, 30, 199 nn. 52,
59
Young, Robert, 178 n.12

Zefferelli, Franco, 196 n.16
Zenocrate, 25–26, 62–64, 70, 71, 72–73,
76–77, 79

This book has been set in Linotron Galliard. Galliard was designed for Mergenthaler in 1978 by Matthew Carter. Galliard retains many of the features of a sixteenth-century typeface cut by Robert Granjon but has some modifications that give it a more contemporary look.

Printed on acid-free paper.